CREATIVE
BIBLE
TEACHING

Revised and Expanded

CREATIVE BIBLE TEACHING

Lawrence O. Richards
Gary J. Bredfeldt

MOODY PUBLISHERS
CHICAGO

ISBN: 0-8024-1644-6
ISBN-13: 978-0-8024-1644-5

We hope you enjoy this book from Moody Publishers. Our goal is to provide high-quality, thought-provoking books and products that connect truth to your real needs and challenges. For more information on other books and products written and produced from a biblical perspective, go to www.moodypublishers.com or write to:

Moody Publishers
820 N. LaSalle Boulevard
Chicago, IL 60610

15 17 19 20 18 16

Printed in the United States of America

To my wife,
Marlene Bredfeldt,
and to our children—
Lynne,
Stephen,
Michael,
and Amy—
whose encouragement and support
have made this project a reality and
whose love has made my life rich

To my parents,
Vivian and Charlotte Richards,
whose quiet living of God's Word
has proven to be His
creative force in my life

CONTENTS

LISTING OF
FIGURES AND TABLES

FIGURES

TABLES

PREFACE

OOK, BOOK, LOOK, TOOK—It sounds like a page from a children's story by Dr. Seuss, but this little memory device has helped shape Bible lessons for nearly three decades. As a student at the Moody Bible Institute in the early 1970s, I was taught Lawrence Richard's framework for lesson construction in my first Christian education course. *Creative Bible Teaching* was the required text in Mr. Omar Brubaker's class dealing with basic principles and methods of Bible teaching. Mr. Brubaker informed us, "These four words might sound corny to you at this moment, but you will never forget them, and you will use them throughout your ministry career as a means of effectively teaching the Bible."

Omar Brubaker was right. He was right when he said that "hook, book, look, took" sound corny. He was also right when he predicted that I would use these four words to effectively teach the Bible. I am certain that no single bit of classroom teaching has so affected my ministry as has this lesson approach.

This is the pattern I received as a Bible college freshman when I was assigned to read Lawrence Richards's book, *Creative Bible Teaching*. Likewise, this is the lesson planning framework given to many students by teachers like Omar Brubaker in Bible college and seminary Christian education courses for several years. It is now a classic means of lesson planning for Bible teachers. It is simple. It is clear. But, most important, it works in a way that affects student learning with the life changing message of the Word of God. Personally, I have used it as a pastor, youth pastor, director of Christian education, and lay Sunday school teacher. Now I teach a new generation of Moody Bible Institute students this tool of teaching effectiveness.

When the editorial staff at Moody Press discussed the possibility of a revision of Dr. Richards's book, I was immediately ready to join in the effort. *Creative Bible Teaching* has been a seminal work for many other texts and popular works in Christian education. It is known by nearly every professor of Christian education as foundational literature for those planning to teach the Bible. But after nearly thirty years it needed to be updated. This edition brings the reader new help in understanding the learner and the lesson preparation process and in the science and art of teaching the Bible. It is designed to be theoretically solid and immediately practical. It is written for both the lay person's use and professional training.

Creative Bible Teaching is far more than a book on lesson preparation. It is designed to aid you as a teacher in becoming the bridge between the biblical world and your students' world. It is a privilege to join with Lawrence O. Richards in submitting this book as a bridge-building resource.

GARY J. BREDFELDT

INTRODUCTION

There is something about a bridge that is fascinating. Take, for example, San Francisco's Golden Gate Bridge, one of the world's longest single-span suspension bridges. Its rust-colored structure is strikingly beautiful when partially shrouded in a morning fog and illuminated by rising sun. Another breathtaking view can be had atop Colorado's Royal Gorge Bridge. The bridge has a total length of 1,260 feet and is suspended 1,053 feet above the Arkansas River, which flows through the bottom of the canyon below. This height makes The Royal Gorge Bridge the world's highest suspension bridge and one of America's most spectacular attractions. But if those two engineering masterpieces are not enough to awe the tourist, try Florida's seemingly never ending Tampa Bay Bridge spanning some seventeen miles on Florida's gulf coast.

How do they do that? How do they build a bridge to connect two land masses thousands of feet, or even many miles, apart over choppy seas or across towering cliffs? It seems almost an impossible achievement. There are answers, of course. Answers that involve elaborate construction processes. A qualified structural engineer specializing in bridge design could tell you of the theory and process of bridge building that are behind such accomplishments. But, for the uninformed or the inexperienced, building a bridge is still a mystery.

In much the same way, effective Bible teaching seems to be a bridge-building task only a few have mastered. Consider the assignment. The Bible teacher must build a bridge from the ancient world of the Bible to the modern world of the student. It is a bridge that crosses both time and cultural boundaries. This bridge must take the student into a society far different from his own and back again. But it must span still further. The student must be able to cross not only to the past but to his own future as well. The teacher must help the student construct a bridge that will carry biblical principles from the world of Abraham, David, Jesus, and Paul to one of stock markets, inner-city housing projects, high school hallways, and the Internet. This is no easy bridge-building project, but it can be done. God's Word is "living and active. Sharper than any double-edged sword, it penetrates" (Heb. 4:12). It is contemporary. It is relevant. But it is the teacher who has the task of aiding the student in seeing Scripture's relevance. Such a bridge-building task demands creative Bible teachers.

THE FIVE STEPS IN BIBLE TEACHING

Just how, then, do teachers accomplish this goal of creative communication? What is the process of bridge building that each Christian teacher must master? How can we build a bridge from the biblical world to the student's world? Answering these questions is the goal of this book. This is a book on biblical bridge building. It reveals a five-step process by which the Christian teacher can construct a bridge across time, geography, and culture. Figure 1 depicts each of the steps in this bridge-building process, the five steps that comprise *The Creative Bible Teaching Model*. Each of the steps in the creative teaching process are developed as a separate unit in this book.

Step I—Studying the Bible

In this section of the book you will develop an understanding of the nature, role, study, and interpretation of the Bible as the first step in lesson preparation. Before one can be a teacher of the Bible, it is essential to become a student of the Bible. This section gives the help you need in preparing biblically accurate lesson plans.

Step II—Focusing the Message

This section addresses matters of student learning and appropriate teaching responses. As you read you will discover how to teach for student learning. In this section, you will be introduced to research in human learning theory and will be given practical help in applying that knowledge to your own teaching ministry. Various examples will help guide you in the process of translating learning theory into lesson preparation.

Figure 1

THE CREATIVE BIBLE
TEACHING MODEL

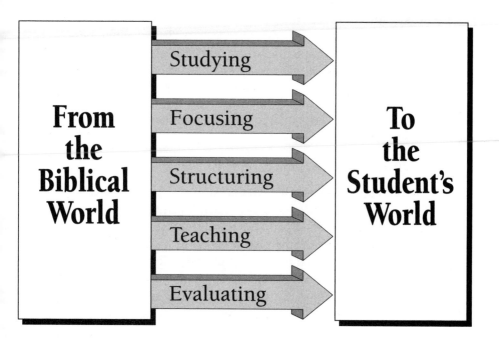

Step III—Structuring the Lesson

In this segment of the book your reading will show you how to actually develop a creative Bible teaching lesson plan using the Hook, Book, Look, Took structure. This is the "nuts and bolts" of the book, and a section that you will find most helpful in increasing your effectiveness as a Bible teacher.

Step IV—Teaching the Class

The fourth step in the creative teaching process is the actual in-class instructional time. This part of the book will provide you with a summary of six practices of truly great teachers. By reviewing these practices, you will discover principles of teaching that can be applied in your own teaching ministry, leading to a more dynamic and satisfying teaching experience. Also included in this section is an overview of the developmental needs of children, adolescents, and adults. Developmentally appropriate teaching strategies are presented in light of understanding human growth and change.

Step V—Evaluating the Results

This section of the book is designed to encourage and enable creative Bible teachers to evaluate their own teaching effectiveness. Improvement requires assessment and appropriate change. You will learn how to assess the outcomes of your teaching. A model for evaluation is presented that can be used to make informed judgments regarding student learning and teaching effectiveness. Finally, we provide assistance and suggestions on how to improve your teaching results by altering the variables in the teaching-learning process.

ONE FINAL WORD

We write this book from a decidedly conservative and evangelical position. We make no apologies for our conviction that the Bible is God's Word. We hold that the Bible is God's special revelation written as the one authoritative guide and rule for faith and conduct. It is our belief that the Bible provides objective, propositional truth about God and stands as an absolute standard and test of truth. Whether or not human beings receive and submit to the Bible's authority does not affect its authoritative role. The entire structure of the teachings developed in this book rests on this presupposition.

Let's build a bridge, shall we?

Figure 2

THE CREATIVE BIBLE
TEACHING MODEL

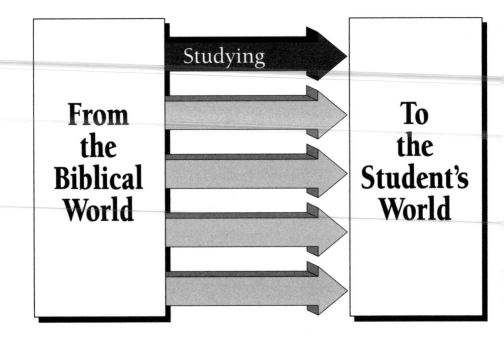

From
the
Biblical
World

Studying

To
the
Student's
World

STUDYING THE BIBLE

Matt was ready to go. He had prepared the room by placing the chairs in groups of four so that he could get the students into a small group discussion. He had prepared some handout sheets with a very interesting case study, and he had a video clip that fit his lesson goals perfectly. He even had a multicolored overhead that he had prepared with his new presentation software program. Matt felt good about the upcoming class. His passage was to be James 3:1–18, the need to control the tongue.

The class proceeded just as Matt had planned. Students were all engaged in discussion, especially when Matt asked them to tell ways they struggle with inappropriate words. All went well, or so it seemed. Then it was time to evaluate Matt's efforts. You see, Matt was taking a course called "Teaching the Bible."

"What did Matt do well? What can we commend him for?" asked the professor. Several students immediately supported Matt's teaching performance with comments about his creativity, choice of methods, and ability to get students engaged. "What could Matt do to improve?" was the next question the professor posed. At this, the entire class raised their hands.

Kate responded. "Well, I would kind of like to see him actually get us into the Bible. We read it and all, and we did share some opinions on what it said, but we maybe spent five minutes with the text at the most. All of his methods were fun, but I don't think we actually studied the Bible. In fact, I don't think we really ever got to the author's point."

Kate was a perceptive listener. Matt did not teach the Bible passage. Matt instead led a class session on everyone's experiences and opinions. He did quite well when it came to the dynamics of teaching, but he failed when it came to teaching with authority. Matt responded to Kate's critique. "Well, I really didn't have a lot of time to study the passage. I had a paper due in another class, so I thought I would just get everyone involved." Matt made a fundamental error in his teaching ministry. He confused involvement with authority. Getting students involved in a class is not the same as getting them involved in the Bible. Authority in teaching the Bible is not derived from the teacher's skill or the methods selected, but only from teaching what the Scriptures teach.

Creative Bible teaching begins with effective Bible study. Before one can be a teacher of the Bible, one must first be a student of the Bible. Although there are no guarantees that those who study the Bible well will also teach well, it is certain that those who do not study the Scriptures with diligence cannot teach well. Why? Because those who teach the Bible well do so with authority. Not an authority that is gained by the use of creative methods or by telling captivating stories. Nor an authority derived from an appealing personality, catchy wit, or stimulating discussion questions. Although all of these things may contribute to an effective class, teachers who teach with the authority of Scripture do so because they first know and then teach only and always what the Word of God intends to teach. In other words, they submit their teaching to the authority of the Bible by teaching what the Bible text teaches. This is possible only if they know what the text teaches. To know, they must study. This unit will help you with this step in creative Bible teaching.

Chapter One

THIS BIBLE:
THE NEED FOR AND
NATURE OF THE BIBLE

It really isn't a very impressive sight. Actually, it's just a small, lily-pad-covered pond like a thousand others in Yellowstone National Park, yet this one is surrounded by a large parking lot. Most of the time the lot is full. Why the attraction? The answer is found on a sign that park visitors stop to read as they take the boardwalk around the lake. The sign tells tourists that this little pond is the "watershed of two great rivers." A few drops of water leaving the pond down a very tiny creek to the west flow through a variety of streams and rivers eventually to reach the Columbia River and finally the Pacific Ocean. Another few drops of water flowing out of the equally tiny creek to the east eventually flow to the Missouri River, on to the Mississippi River, and, finally, to the Gulf of Mexico.

A watershed is the elevated point at which water flows in one direction or another. The Bible, or more accurately our attitude toward the Bible, is a watershed issue in Christian teaching. The Bible teacher's view of Scripture will serve to determine the direction and purpose of his teaching ministry. If the Bible is regarded as a purely human book with doubtful stories told by pre-scientific persons in an effort to understand their world, the teacher will most likely approach the Bible seeking to demythologize its message. On the other hand, if the Bible is regarded as the inspired, inerrant revelation of God to human beings in a specific time and place, then the teacher's approach to the Bible will entail admiration, respect, and even a mandate for obedience to its teachings.

How have Bible teachers understood this Bible we teach? In which directions have their understandings taken the flow of their teaching? What is the nature of the Bible, and how does its nature affect how we teach it? To answer these questions, we must first consider the need for the Bible. Why did God give us this Bible in the first place?

THE NEED FOR THE BIBLE

Consider the words of J. I. Packer.

> What were we made for? To know God. What aim should we set for our lives? To know God. What is the "eternal life" that Jesus gives? Knowledge of God. . . . What is the best thing in life, bringing more joy, delight, and contentment, than anything else? Knowledge of God.[1]

Packer's point is absolutely correct. Nothing could better describe the purpose of mankind than to know their Creator in an intimate and personal way. But how does one know God? An even more difficult question is this: How does one know that one knows God? Figure 3 depicts two foundational views of what is meant by "knowing God." These two primary views of knowing God are both embraced in our day.

Two Views of Knowing God

The immanence view. The first of these concepts of knowing God sees knowledge of God as the result of a search within the seeker. We might term this view an immanence view of God. The word *immanence* means "within" and carries the idea of something completely immersed in another thing. Those who hold this view contend that God is one with His creation. God is believed to be of the same essence as His creation. Immanence views of God understand God to be a force or power and impersonal in nature. God cannot be separated from creation and, in fact, is found within the created order of things. It is contended by immanence proponents that something of the divine spark or force is found in each person. Therefore, to know God, the seeker must know himself and discover within "the self" the qualities of God.

This position has its historic roots in Eastern mystic religions such as Hinduism and Buddhism, but today it finds its expression most prominently in the New Age Movement. Several books have helped to popularize this view of God. Author and actress Shirley MacLaine, through her book *Out on a Limb*, brought increased public attention to the New Age view of God as immanent. And more recently, the runaway best-sellers *Embraced by the Light* and *The Celestine Prophecy* have contributed to the widening acceptance of New Age thinking. Prominent

Figure 3

TWO VIEWS OF
KNOWING GOD

Immanence View: God Within

God Is Discovered Within the Seeker

Transcendence View: God as Other

God Must Make Himself Known Through Revelation

physician Larry Dossey described the immanence view of God in *Healing Words*, his best-selling book on prayer, as the "modern model" for understanding God and prayer. After explaining that prayer is "nonlogical" and "evidence for shared qualities with the Divine—the Divine Within"—he writes,

> The way prayer is conceived by most Western religions is far different from this: God is installed outside us, usually high above, as if in stationary orbit, functioning as a sort of master communications satellite. . . . God up there, us down here . . . isolated creatures of the moment locked into a linear, flowing time, confined to the body, and awaiting death, ultimately sinful and unworthy, and whose only hope is to be redeemed by the merciful act of a Supreme Being. Although this version may be comforting for millions of people—those who are convinced they are "saved" or "chosen," or who belong to some religious in group—it causes immense confusion and guilt for others, and has been the source of untold nastiness in human affairs throughout recorded history. When compared with other religious views worldwide, this exteriorization of God . . . appears to be "pathological mythology." . . . The old biblically based views of prayer, which are still largely in vogue, were developed when a view of the world was in place that is now antiquated and incomplete.[2]

For those who hold the immanence view, knowing God does not involve knowing objective information about God or even knowing God as a person. Knowing God involves a communion with an inner force, the "Divine Within." In the process, the seeker reaches a state of tranquillity and peace. Since knowing God does not involve propositional knowledge about God, knowing God is a personal and undefinable experience that is distinct for each seeker. God does not reveal Himself to the seeker; He instead is revealed by the seeker through a personal search for a God-consciousness.

Those who hold to the immanence view of knowing God have a very definite view of the Bible. To them, the Bible is not God's revealed and inspired Word. The Bible is a record of human beings' quest for wisdom and divine consciousness. The Bible is a wise book, among many wise books, but it is to be no more revered than any other book of human sayings and truisms. If one embraces this view of the Bible, teaching the Bible would take on a far different role and nature than it would for those who embrace the Bible as the written revelation of the living God. For those who hold to the immanence perspective, teaching the Bible is simply using the Bible for its illustrative value in showing the learner how to reach a God-conscious state of inner tranquillity.

The transcendence view. The opposite and alternative view of knowing God could be termed a *transcendence* perspective. This is the view that is embraced by historical Christianity. This theological truth proclaims God as different and distinct from His creation in essence. He is considered to be "totally other" than that which He has created. "Totally other" does not mean that He cannot be known by human seekers at all, but that He cannot be found in His creation. He does not reside in creation. He is distinct, and He is not dependent on His creation for His continued existence. He is higher and greater than anything He has created, and, therefore, all human efforts to fully understand Him and contain Him are fruitless. Rather, God must make the first move if He is to be known. God truly is immanent as well as transcendent, but it is because He chooses to be; "immanence" in the Christian sense of the word means that God is close to His creation, not that He is part of it.

Imagine taking a stroll through a famous art museum or institute. On each wall is a priceless painting, and throughout the halls are sculptures—all created by one highly gifted artist. As you pass through each hallway and exhibit area you gain an ever greater appreciation for the handwork of the artist. By the time you leave the museum you feel you almost know the artist. You have detected something of his heart and even his attributes. Surely, by studying the artist's creation you can learn much about the artist. But do you know the artist? Is this kind of intuitive knowledge of the artist the same as a personal knowledge of the artist? What if the artist were to make himself known to you by making contact with you? What if he were to send a representative or a letter telling you of his purpose in creating each painting or sculpting each statue? Would you know more of the artist than you did merely looking at his creations? What if he went still further and entered the art museum? What if he actually walked the halls of the institute with you? Would this not produce a greater knowledge of the artist?

Bible believing Christians insist that this is exactly what God, the Creator-Artist, did. Although it is true that He made Himself known through His creation in what theologians call *natural* or *general revelation,* He did more than that. He communicated with us. He communicated to His creatures in a means known as *special revelation.* Through special revelation God makes known those things about Himself that otherwise could not be known. He does this in two primary ways. First He reveals Himself through His written Word, inscribed in the pages of the Bible. Second, He also reveals Himself in the incarnate Word, the person of Jesus Christ who became flesh and dwelt among us.

By a careful study of the creation, the seeker will come to know something of God's divine nature and His invisible attributes. This is a knowing about God. But, through the special revelation of the Bible and in the person of Jesus Christ, God can be known in a personal and intimate way, that is, in a relationship. The transcendence view is a revelatory view. It holds that God is a personal being who transcends His creation and must reveal Himself if He is to be known at all. Apart from divine revelation, God would remain the unknown God. This then is the role of the Bible, *to make God known.*

The Unknown God

If God has revealed Himself in both natural revelation and special revelation, why is it that people do not know Him? Why is God the unknown God? God is unknown to us for two basic reasons—His nature and our nature.

His nature makes Him unknown to us. Isaiah quotes God as He describes His own lofty and distinct nature in these words: "'For my thoughts are not your thoughts, neither are your ways my ways,' declares the Lord. 'As the heavens are higher than the earth, so are my ways higher than your ways and my thoughts than your thoughts'" (Isa. 55:8-9). God is unlike us in His cognitive capacity. We cannot understand His rationale for His actions. God must come to us, for we certainly could not come to Him given this kind of gulf of understanding. In a similar way, God explains Job's limitations in comprehending and knowing the God of creation. "Can you fathom the mysteries of God? Can you probe the limits of the Almighty? They are higher than the heavens—what can you do? They are deeper than the depths of the grave—what can you know?" (Job 11:7-8). "How great is God—beyond our understanding! The number of his years is past finding out" (Job 36:26). God is by nature impossible for us to probe. He is the unknown God because He is higher, deeper, and beyond human search. But He is not limited in His ability to find us and make Himself known to us.

Our nature makes Him unknown to us. Not only is God beyond us, we are limited by our own sin and our tendency to suppress any of the truth God has made known. Paul reminds us that sin has blinded us to revelation from the Spirit of God. "The man without the Spirit does not accept the things that come from the Spirit of God, for they are foolishness to him, and he cannot understand them, because they are spiritually discerned" (1 Cor. 2:14). Satan too has a part in blinding us from seeing and comprehending divine truth, including the gospel of Jesus Christ: "The god of this age has blinded the minds of unbelievers, so that they cannot see the light of the gospel of the glory of Christ, who is the image of God" (2 Cor. 4:4).

God has indeed made truth about Himself known, but human beings suppress that truth, choosing to believe lies instead of the revelation given by God in nature. In a passage of profound importance, Paul wrote,

> The wrath of God is being revealed from heaven against all the godless-ness and wickedness of men who suppress the truth by their wickedness, since what may be known about God is plain to them, because God has made it plain to them. For since the creation of the world God's invisible qualities—his eternal power and divine nature—have been clearly seen, being understood from what has been made, so that men are without ex-cuse. For although they knew God, they neither glorified him as God nor gave thanks to him, but their thinking became futile and their foolish hearts were darkened. Although they claimed to be wise, they became fools and exchanged the glory of the immortal God for images made to look like mortal man and birds and animals and reptiles. Therefore God gave them over in the sinful desires of their hearts to sexual impurity for the degrading of their bodies with one another. They exchanged the truth of God for a lie, and worshiped and served created things rather than the Creator—who is forever praised. Amen. (Rom. 1:18–25)

God is, for all intents and purposes, the unknown God. Not un-knowable, for God can make Himself known, but unknown because of our state and condition. How then does the unknown God make Him-self known? Through special revelation, through His Word, inscribed in the Bible and incarnate in Jesus Christ, God has acted and willed that He be knowable.

God Made Known

In nature God has left a calling card. He uses it to draw our atten-tion so that He can make His clearer and more personal revelation plain. Paul spoke to this in Acts 17 when he addressed the Athenian philosophers:

> The God who made the world and everything in it is the Lord of heaven and earth and does not live in temples built by hands. And he is not served by human hands, as if he needed anything, because he himself gives all men life and breath and everything else. From one man he made every nation of men, that they should inhabit the whole earth; and he determined the times set for them and the exact places where they should live. God did this so that men would seek him and perhaps reach out for him and find him, though he is not far from each one of us. "For in him we live and move and have our being." As some of your own po-ets have said, "We are his offspring."
> Therefore since we are God's offspring, we should not think that the divine being is like gold or silver or stone—an image made by man's

design and skill. In the past God overlooked such ignorance, but now he commands all people everywhere to repent. For he has set a day when he will judge the world with justice by the man he has appointed. He has given proof of this to all men by raising him from the dead. (Acts 17:24–31)

Through God's natural revelation we come to know about God. We learn of His divine nature, His creative role, and His invisible attributes. But it is in the person of Jesus Christ that God makes Himself known in an intimate and personal way. Through God's special revelation in Christ we actually come to know God. John tells us of the incarnation of the Word of God. God became flesh that we might know Him.

> In the beginning was the Word, and the Word was with God, and the Word was God. He was with God in the beginning. Through him all things were made; without him nothing was made that has been made. In him was life, and that life was the light of men. The light shines in the darkness, but the darkness has not understood it. . . . The Word became flesh and made his dwelling among us. We have seen his glory, the glory of the One and Only, who came from the Father, full of grace and truth. . . . No one has ever seen God, but God the One and Only, who is at the Father's side, has made him known. (John 1:1–5, 14, 18)

According to the author of Hebrews, Jesus is no mere reflector of God's glory and nature as the moon would reflect the sun. He is like the sun giving forth its light. He radiates the very glory of God, the Father. He is the exact representation of His being.

> In the past God spoke to our forefathers through the prophets at many times and in various ways, but in these last days he has spoken to us by his Son, whom he appointed heir of all things, and through whom he made the universe. The Son is the radiance of God's glory and the exact representation of his being, sustaining all things by his powerful word. After he had provided purification for sins, he sat down at the right hand of the Majesty in heaven. So he became as much superior to the angels as the name he has inherited is superior to theirs. For to which of the angels did God ever say, "You are my Son; today I have become your Father"? Or again, "I will be his Father, and he will be my Son"? (Heb. 1:1–5)

Paul summarizes this truth for us in his Colossian letter and adds a further point. In Christ we are reconciled to God and can know Him in a new relationship untainted by the power of sin.

He is the image of the invisible God, the firstborn over all creation. For by him all things were created: things in heaven and on earth, visible and invisible, whether thrones or powers or rulers or authorities; all things were created by him and for him. He is before all things, and in him all things hold together. And he is the head of the body, the church; he is the beginning and the firstborn from among the dead, so that in everything he might have the supremacy. For God was pleased to have all his fullness dwell in him, and through him to reconcile to himself all things, whether things on earth or things in heaven, by making peace through his blood, shed on the cross. (Col. 1:15–20)

Paul says that Jesus is the God of creation. He holds all things together by His power. He is supreme, and He supremely reveals the divine character of God. Remarkably, He makes peace with God through His atoning blood sacrifice on the cross, allowing us to know God.

Through God's natural revelation we come to know about God. Through God's special revelation in Jesus Christ, we come to know God. What, then, is the purpose of the Bible as special revelation? It is this: Through God's written revelation we come to know and believe in Christ, the Messiah. Then, by Scripture's objective truth, we are able to confirm the validity of our knowledge of Him. John puts it this way: "Jesus did many other miraculous signs in the presence of his disciples, which are not recorded in this book. But these are written that you may believe that Jesus is the Christ, the Son of God, and that by believing you may have life in his name" (John 20:30–31). This is the reason we need the Bible—that we might believe and, by believing, that we might come to know Him.

THE NATURE OF THE BIBLE

How is it that a book, given by God to transform, seems so unproductive when taught in the very churches where it is most honored and best known? Our Christian education has often produced warped personalities; our teaching has often failed to straighten twisted lives. Warping is so common that we've become used to it! Used to shaking our heads about "lost faith" in high school and college students. Used to congregations and individuals without vitality or dedication or reality in their walk with Christ. Used to an exploding population and a sputtering evangelism. Used to living day after day with men and women who need the Savior, and used to saying nothing to them about Him. Used to reading and studying and teaching the Bible without seeing God use it to transform. Have we been successful in reproducing the biblical faith in our modern world? Have we "turned the world upside down" as did the early church? Are our churches filled with spiritual giants?

Hardly! Teaching the Bible as we teach it has not transformed men as our theology says the Word of God should. But why not? Is it possible that we haven't really understood the nature of the Bible we teach? Is it possible that we haven't been teaching the Bible in a way that harmonizes with God's purposes in giving it?

Views of Scripture

The conservative view. What we call a conservative view of Scripture —that it is God's revealed and authoritative written Word—dominated Protestantism after the Reformation. The conservative has always believed that in the Bible God communicates with humans. He communicates information, truth, that we could not otherwise know. Because God has communicated His viewpoint to us in words, we need not guess what He is like or what He gives us in Christ. God has communicated with us in words, in just the way we communicate with other people.

For this speaking, God chose certain men and superintended their writing by His Holy Spirit, so that the product, our Bible, is His message. Its accuracy and infallibility are guaranteed. Of course, God didn't blank out the mind of each writer and use his hands as we would a puppet's. He didn't simply dictate. He worked through the consciousness and personality of each writer, through his feelings and patterns of expression. Yet the end result is God's message, His truth, His Word. So the conservative believes.

But in this century other approaches to the Bible have become popular and even dominant. People have suggested entirely new understandings of the nature of Scripture and new understandings of the place the Bible has in our relationship with God. These new views have led to new approaches in teaching, Christian nurture, and Christian education.

The liberal view. This view dominated the thinking of religious educators of most denominations from the twenties through the thirties. Men like George A. Coe and William C. Bower drew from liberal theology and the progressive school of education and proposed a new approach to Christian training. And they modified completely the role of the Bible in Christian teaching.

Briefly, men of this school viewed God as One who acts in our world of today just as He acted in the biblical world. God, therefore, should not be sought in a book, but in life. To these men, however, God's activity was not supernatural in the sense of miraculous. It was natural. God worked through the natural processes of individual and societal life.

What then do they say about the Bible? In a basic sense, the Bible was considered to be unneeded. It did not, to these men, contain truth about God or truth from God. Instead it recorded human experience. It was the story of men and women who looked for God in the normal events of their lives and times, and who believed that they had found Him. Today, they said, we are to look for God not in the events of the past but in the events of our own society. "God is at work today!" was their exciting cry. "Let's leap into life and meet Him."

And so the Bible was discarded as a source book of truth and values and authority, and human values and relationships moved onto center stage. The goal of Christian training became the enrichment of human life, the process of guiding people to discover the "higher Christian meanings" of their experiences. It was only in living life that God could be found, and found to be meaningful.

So religious educators and church leaders turned to the development of ways in which experiences could be guided and learners helped to grow in their ability to live meaningfully as individuals and in groups.

The neo-orthodox view. "Not Christian" was the charge raised against liberal religious education by H. S. Smith in his *Faith and Nurture.*[3] The Christian faith, said Smith, is rooted in something deeper than "growing values." It is rooted in a Christian revelation. It is rooted in a sovereign God, who stands outside of history, yet who disclosed Himself in a historical Christ. Liberal religious education, without a God who discloses Himself and encounters individuals supernaturally, cannot claim to be Christian.

Unlike the complete disregard for the Bible by liberal theologians, neo-orthodoxy recognizes the Bible as containing the Word of God. For the neo-orthodox theologian, the Scriptures are time-bound and culturally conditioned. Neo-orthodox theologians hold that, because the writers of the Bible were real, historical men as we are, and therefore sinful, they were capable of, and actually guilty of, error as they prophesied and recorded Scripture. In spite of this fact, neo-orthodox teachers believe, God speaks through the text of the human fallible Scripture. Neo-orthodoxy takes an approach to theology that places the religious experience of the believer as primary. The Bible stimulates such an experience. When it does so, they believe that it "becomes the Word of God" for that reader. So, neo-orthodoxy holds that the Bible becomes the Word of God to the individual reading it when the reader encounters God in the pages of Scripture, not that it is intrinsically the Word of God.

In a short time the neo-orthodox viewpoint dominated theologically and educationally. Paul Vieth's *Church and Christian Education*[4] reflects the changing climate. Soon Christian educators like James D.

Smart, Lewis J. Sherrill, and Randolph Crump Miller appeared. They attempted to develop a philosophy of Christian teaching based on the neo-orthodox theology. Today their influence is still seen in the curricula of major denominations and publishing houses, and the basic concepts they developed are reflected in many books on Christian education and in religious education publications.

The neo-orthodox influence was a healthy corrective to the liberal viewpoint. Neo-orthodox educators saw people as sinful (though this was variously defined). Human beings needed to know God, according to the neo-orthodox educator. God's revelation is channeled through the Bible, these educators believed, and so the Bible did have a place in Christian training. To the neo-orthodox educator, however, the Bible was not the Word of God, but instead, it became the Word of God as people encountered God in the Scriptures. Neo-orthodox educators argued that the text itself was nothing more than a human record of God's encounters with humanity. But when the Bible causes the reader to encounter God it becomes the Word of God to the believing person. In this sense, the Bible is an indirect revelation of God.

Neo-orthodox teachers held a distinctive concept of what revelation is, what the place of the Bible is in revelation, and how the Bible should be taught. To them, the Bible could not be taught as simply facts about God, but as human encounters with God. And in this respect we have been done a service. For development of this theory has forced us to look honestly at our own Bible teaching and to ponder why the teaching of the Bible in our churches has been so unproductive in terms of transformed, dedicated, Christ-centered lives if, as we believe, the Bible is the written Word of God. We have been forced to ask theological questions about our teaching of the Bible.

How we need this! How we need not merely to assert the fact of propositional revelation, but to understand the nature of that revelation and to see its implications for our Bible teaching. Remember, the purpose of the Bible is to reveal truth about God and to enable our students, through that revealed truth, to know God. It is not merely a book of facts to be learned or verses to be memorized. That kind of teaching falls short of a genuine understanding of the nature and purpose of the Bible.

Words Mean Something

Rush Limbaugh likes to make the statement, "Words mean something!" By this statement he is chastising the current approach to language that allows words to take on whatever meaning the reader or hearer wants to assign them. Whether applied to human conversation, interpreting the United States Constitution, or our understanding of biblical authority, such a view of words leaves the meaning of words strictly in the mind of the receiver. This is not the perspective held by the authors of Scripture with regard to its words. They were certain that "words mean something!"

Just glance through the Bible and it strikes you that the writers were not only sure they knew God; they were sure they knew a lot about Him. They thought they knew what God had done in human history; they labeled events as His acts, such as His overshadowing Mary so that her child was fully human and fully God (Matt. 1:18; Luke 1:35). They said God caused the Flood, that He led Israel out of Egypt. They said national emergencies, the invasions of Israel by pagan nations, were God's chastising acts (Isa. 10:5–6). Peter said that God caused, in the sense of ordaining, Christ's crucifixion (Acts 2:23).

And the writers went beyond events. They claimed to know God's motives and outcomes of events that simply could not be observed. They tell, for example, why Christ died, and what His death accomplished. Christ died for our sins (Rom. 15:3) to reconcile us to God (2 Cor. 5:18) in order that we might have God's forgiveness (Eph. 1:6) and be given immortality (2 Tim. 1:10) and eternal life (Titus 1:2). Christ's death means other things, too, and the writers thought they knew what the meaning was for the entire universe (Rom. 8:19–22) and for Satan (Heb. 2:14).

The Bible writers even dared to talk about what God will do in the future, giving details of Christ's physical return (1 Thess. 4:14–17), of the end of the earth (2 Peter 3:7), of humanity's final rebellion under the "man of sin" (2 Thess. 2), and of the final judgment on unbelievers (2 Thess. 1:7–10). And of God's plans for the future, Bible writers dare to say "the Spirit clearly says" (1 Tim. 4:1)!

No one can read things like this without being sure that these writers felt that they had received—and were communicating—information about God and from God. The writers expressed this information in words. Obviously, if information (as distinct from raw data) is going to be communicated, words play a part. Thus, a valid understanding of the nature of the Bible must focus on the words of the Bible.

Revelation from the Spirit of God

However, as it is written: "No eye has seen, no ear has heard, no mind has conceived what God has prepared for those who love him"—but God has revealed it to us by his Spirit. The Spirit searches all things, even the deep things of God. For who among men knows the thoughts of a man except the man's spirit within him? In the same way no one knows the thoughts of God except the Spirit of God. We have not received the spirit of the world but the Spirit who is from God, that we may understand what God has freely given us. This is what we speak, not in words taught us by human wisdom but in words taught by the Spirit, expressing spiritual truths in spiritual words. (1 Cor. 2:9–13)

Paul, writing in 1 Corinthians 2, gives a striking portrait of divine revelation in Scripture. Let's note the most significant ideas.

Revelation gives information not otherwise known. All of us draw conclusions from our experiences. We watch another person for a time, and we get ideas of why he acts as he does. We assign motives and even predict behavior. This much we deduce from experience. In this passage Paul is talking about something a little different. He's talking about God's plans, "God's secret wisdom, a wisdom that has been hidden and that God destined for our glory before time began" (1 Cor. 2:7). It's information about these plans that Paul says is now revealed.

Now, in what possible way could men discover God's hidden plans? Paul quotes the Old Testament to nail down the fact that the source of such information is not in the realm of human experience. No eye saw it. No ear heard it. No one imaginatively figured it out. These ideas did not develop as a human interpretation of a "revelation experience." Such information had to be directly revealed by God.

The Spirit reveals. It's one thing to deduce from observed behavior, and another entirely to know by revelation. No one on the outside can get down into another person's mind and know his thoughts. The person has to tell his thoughts if they are to be known. But, Paul points out, the Holy Spirit is God. So He can comprehend the thoughts of God, "even the deep things of God." Revelation, to Paul, is a work of the Spirit by which He communicates information from God to men. And the initial purpose of this communication isn't said to be "to bring men to encounter." It's that we might understand God's gifts to us.

Communication is by words. After all, God wants us to understand, to know, not to guess. And so He communicates to us in the way that we communicate, in a way that we can understand, by words. In the passage Paul says we impart (communicate) God's revelation in "words taught by the Spirit" (2:13).

What view of revelation does Paul present? The passage looks at revelation like this: (1) The source of revelation is the Spirit; (2) The content of revelation is information; and (3) The medium of revelation is language.

The idea that God speaks to us in words is not peculiar to Paul. The Old Testament prophets spoke words that they claimed were God's, not theirs. The writer of Hebrews talks constantly of the Old Testament as what "God said" or "the Holy Spirit says" (Heb. 1:5–14; 4:7; etc.). The consistent biblical picture, then, is that information is communicated to us by God in human language, in words. And "revelation" is a label for that information.

WHAT ABOUT THE BIBLE?

Probably the simplest thing to say about the Bible is that the words imparting God's revelation are written there. Because the revelation is in words, evangelicals often say that the Bible itself is God's revelation. They claim that it does not *contain* the Word of God; it *is* the Word of God. Failure of the teaching of the Bible to transform must lie somewhere other than in the Bible itself or its literal interpretation. For the Bible is given to be understood. We are to take God at His word. The problem then in teaching does not lie in the authority of the Bible but it must lie in the teacher, the student, the method of teaching, or some combination of the three. In order to teach the Bible creatively and with authority so as to change lives, we must begin with a high view of Scripture. Such a view mandates that the Bible teacher recognize the inspiration of Scripture and understand something of the literary nature of the inspired text. We will turn our attention to these matters in the next chapter.

NOTES

1. J. I. Packer, *Knowing God* (Downers Grove, Ill.: InterVarsity, 1973), 29.
2. Larry Dossey, *Healing Words* (New York: HarperCollins, 1993), 6–7.
3. H. S. Smith, *Faith and Nurture* (New York: Scribner, 1941).
4. Paul Vieth, *The Church and Christian Education* (St. Louis: Bethany, 1963).

Chapter Two

INSPIRED BY GOD:
THE DIVINE AUTHORSHIP AND
HUMAN LITERATURE OF THE BIBLE

The Bible has both a divine quality and a human side to its design. It is inspired by the Spirit of God so that it records, in its very words, God's special revelation concerning His dealings with human beings. Yet it does this using the writing styles and selected genres of its human authors. Written in three different languages, the sixty-six books of the Bible span some 1,500 years of human history. God expresses His Word in varieties of vocabulary and writing styles as well as in diverse cultures and historic settings, while still maintaining a consistent theme and purpose. The Bible is unique among books for its message, its diversity, its survival, and its power to change lives. When we teach the Bible, we teach a God-breathed text that retains human attributes.

INSPIRATION: THE DIVINE AUTHORSHIP OF THE BIBLE

The Word and Words of God

We call Jesus Christ "the Word." John uses the term "logos" or "word" for Jesus in his opening chapter, where we read, "The Word became flesh and made his dwelling among us" (John 1:14). "The Word" often refers to Jesus Christ. He is God's revelation, incarnate in human flesh. And the Bible is "the Word," for it too is God's revelation, inscribed in human language.

Two incidents in the life of Christ show how fully He regarded the text of Scripture to be the inspired and revealed Word of God. Once He warned His listeners, "Do not think that I have come to abolish the Law or the Prophets; I have not come to abolish them but to fulfill them. I tell you the truth, until heaven and earth disappear, not the smallest letter, not the least stroke of a pen, will by any means disappear from the Law until everything is accomplished" (Matt. 5:17–18). Christ was talking about the Old Testament, using the common designations of the Law and the Prophets. He declared that the Old Testament communication was sure and unchanging. It is not open to reinterpretation. God said what He means, and that settles it. The Law and the Prophets stand as God's revealed Word and, as such, stand with eternal authority.

Another time Christ rebuked some Sadducees, Jewish religious leaders who denied the resurrection. In doing so He quoted God as saying in the Old Testament, "I am the God of Abraham, the God of Isaac, and the God of Jacob." His rebuke hinged on the *tense* of a verb: *am*. God did not say *"was."* Therefore Jesus concludes, "He is not the God of the dead but of the living" (Matt. 22:32).

These two incidents indicate something remarkable about Jesus' view of the Scriptures. What kind of book is unchangeable and so reliable that proof of a vital doctrine can be advanced by pointing out the tense of a verb? Only a book in which the words are God's words, not the words of human beings. Jesus recognized the Bible as the unchanging Word of God.

No wonder, then, that emphasis is made in the epistles and elsewhere on remaining true to the words! Believers are to "agree to the sound instruction of our Lord Jesus Christ and to godly teaching" (1 Tim. 6:3). They are to "keep . . . the pattern of sound teaching" (2 Tim. 1:13), "hold firmly to the trustworthy message as it has been taught" (Titus 1:9), and hold "to the teachings [*paradosis*], just as I passed them on to you" (1 Cor. 11:2). Why these calls to regard the teachings of Scripture? Because the teachings are God's words!

Men Spoke from God

How were God's words given in the first place? The Bible doesn't explain the mechanics. Second Peter 1:21 gives the clearest picture of the process. "For prophecy [expression of a divine revelation] never had its origin in the will of man, but men spoke from God as they were carried along by the Holy Spirit."

Because the authors of Scripture were "carried along by the Holy Spirit," Peter finds Scripture more convincing than his eyewitness experience of Christ's glorification (2 Peter 1:16–18) or the fact that he himself heard a voice from heaven that identified Christ as God's Son! Why the greater confidence in the written, revealed Word of God? Because what we think happened and what actually happened can be two different events. Experiences can be colored by our own emotions and presuppositions. God's Word cannot. God records truth truly.

"Carried along," as the NIV puts it, or "moved," as translated in the KJV, can be translated "inspired." The Greek word pictures a boat, with sails filled by the wind, being carried along over the seas. So too, the writers of the Bible, filled with the Spirit, were carried along. The result: the words and thoughts recorded are guaranteed to be God's. The writings are true and accurate, and the information authoritative beyond question. And, according to Paul, all Scripture is inspired by God (2 Tim. 3:16).

Biblically and theologically, then, *inspiration* refers to the influence God exerted over the human writers of Scripture. By inspiration, He guarantees that the result accurately expresses that which He intends to communicate.

Of course, inspiration guarantees only the accuracy of the original writings, not of later copies or modern translations. But the science of textual criticism has proven what we would expect if God is continuing to watch over His Word: that the degree of accuracy with which the biblical text has been transmitted is fantastic. We can be confident that in the Bible we have the Word, and the words, of God.

Nonverbal Revelation

Is the truth given by revelation limited to biblical statements expressing information in words? Or can revelation in the Bible extend beyond the words spoken in the Bible? The Bible shows that God has spoken to men and women through more than words. How? Through events, like the plagues of the Exodus period. Through things, like the tabernacle and its furnishings. Through experiences, like the sacrifices ordained in the law. But we must exercise caution here. *The meaning of these nonverbal forms is interpretable only because of other revelations in words.*

God showed His power overwhelmingly in the plagues. But the Bible doesn't simply record the events; it offers information as to why God acted as He did. Exodus assigns three reasons for the plagues: (1) that Israel should see and know "that I am [Jehovah] your God" (6:1, 7), (2) that the Egyptians should "know that I am [Jehovah]" (7:5), and (3) that judgment might be executed on Egypt's gods (12:12).

But an even larger context is needed for understanding. Why did God act this way for Israel? Why did He choose Israel? What were, and are, His purposes? Here the whole pattern of Old Testament revelation is relevant. God made a covenant with Abraham; He honored that covenant.

God set His love on Israel by sovereign choice, not because they were better or holier than others. Through them God determined to glorify Himself, to show His power, and to establish His salvation and rule on the earth. For interpretation, events require more information than they convey! They require words.

The same may be said of objects that communicate. According to Hebrews, God used the veil of the temple to signify that the way into the holiest was not yet open. Note the phrase "the Holy Spirit was showing" (9:7–8). God is communicating by symbol. Yet this too needs a verbal key for interpretation. And the Bible gives it (cf. Heb. 8–9). How about the sacrifices? Leviticus 17:11 explains that "the life of a creature is in the blood, and I have given it to you to make atonement for yourselves on the altar; it is the blood that makes atonement for one's life." Thus, verbal interpretation makes the meaning of the sacrificial act clear, long before history reveals that the blood of animals shed for sin only pictures the lifeblood of God's Son, poured out in expiation on Calvary.

It is important to realize, then, that while the Bible describes nonverbal revelations, it retains the right to interpret them verbally. When you look for the meaning of an act or symbol, you will find that meaning in Scripture. Revelation is not left open to careless or subjective explanation. Again, the words of Scripture are essential to comprehend the nonverbal messages of Scripture. The concept of the verbal inspiration of Scripture is foundational to an objective understanding of nonverbal revelation.

Varieties of Verbal Inspiration

Nonverbal revelation is only part of the matter. As any reader of the Bible knows, the Bible isn't all statements or all assertions. Much of the Bible gives information about God in purely propositional form, but not every passage does so. Scripture presents truth to the reader through a variety of genres, including poetry, narrative, and historical description.

Poetry in the Bible often expresses human emotions. In the Psalms we read of and feel worship, fear, love, anger, doubt, trust—the full range of emotions that torment us and yet raise life to the sublime. In what sense are such psalms revelation, or inspired? How are they the words of God?

Or look at the extended description of lives and national histories. Chapter after chapter tells incidents in the lives of Abraham and Isaac and Jacob. Whole books describe the life of Christ on earth, and great sections of these books communicate no information that could not be seen by the human eye. They simply record what men observed, what

Jesus did and said, how His friends and enemies reacted. Yet this is part of the Bible and is called God's Word. What does it all mean?

First, the form or genre of Scripture does not change the fact of inspiration. The writing of poems, history, and description was superintended by the Holy Spirit, and these are God's Word. God inspired writers to use their own unique styles and perspectives, as well as their choice of literary genre to communicate in words His revealed message. By God's Holy Spirit, He superintended the very words of the Scripture including its variety of genres. He did not do this in the form of dictation, but He did define, and ultimately control, the outcome. As a contractor supervises a construction site, God supervised the recording of His Word. The human authors were personally involved in the process, yet their product was the result of the work of the Holy Spirit in inspiration.

Second, when we call the *whole* Bible inspired and claim the whole Bible to be God's divine revelation, we're not using the term "revelation" in the sense of making known that which was secret and hidden. We mean that in every word of the Word, God speaks to us and that every word is recorded as God superintended.

This speaking need not be wholly informational. After all, we're not disembodied minds—cerebral computers designed to sift and store facts. Our capacity to understand is matched by our capacity to feel. The Bible speaks to this capacity too; it communicates to every aspect of our personality, that in every way we might know and respond to God. Inspiration, relating to genres like poetry, guarantees both that feelings are accurately portrayed and that God included them in His Word for a purpose.

The same can be said about description. Inspiration guarantees the events presented as historical to be historical; to really have happened, and in the way described. Inspiration also guarantees that God included them for a purpose.

Third, the reason God inspired such diversity of genres is discoverable in the genres themselves. God spoke as men speak, in a variety of literary means. The key to interpretation is taking the words in their normal usage in the form used. (If figuring out what normal usage means sounds like hard work, it is; but we'll try to make it a little more approachable later in this chapter.) The Bible is a literary anthology. It is comprised of many different literary forms and devices. We say that not to make the task of interpretation more difficult, but simply to say that God communicated to us as we communicate to each other. Various literary forms and genres are part of human language, and so they are used in the language of the Bible. Why? Because this is characteristic of God's creative nature. The Bible is not a dry list of statements about God. It is reflective of the creative nature of the living God.

Take a phrase from a poem, such as this one in Habakkuk 3:6: "He stood, and shook the earth; he looked, and made the nations tremble. The ancient mountains crumbled and the age-old hills collapsed. His ways are eternal." Does this verse say that at a particular point in time God stood and looked at the earth in such a way as to cause earthquakes that shook nations and broke up and scattered mountains? Not necessarily. This is poetry. The words have *poetic* meaning. In the context of Habakkuk's vision of coming judgment, in which he sees God as the awful judge, poetry conveys the sense of terror and majesty far better than any journalistic assertion. After all, this is the way we use words in poetry. God uses words as we do, and their meaning is determined by the literary form in which they're used. If we approach the Bible as literature, our task of understanding it will be simplified, as long as we keep in mind that this literature is recording truth; it is not written primarily to entertain.

Or take the description of events recorded in John's gospel. How are these to be understood? How are we to learn from them? John provides the key to interpretation himself (20:30–31). The book was written that its readers might believe that Jesus is the Christ, the Son of God. Events from Christ's life are carefully selected to demonstrate this theme (about 92 percent of the material is unique to John), and much material is omitted. From the opening verses, the demonstration of Christ's deity is focal.

Within the framework of this purpose, told plainly and simply, the reader can draw conclusions and make applications that are not specifically stated in the text but are supported by Scripture taken as a whole. And this is clearly God's intention, for all Scripture is profitable to equip the man or woman of God (2 Tim. 3:16–17).

The Bible says that the experiences of individuals and peoples "happened to them as an example, and they were written for our instruction" (1 Cor. 10:11 NASB). And abundant New Testament interpretations of Old Testament experiences give us clear guidelines as to how to draw out the intended lessons (cf. 1 Cor. 10:6; Heb. 3:7–4:6).

Needless to say, no major doctrine rests on this indirect form of expression for its communication. Events may illustrate, but God has taken care that the basic tenets of our faith are clearly and plainly *stated* in His Word.

What All This Means

What can we say, then? First, that the Bible communicates that which is objectively and historically true. It describes accurately events that really happened. It shows feelings that men and women of God really had. It communicates in words revealed information about God and from God to which we have no other access. It does this because of the work of the Holy Spirit known as inspiration.

And the words in which all this is communicated do have "cash value"! They mean what they say; they say what they mean. They're to be taken and understood as all human speech, and they can be interpreted literally in the context of the grammatical and historical situation. And so they must be taught.

It's clear, then, that the Bible teacher does communicate information. We can't say that the failure of people to be transformed by the truth of God stems from our communicating information as literally true. To teach truth and fact, to give information about God, is exactly what the Bible is designed to do through inspiration.

LITERARY GENRES: THE HUMAN LITERATURE OF THE BIBLE

The word *Bible* means "little books." Many misunderstand the Bible to be a single book. More accurately, it is a collection of many books woven together by God around the central theme of reconciliation with God. The Bible is, in fact, a sixty-six-book library of small volumes. The Bible's rich variety of literary genres includes, but is not limited to, history, narrative, legal codes, comedy, drama, poetry, satire, proverbs, parables, epistles, allegory, and prophecy. God did not inspire the Bible to be a flat book giving only factual statements or theological proof texts. He made it a living book, filled with the diversity of genuine human experience, thought, emotion, and expression. To teach the Bible is to teach an artistic treasure as well as to teach the very Word of God. But such variety does present the Bible teacher with a problem. Different genres require different "rules" of interpretation, and different genres mandate different approaches to teaching.

Interpreting Different Writing Types

Those who study and teach the Bible must approach the Bible in a literal fashion. But literal interpretation does not mean that we take every word to be literal, but that we look at each book and passage of Scripture according to its natural and normal literary meaning. How can those two statements be reconciled? And how does one study, interpret, and teach the Bible in light of literary genres?

For example, historical accounts are not the same as parables. In Mark 10:46 we read that Jesus and His disciples "came to Jericho." This is meant to be taken by the reader as historic fact. It is stated by the gospel author to give a historic and geographic reference point for understanding the chronological flow of Jesus' ministry. In Luke 10:30 we read, "A man was going down from Jerusalem to Jericho." In this case, the indication of travel to Jericho is not included for historic purposes. It is part of a parable and is included to set a dramatic stage in the mind of the hearer. In all likelihood, there was no such man. This is a parable, a story, and it should be interpreted as such. Parables are to be taken as stories with a meaning or moral, not necessarily historical accuracy.

A second example of the need to interpret and teach the Scripture in light of its literary genres is that of Job. Job is a kind of historic poetry. Although the Bible presents Job as a real person, the intent of Job is not to be a historical record. Rather, Job is a poetic writing that deals with the question of suffering and the sovereignty of God. It is not likely that Job's friends argued in a highly complex Hebrew poetic form. The author was certainly using poetic license when he recorded the conversations that took place. As a result, their words and Job's responses are rich in metaphoric imagery that continues to powerfully teach what God intended through the inspired words of Scripture. To miss the poetic nature of the book is to miss much of the message of the book.

How does one interpret a passage of Scripture if the type of genre impacts the meaning of the passage? The answer is found in the passage itself. The Bible teacher should ask, "What was the intent of the author? Does the passage give hints as to its genre?" The Bible teacher should remember that the biblical author will often provide clues so that the reader knows what type of literature is being read. Otherwise, how would the reader ever understand the writer's meaning? The biblical interpreter should examine the passage to see if it gives any such indication of its intended genre. An example of this might well be the story of the Prodigal Son.

The story of the Prodigal Son is a parable. It is never identified as such directly, but it gives evidence of parabolic genre in context and style. In Luke 15:3, where Jesus tells His listeners the parable of the lost sheep, we read that "Jesus told them this parable." Then verse 11 says, "Jesus continued: 'There was a man who had two sons.' " It is clear from both the context and the passage itself that this is a story told to communicate a principle. It is the principle that is the driving purpose of the story, not all of the details of the story. Rather than getting lost in trying to interpret a hidden meaning in the details, the reader should look for the larger principle as the goal of study.

But some parables do have allegorical qualities. Again, the reader should look for hints in the passage or its context to determine if this is the case. For example, the parable of the wicked vineyard tenants (Matthew 21:33–41) is intended to speak allegorically of the Pharisees.

The Pharisees recognized the parable as having an allegorical point and as a result took offense at Jesus' teaching. This fact should serve as a significant hint to the reader, and the reader should have little difficulty recognizing the allegorical nature of the genre. Likewise, the parable of the sower (Luke 8:1–15) has allegorical qualities. Interpretation of the parable is added by Jesus. He provides an extended explanation of the primary characters and details of the allegory. These examples show that the Bible does contain allegory, and that genre should be interpreted as such. But the majority of the Bible should not be interpreted allegorically. To do so will mean that the reader finds hidden meanings in the text where they are not intended.

Where does one find guiding principles for interpreting the various genres of the Scriptures? Of particular help is Fee and Stuart's book entitled *How to Read the Bible for All Its Worth*.[1] Fee and Stuart provide individual chapters on the various genres of the Bible and give input to the reader for interpreting each genre. Every teacher of the English Bible should become familiar with their book. We have also found the chapter entitled "Biblical Genres" in Dan McCartney and Charles Clayton's book *Let the Reader Understand*[2] to be useful in this regard.

YOU'RE MAKING PROGRESS

We have examined some weighty background material to creative Bible teaching. Let's face it, you are undertaking a significant task. You do need to have a solid background understanding of the Bible you plan to teach. That means you must understand something of the need for, and the nature of, the Bible. Additionally, you must understand what is meant by the inspiration of the Bible and must recognize the diversity of the literature of the Bible. All of these concepts are important for you to grasp if you are going to become the kind of Bible teacher you desire to be. But we have one more subject to address before you launch into your preparation to teach. We must examine the overall message of the Bible and its specific role in affecting your students' lives. So let's take your quest to become a creative Bible teacher still further as you read the next chapter in this section dealing with studying the Bible.

NOTES

1. Gordon D. Fee and Douglas Stuart, *How to Read the Bible for All Its Worth* (Grand Rapids: Zondervan, 1982).
2. Dan McCartney and Charles Clayton, *Let the Reader Understand* (Wheaton: Victor, 1994).

Chapter Three

PERSON TO PERSON:
THE MESSAGE AND
ROLE OF THE BIBLE

One Sunday morning, after sitting in an adult Sunday school class at church, Dave asked his teacher, Jim, "Have you ever taught a Bible study for a group of seekers?" Jim wasn't exactly sure what Dave was getting at, so he asked him to be more specific. "Seekers," Dave said, "You know, people who aren't yet Christians but who are interested in what the Bible teaches. I work at the Chicago Board of Trade, and one of my coworkers and I thought we could get a group of people together to study the Bible. We have discussed Christ with a number of people, but we keep running into doubts about the Bible. We thought that we would offer a study on the Bible itself. You would be just the person to lead the study."

Jim considered the request and agreed to try. His task was to explain the message of the Bible in one session and then defend its reliability in a second session. If the two sessions sparked interest, the study would be continued for those who wanted to learn more.

Jim sat down to prepare, and the nature of the task began to concern him. *How exactly can I summarize what the Bible is all about?* he pondered. *Sure it's about God, but what does it say about God? What is its unifying theme? How can I present the entire message of the Bible in just one session to a group of people who know very little about the Bible?*

If you were Jim, what would your Bible study focus on? How would you summarize the message of the Bible? What is the unifying theme of the Bible that makes it more than simply a collection of short books?

THE MESSAGE OF THE BIBLE

The message of the Bible is rooted in history. It is not a story given in a vacuum. It records events in lives of individuals and groups of people, living in specific places, at particular times. But it is not a record of world history as men would write it. It is a sacred history. It is history from God's vantage point. It is the story behind history, for it gives the meaning to history. You see, this is a history of God's dealings with human beings. Because of this, it is a rather unique presentation of human history. It was penned by men, but it was written under the inspiration of the Holy Spirit. The historic record of the Bible reveals more than significant events, important personages, or great ideas and advances. It reveals God's plan and purpose for His creation and, in particular, for human beings. John R. W. Stott describes the biblical account of human history as recorded by the writers of Scripture in these words:

> Therefore, they were selective in their choice of material and (the secular historian would add) unbalanced in their presentation of it. For example, ancient Babylonia, Persia, Egypt, Greece and Rome—each a mighty empire and rich civilization—are only included as they impinge on the fortunes of Israel and Judah, two tiny buffer states on the edge of the Arabian desert, which hardly anybody had heard of. The great thinkers of Greece, like Aristotle, Socrates and Plato are not so much as mentioned, nor are national heros like Alexander the Great (except obliquely) and Julius Caesar. Instead, the scriptural record concentrates on men like Abraham, Moses, David, Isaiah and the prophets to whom the word of God came, and on Jesus Christ, God's Word made flesh.[1]

Stott believes the central theme of the Scriptures is salvation. He underscores the idea that the historic record accounted in the Scriptures is incomplete. Stott continues,

> For the concern of Scripture is not with the wisdom, wealth or might of the world, but with the salvation of God. Biblical history is *Heilsgeschichte*, the story of salvation. . . . The sweep of this sacred history is magnificent. Although it omits great areas of human civilization which would feature prominently in any history of the world, from God's point of view it tells the whole story of man from start to finish, from the beginning when "God created the heavens and earth" to the end when He will create "a new heaven and a new earth."[2]

Habermas and Issler provide another "unifying motif" for understanding the message of the Bible. In particular, they focus on the theological concept of reconciliation. They picture the storyline of the Bible as a three-act play. Each act presents a phase in the unfolding drama of God's plan for reconciling estranged image bearers with the Creator God through Christ's atoning sacrifice. Figure 4 on the next page depicts Habermas and Issler's dramatic model of God's plan for reconciliation.[3]

In Habermas and Issler's model, the biblical story centers around the matter of the image of God in men and women. They write, "Being created in God's image sets the critical theological tone for biblical anthropology."[4] Act one in their scenario of human history begins with "Righteous Reflection." Adam and Eve were flawlessly created to perfectly mirror the image of God. In this perfect state, these first humans enjoyed a righteous relationship with their creator.

When the curtain rises on the second act of the divine drama, the fall of Adam and Eve is in view. In this act the devastating impact of sin is experienced. Because of Adam and Eve's willful rebellion, the once harmonious relationship between God and His human creation is broken. In fact, not only is the image of God marred by sin, relationships between human beings are distorted as well. Habermas and Issler describe this act as "Refracted Reflection." They liken the distorted image of God in fallen persons to the image one sees in an amusement park mirror. Although the image of God remains, the image is a flawed reflection of the nature and character of God. As such, our union with the perfect God is broken. Along with the warping effect of sin in our vertical relationship with God come other results as well. Guilt, fear, pain, discord, strife, death, satanic affliction, and even the cursed ground are among products of the refraction of sin.

The final act Habermas and Issler name "Rejuvenated Reflection." This act is subdivided into three scenes. The first scene of this act, "Initial Reconciliation," involves the believer coming to right relationship with God through personally trusting in Christ as the sacrificial offering to make peace with God. The second scene, "Daily Reconciliation," describes the process of becoming like Christ in the pilgrimage of life. The last scene of this third act is called "Ultimate Reconciliation" and refers to the coming day when all that we are declared to be in Christ positionally is achieved experientially. Ultimate reconciliation will occur when Christians are presented to God "holy . . . without blemish and free from accusation" (Col. 1:22).

John F. Walvoord agrees that Christ's work of reconciliation is an appropriate overarching concept for the entire work of Christ in salvation. He writes, "Few doctrines are more important in a total theology than the doctrine of reconciliation."[5] Walvoord continues, "In the broadest sense, the work of reconciliation extends to the total work of

Figure 4

GOD'S PLAN FOR RECONCILIATION

The Storyline of the Bible

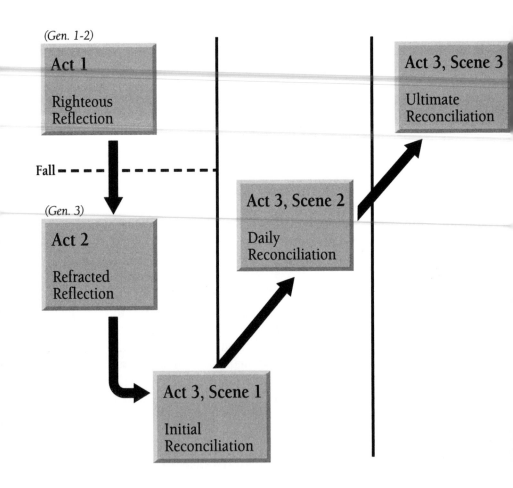

(Gen. 1-2)

Act 1

Righteous
Reflection

Fall

(Gen. 3)

Act 2

Refracted
Reflection

Act 3, Scene 1

Initial
Reconciliation

Act 3, Scene 2

Daily
Reconciliation

Act 3, Scene 3

Ultimate
Reconciliation

Birth   Salvation   Death and Resurrection   Eternit

God on behalf of the believer. . . . Reconciliation, then, deals with man's total need and total restoration."[6]

Vincent Taylor also prefers the concept of reconciliation as presented in the New Testament as the unifying theme of Scripture. The message of the Old Testament is one of atoning sacrifice. That concept is continued in the New Testament with the ultimate sacrifice of Christ, the perfect Lamb of God. Taylor holds that reconciliation is "the best New Testament word to describe the purpose of the Atonement."[7]

A. H. Strong includes the totality of God's salvation work on behalf of mankind in his use of the term *reconciliation*. Strong enfolds election, calling, union with Christ, regeneration, conversion, justification, sanctification, and perseverance into the doctrine of reconciliation.[8]

It seems, then, that the message of the Bible can be summarized in this one word—*reconciliation*. It is a term that bridges the Old Testament promise of atonement with the New Testament fulfillment in the person of Jesus Christ. It is a term that demands further definition and exploration.

Reconciliation: Peace with God

The English word *reconciliation* is derived from the Latin word *concillium*, meaning "a gathering" as a noun or "to unite together" in its verbal form. We get our English words *council* and *conciliatory* from the same Latin term. Reconciliation is the word used by translators of the Bible in five New Testament occurrences of the Greek word *Katallosso* (Rom. 5:10; 1 Cor. 7:11; 2 Cor. 5:18, 19, 20). In the noun form (*katallage*) it is used four times (Rom. 5:11; 11:15; 2 Cor. 5:18–19). Another form of the verb (*apokatallasso*) occurs three times in two passages (Eph. 2:16; Col. 1:20–22) and is translated with some form of "to be reconciled."

The Greek word carries a far deeper meaning than does the English word. The Greek verb means "to exchange one thing for another."[9] The exchange results in peace and harmony between estranged parties. In the case of biblical reconciliation, Jesus Christ is the substitutionary sacrifice exchanged for the sin of Adam. In Christ, God makes provision for all people, but His provision becomes effective only for those who believe (2 Cor. 5:19–20).

Reconciliation: Plan of God

No event in all of recorded history compares to the death, burial, and resurrection of Jesus Christ. Through this act of God, atonement is made, putting the sin of all human beings who choose to believe out of God's sight. It is through this act of atonement that God and mankind are reconciled.

Atonement means "to cover." It is a word etymologically derived from the three syllables "at-one-ment," meaning "to make one" or "to reconcile."[10] This is God's plan for men and women, that each be personally reconciled to God through the atoning work of Christ. This is the message that links the Bible from cover to cover. It is a message promised in the Old Testament and fulfilled in the New Testament. Three key New Testament passages present reconciliation as the plan of God for history.

Romans 5:6–11. Paul points out the utter need that all persons, men and women, have for a reconciled relationship with God through Christ. He writes,

> You see, at just the right time, when we were still powerless, Christ died for the ungodly. Very rarely will anyone die for a righteous man, though for a good man someone might possibly dare to die. But God demonstrates his own love for us in this: While we were still sinners, Christ died for us. Since we have now been justified by his blood, how much more shall we be saved from God's wrath through him! For if, when we were God's enemies, we were reconciled to him through the death of his Son, how much more, having been reconciled, shall we be saved through his life! Not only is this so, but we also rejoice in God through our Lord Jesus Christ, through whom we have now received reconciliation. (Rom. 5:6–11)

What is Paul saying about our need for the atoning sacrifice of Christ? First, we learn that the sacrifice of Christ occurred "at just the right time" (6), indicating that this was indeed God's plan all along. Second, he makes clear that we lacked the strength necessary to reconcile ourselves to God by saying that it was God who acted "when we were still powerless" (6). Third, we discover that reconciliation is not the result of our character or actions, for "Christ died for the ungodly" (6) and that it was "while we were still sinners, Christ died for us" (8). Fourth, we find that we were, in fact, "God's enemies" (10). The indictment is clear in Romans 5. We cannot reconcile ourselves to God. The conclusion is then made plain. "We were reconciled to him through the death of his Son. . . . Not only is this so, but we also rejoice in God through our Lord Jesus Christ, through whom we have now received reconciliation" (10, 11).

Ephesians 2:15–16. In Romans 5 we learned of our need for reconciliation. In Ephesians 2:15–16 we find that the results of reconciliation extend beyond our relationship with God to relationships between people groups. Through the reconciliation accomplished by the atoning sacrifice of Christ, a united body of Christ is established, and that is the church.

His purpose was to create in himself one new man out of the two, thus making peace, and in this one body to reconcile both of them to God through the cross, by which he put to death their hostility. (Eph. 2:15-16)

Colossians 1:19-22. This passage expands the extent of reconciliation still further as it indicates that reconciliation has some form of universal result. Here Paul writes of God's plan to reconcile all things to Himself.

For God was pleased to have all his fullness dwell in him, and through him to reconcile to himself all things, whether things on earth or things in heaven, by making peace through his blood, shed on the cross. Once you were alienated from God and were enemies in your minds because of your evil behavior. But now he has reconciled you by Christ's physical body through death to present you holy in his sight, without blemish and free from accusation. (Col. 1:19-22)

Through the act of reconciliation, God makes universal provision for sin and makes possible the reconciliation of any and all individuals who believe (Col. 1:3-6; 2:6). Clearly, reconciliation is intended for all but is limited in its application to those who believe.

Reconciliation: Purpose of Ministry

We have learned that the message of the Bible is one of reconciliation. We discovered that reconciliation is something we could not accomplish ourselves. It is a work of God whereby He makes peace between Himself and His creation based upon the atoning sacrifice of Christ. Further, we discerned that the provision of peace with God, that is, reconciliation, is applied to those who believe. We now turn our attention to the creative Bible teacher's purpose in ministry.

What motivation can drive and sustain creative Bible teachers in their ministry of the Word? Is it that they are well paid? Hardly! Most who teach the Bible are volunteers. Is it the recognition they receive for their efforts? For many, such recognition is occasional at best and nonexistent at worst. Is it the sense of obligation or duty? These have some motivational value to be sure, but they fall short in the long haul. What, then, motivates and sustains creative Bible teachers? It is the awareness that they are actually instruments in the hands of God being used to achieve His work of reconciliation in this world. That is Paul's perspective when he recaps the ministry of reconciliation in 2 Corinthians 5. Here we read,

Therefore, if anyone is in Christ, he is a new creation; the old has gone, the new has come! All this is from God, who reconciled us to himself through Christ and gave us the ministry of reconciliation: that God was reconciling the world to himself in Christ, not counting men's sins against them. And he has committed to us the message of reconciliation. We are therefore Christ's ambassadors, as though God were making his appeal through us. We implore you on Christ's behalf: Be reconciled to God. God made him who had no sin to be sin for us, so that in him we might become the righteousness of God. (2 Cor. 5:17–21)

Habermas and Issler describe this passage as the "Magna Charta for all believers, our authority, directive, and liberation."[11] Why do they offer such a towering analysis of this passage? Because in this passage Paul summarizes the atoning work of Christ, the life changing impact of that work for those who believe, and the believer's role in furthering the work of reconciliation in the world. Four specific points made in the passage by the apostle are worth noting here.

Metamorphosis of reconciliation. Paul begins with the end. That is to say, he begins with the results of reconciliation in the life of the believer. He declares all reconciled believers to be "new creations" (17). Habermas and Issler call this "the metamorphosis of reconciliation."[12] Those who are reconciled to God through Christ are changed or transformed. But what actually changes when one comes into fellowship with God? Wouldn't it be nice if when we became Christians our IQ went up twenty points or we could instantly play the piano like a concert virtuoso? Imagine if every negative aspect of our personality instantly vanished or every one of our undesirable habits was vanquished. Even if we just lost thirty pounds the transformation would be impressive! But it seems that the "new creation" spoken of by Paul must be describing something other than outward aspects of a person. Paul is referring instead to our new standing before God. No longer are we dead in our sins and separated from God. Now we are alive in Christ and seen as righteous before God because of the atoning sacrifice of Christ (21).

Ministry of reconciliation. Paul makes a second essential point in this segment when he refers to the "ministry of reconciliation." He tells his readers that "God . . . reconciled us to himself through Christ and gave us the ministry of reconciliation" (18) and "has committed to us the message of reconciliation" (19). Paul's emphasis is on our role in carrying out God's plan. The amazing fact is that God has chosen to use His children to carry out His work. He did not have to do this, but this is His plan. We are His instruments in this great work. As a teacher of the Bible, you possess a ministry and a message given by God. Your efforts to teach the truth of God's Word are no small undertaking. You are an agent of reconciliation. What a calling! What a privilege! Now there is a reason to teach the Scriptures this week.

Messengers of reconciliation. Paul's third point takes us a step further. He refers to himself and his co-laborers in the gospel as "Christ's ambassadors" (20). Many read these words through our modern understanding of the role of an ambassador. They picture the ambassador simply as a national representative bringing goodwill between countries. But that is not the concept Paul has in mind. In Rome, an ambassador had a far different function. Ambassadors were messengers sent from an overpowering army to one that was about to be destroyed. As was military custom, the messengers brought terms of surrender and, thus, peace to the army that was about to be overwhelmed. It was a final offer before utter devastation. That is what is in view here.

It is something like an incident, under the Clinton administration, that involved an impending invasion of Haiti. In October 1994, retired general Colin Powell served as an eleventh hour envoy to the Haitian dictator. Powell's message was one of impending destruction. He informed the dictator that if he did not agree to the United States' terms of peace, an invasion would immediately take place. As a matter of fact, the invasion force was in place and, at the word of the president, utter destruction was only minutes away. This is the nature of the ambassador spoken of in 2 Corinthians 5. We are messengers with a message of good and bad news. The bad news is that destruction is imminent. The good news is that God has provided terms of peace. But the outcome is certain! If we do not tell the message of reconciliation, people will remain lost and will face a terrible future. Paul says it is "as though God were making his appeal through us" (20).

Means of reconciliation. Paul's fourth point focuses on how reconciliation was accomplished. Paul writes, "God made him who had no sin to be sin for us, so that in him we might become the righteousness of God" (21). This is the exchange that reconciled us to God. By the atoning sacrifice of Christ, our sin was placed upon Christ while His righteousness was imputed to us. Reconciliation, then, is the New Testament message of atonement.

How can creative Bible teachers serve Jesus Christ as His educational ambassadors? Since reconciliation is the key to the Scripture, the purpose of educational ministry from a Christian perspective is to bring the learner into a reconciled relationship with God through Jesus Christ and to enable the learner to order all of life and learning around that relationship.

THE ROLE OF THE BIBLE

What role does the Bible play in the ministry of reconciliation? To answer this question, we must consider three basic functions of the Bible.

The Bible Enlightens

Consistent with the revelatory nature of the Bible, one of the basic functions of the Bible is enlightenment. The Bible makes truth known to the reader that can be discovered from no other source. That fact allows the reader to order life in a meaningful way. The psalmist puts it in these words in Psalm 19:7–11:

> 7The law of the Lord is perfect, reviving the soul. The statutes of the Lord are trustworthy, making wise the simple. 8The precepts of the Lord are right, giving joy to the heart. The commands of the Lord are radiant, giving light to the eyes. 9The fear of the Lord is pure, enduring forever. The ordinances of the Lord are sure and altogether righteous. 10They are more precious than gold, than much pure gold; they are sweeter than honey, than honey from the comb. 11By them is your servant warned; in keeping them there is great reward.

God's word gives "light to the eyes" (8). Because of its ability to guide, give wisdom, provide understanding, and warn, the Bible has a priceless quality about it. It is only in the pages of the Bible that one can find the true purpose of life and the plan of God by which that purpose can be achieved. The Bible reveals the plan that leads to reconciliation. It makes known the mind and character of God. By reading it and heeding it, one indeed finds "great reward" (11). In a similar vein, the psalmist proclaims, "Your word is a lamp to my feet and a light for my path" (Ps. 119:105).

The Bible Exposes

Enlightenment has both a positive and a negative side to it. The Word of God sheds light into the dark recesses of our understanding, making wise the simple. That is positive. But it also sheds its light into the dark corners, the hidden places of our heart. It exposes as well as enlightens, and that can be negative, depending on how we choose to respond to its probing and penetrating power.

A young pastor of a church located in the mountains of Colorado found that the parsonage needed quite a bit of regular maintenance. The most recurring problem was an unreliable water system. His home was built over an old mine. Water was pumped from the mine to a holding tank under the living room floor to be used for daily needs. On more than one occasion the pastor had to climb down into the cellar, a four-foot deep, dirt-floored crawl space, in order to repair the pump. Each time the breakdown occurred, the pastor ventured into the dark crawl space with flashlight and tools in hand, but he never relished the task. Beyond the fact that the faulty pump was an annoyance, the pastor had a phobia about spiders, and the cellar was just the place to find these little creatures.

One day when the pump broke down for what was probably the sixth time, the pastor had an idea. He decided that it would be wise to install an electric light in the cellar to make his repair task a bit easier. He reasoned that if he had to do this repair every few weeks, he might as well have some light to work by. So, taking his flashlight, he shone the light around the cellar in search of an appropriate place to hang the light fixture. As he moved the beam, a clump of spider webs caught his eye. Something was hanging from the ceiling, almost totally encased in the webs. Slowly he pushed away the webs uncovering what they hid—a light bulb! He pulled the string and the entire cellar was illuminated. He was unnerved to discover that all around him were spiders. Well, this pastor did what any wise person in such a situation would do: He extinguished the light, finished his task, and got out of that cellar.

As the light illuminated the cellar of the pastor's house, exposing the webs and spiders, so too does the light of Scripture expose the webs and spiders in the cellar of our lives. And often, as the pastor did, we simply choose to extinguish the light rather than clean the cellar. One of the functions of the Bible is to be an exposing light in our lives. The Bible is a unique book in that it can shine into the very depths of the heart.

The author of Hebrews recognized this quality about the Scriptures. He used the metaphor of a two-edged sword to describe its penetrating and exposing nature.

> For the word of God is living and active. Sharper than any double-edged sword, it penetrates even to dividing soul and spirit, joints and marrow; it judges the thoughts and attitudes of the heart. Nothing in all creation is hidden from God's sight. Everything is uncovered and laid bare before the eyes of him to whom we must give account. (Heb. 4:12–13)

One cannot hide from the probing Word of God. God uses it like a surgical instrument to reveal and expose the inner motives and attitudes we possess. Everything about us is in view before Him. The Scripture has a way of powerfully probing into our lives, not like a dead book of history, but as a living, active tool in the hand of God.

The Bible Equips

God's ultimate goal in giving us biblical revelation is not punitive. He desires that His Word equip us for His service. Its message brings us reconciliation through the work of Christ. Its probing exposes our need for a reconciled relationship with Him. And then His Word gives us the tools we need to actually experience that reconciled relationship on a daily basis. This is what Paul told Timothy about the role of the Bible: "All Scripture is God-breathed and is useful for teaching, rebuking, correcting and training in righteousness, so that the man of God may be thoroughly equipped for every good work" (2 Tim. 3:16–17).

Paul used four words to delineate the role of the Scriptures in equipping believers. First he used the word *teaching*. This word has the idea of guidance or instruction. It suggests that the Bible serves to give direction to believers in the path they are to follow. Second, he used the word *rebuking*. Rebuking involves pointing out one's error. In other words, God uses the Bible not only to identify the correct path we should walk, but to point out when we are not on that path. Next he uses the term *correcting*. Correcting involves the concept of returning to the path. God uses His Word to provide the information and assistance we need to get back on the path once we stray. Finally, Paul says the Bible is useful for training. *Training* is a word used primarily for nurturing and instructing children. It carries the idea of helping one stay on track. It can include the concept of discipline and the setting of limits.

Here, then, is the message and role of the Bible. First, the Bible presents the message of reconciliation thematically from cover to cover. It specifically lays out that message in the New Testament as a fulfillment of the promises of the Old Testament. Second, it provides the means by which the believer can experience daily the reconciled relationship that belongs to the Christian positionally. The Bible is both the story of reconciliation and the tool for experiencing the story firsthand.

Remember Jim, the Bible study teacher who was asked to give the message and reliability of the Bible at the Chicago Board of Trade? Well, Jim led his two sessions and several more that followed because of the group's response. About thirty people came regularly to the Bible studies. The most rewarding of all the sessions Jim taught was the one on the theme of the Bible—the one he was most concerned about. At that session, one person, Mike, came up afterward to comment: "Now the Bible finally makes sense to me. I don't mean I understand it all, but that theme you mentioned, the idea of reconciliation, makes sense! That's the real problem in the world today. There's a barrier between God and people. That's why there are so many problems between people. Now I understand why Jesus came." Mike was right. In the moments that followed Jim had an opportunity to explain the gospel to Mike. That day Mike became reconciled to God through the work of His Savior, Jesus Christ.

NOTES

1. John R. W. Stott, *Understanding the Bible* (Grand Rapids: Zondervan, 1976), 60.
2. Ibid.
3. Ronald Habermas and Klaus Issler, *Teaching for Reconciliation* (Grand Rapids: Baker, 1992), 33–46.
4. Ibid., 38–41.
5. John F. Walvoord, *Jesus Christ Our Lord* (Chicago: Moody, 1969), 177.
6. Ibid., 89.
7. Vincent Taylor, *The Atonement in New Testament Teaching* (London: Epworth, 1941), 191.
8. A. H. Strong, *Systematic Theology* (New York: Armstrong, 1902), 886.
9. William Barclay, *New Testament Words* (Philadelphia: Westminster Press, 1964), 165.
10. Walvoord, *Jesus Christ Our Lord*, 154.
11. Habermas and Issler, *Teaching for Reconciliation*, 36.
12. Ibid.

Chapter Four

RIGHTLY DIVIDED:
THE STUDY OF THE BIBLE

Composed of 73,000 tons of steel, its structural frame would make more than 50,000 automobiles. It contains more than 1,500 miles of electrical wiring and 250 miles of pipes. It has 16,000 panes of bronze tinted glass, 640,000 square feet in all. It towers some 1,468 feet into the air, or 110 stories. It has 4.4 million square feet of floor space, equal to 101 acres or 16 Chicago city blocks. It uses 625,000 kilowatt hours of electricity in just one day, equivalent to a community of 2,500 persons. Its total weight is 445 million pounds.

We are describing the United States' tallest building, Chicago's Sears Tower. But, as impressive as its superstructure appears, the unseen aspects of the Sears Tower are the most essential. A building like the Sears Tower depends on a strong foundation. Designed to withstand the winds of Chicago, the Sears Tower is built on caissons anchored in bedrock. Each caisson is 65 feet long and has a permanent steel shell liner. All of the caissons are tied together by a 54-inch deep concrete mat that covers the floor area of the Sears Tower basement. Built on two million cubic feet of concrete foundation, the concrete in the Sears Tower's foundation walls could pave an eight lane expressway for four miles.

Why all this data on a skyscraper? Because we know that a solid foundation is essential to a strong, secure, and stable building; and, in a similar way, Bible study serves as the secure foundation to creative Bible teaching. What your students see when you teach is the superstructure of the class lesson. What they do not see is the foundation—your diligent study of the Word of God. Bible teaching that affects people's lives begins with effective study of the Bible.

THE BASIS OF AUTHORITY IN TEACHING

Paul told Timothy, "Do your best to present yourself to God as one approved, a workman who does not need to be ashamed and who correctly handles the word of truth" (2 Tim. 2:15). Correctly handling the Word of Truth is an essential issue for the creative Bible teacher. Creative Bible teachers have a high regard for the Scriptures, and they see their ministry as a sacred trust. They are servants of God used to communicate His Word in a timely and relevant manner. As such, they desire to be faithful to its teaching in their teaching.

John H. Walton, Laurie Bailey, and Craig Williford warn their readers of "an authority crisis" in Bible teaching and in Bible-based curriculum. By this they mean that curriculum producers and Bible teachers often use the Bible to teach to their own developmental and behavioral objectives rather than actually teaching what the Bible teaches. They are concerned that the Bible is merely being used as a jumping-off point for teaching. Much of Bible teaching simply uses the Bible to teach ideas that are only loosely related to the teaching of Scripture. The result, they contend, is teaching marked only by human authority, teaching unable to change lives by the power of the Word.

> If the Bible is used only as a jump-off point for one's own objectives, the Bible's authority is being bypassed, because if a passage is not being used to teach what the Bible is teaching, the teacher stands only in his/her own authority. Too much of today's curriculum teaches only with human authority rather than with the authority of God. This then is the authority crisis in curriculum.[1]

Walton, Bailey, and Williford argue that authority in Bible teaching can only come from the authority of Scripture, and that authority is found in teaching what the authors of the Bible intend to teach. A second quote illustrates this point.

> It is only the things that Scripture intends to teach that carry the authority of the text. For example, it is very possible to learn much about leadership from a study of Nehemiah. In the end, however, there is no indication that the author of Nehemiah was preserving or presenting his material so that readers could be instructed in leadership. That being the case, when leadership is taught from the book and life of Nehemiah, the authority of Scripture is not being tapped. . . . If someone desires to claim biblical authority for what he/she teaches, Scripture must be used only and always to teach what it intends to teach.[2]

Walton, Bailey, and Williford's point is an important one. But how can teachers be certain they are teaching what the author intended? The answer to that question is found in the process of Bible study. Through careful exegesis (reading the meaning out of the passage) using some foundational rules of hermeneutics (the rules of Bible interpretation), the student and teacher of the Bible can indeed come to an understanding of the biblical author's central principle. That principle can then be applied in appropriate ways today. The central principle of the passage or, as Haddon Robinson terms it, the big idea,[3] serves as the bridge principle from the "then and there" world of the Bible to the "here and now" world of today.

We have found the inductive method of Bible study to be the most reliable means of identifying the bridge principle or central idea of the passage. By the use of the inductive approach, the Bible student allows the authors of Scripture (both human and divine) to communicate the intended message.

THE CREATIVE BIBLE TEACHER'S INDUCTIVE STUDY METHOD

The word "inductive" means to go from specific details to a general principle. We use inductive reasoning in scientific and mathematical study to develop laws and theories from a collection of data. For example, one could study several right triangles (triangles that have one angle equal to 90 degrees) and eventually conclude that all right triangles have a common property. You might state your finding in the formula $A^2 + B^2 = C^2$ or by stating that "the sum of the square of the sides of a right triangle is equal to the square of the hypotenuse of the triangle." What you would have just stated is known as the Pythagorean theorem. Deductive reasoning reverses the process. Here, one begins with a general principle and moves to specific application of that principle. For example, one could begin with the Pythagorean theorem. Using the theorem of right triangles, one could determine the diagonal dimension of a rectangular room by only knowing the length and width of the room.

For the creative Bible teacher, biblical study should begin with inductive study. Inductive Bible study is a study method that seeks to be objective and impartial in its approach to the text of the Scriptures. Typically, the inductive method demands that students of the Bible follow three steps in the study process—observation, interpretation, and application. For those who plan to teach the Bible as a result of their study, we have expanded the inductive process to include two more essential steps that make the link to teaching more direct. One of these we term "generalization." The other we call "implementation" (see Figure 5).

Figure 5

THE CREATIVE BIBLE TEACHER'S INDUCTIVE STUDY METHOD

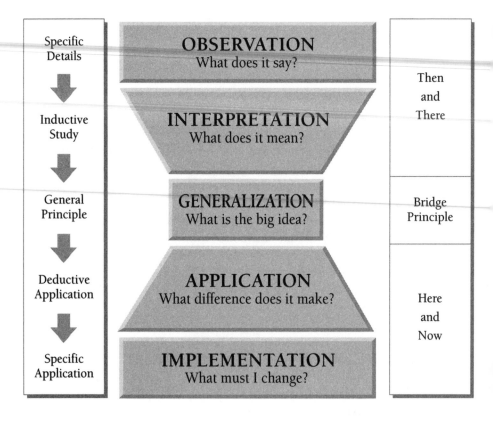

Figure 5 depicts the inductive method that creative Bible teachers will want to employ in their preparation to teach. This model involves five stages in the process of study. These stages, in order, are observation, interpretation, generalization, application, and implementation. Each stage focuses on a specific overarching question. The first two stages in the process deal with the biblical world, that is, the "then and there." The third stage serves as the bridge between worlds. The fourth and fifth stages deal with our world today, or the "here and now." You will note that the model progresses from specific details to general principles in stages one through three. This is where inductive logic is employed. It then moves from general principle to specific application using deductive logic. The hourglass shape of the diagram represents a progression in time from the world of the Bible to our modern world. This method of study is not the only approach a creative Bible teacher can use, but it is well suited to lesson preparation.

Observation: What Does It Say?

The observation stage in the study process takes us back to the biblical world—the "then and there" side of Bible study. The goal of this stage is simply to identify what the author actually said to the original recipients of the text. Remember, the Bible was written in a historic time frame to real people. In a sense, we are reading someone else's mail. It is important to understand what was happening when the mail was originally sent to really grasp the message of the letter. In other words, to understand the message of the text, we must understand the world and the events that surround the text then and there so that we do not misapply the text here and now.

The overarching question of the observation stage is, "What does it say?" The observation stage requires careful attention to the specific details of the passage. This is most effectively accomplished through the use of some basic questions. By asking a consistent list of study questions, the student will begin to gain skill in probing the depths of the biblical text. We would suggest three lines of questioning.

Setting Questions
1. Who is the author or speaker?
2. Why was this book written? What was the occasion of the book?
3. What historic events surround this book?
4. Where was it written? Who were the original recipients?

Context Questions
1. What literary form is being employed in this passage?

2. What is the overall message of this book, and how does this passage fit into that message?

3. What precedes this passage? What follows?

Structural Questions

1. Are there any repeated words? Repeated phrases?
2. Does the author make any comparisons? Draw any contrasts?
3. Does the author raise any questions? Provide any answers?
4. Does the author point out any cause and effect relationships?
5. Is there any progression to the passage? In time? Action? Geography?
6. Does the passage have a climax?
7. Does the author use any figures of speech?
8. Is there a pivotal statement or word?
9. What linking words are used? What ideas do they link?
10. What verbs are used to describe action in the passage?

By this point, some structure or flow to the passage will probably become apparent. You may want to note any structure or logical sequence of thoughts you believe the author was using when he wrote the passage. Your observation may serve as a clue that will help you later in the interpretation and generalization stages. We will actually try the observation process together as we look at a passage in the next chapter. Also, note that Table 1 at the end of this chapter recommends several helpful Bible study tools.

Interpretation: What Does It Mean?

At this point you are ready to draw some interpretive conclusions about what you have been studying. The overarching question in this stage of inductive Bible study is, "What does it mean?" Although the Scripture may have many different applications it can only have one correct interpretation. The correct interpretation is the one that the author intended the reader to come to understand. The task of the Bible student is to discover the original intended meaning. Despite the temptation to jump from observation to application, care must be taken to hear the Word of God as the original readers or hearers did and to find out what the Spirit of God was teaching them.

You do not need a seminary or Bible college degree to discover the intended meaning of the Scriptures. Often it is stated directly by the author or it can be discerned from the structure and emphasis of the passage. The Bible is written so that ordinary people can read and comprehend it. Although there are debated passages and some difficult ones, most of the Scripture is easily understood when its literary form and general theme is known.

A rather remarkable incident happened in the book of Acts. It seems that an Ethiopian official in charge of the queen of Ethiopia's treasury was on his way home from worshiping in Jerusalem. Apparently he had stopped his chariot to rest and was reading from the book of Isaiah. Specifically, he was reading the fifty-third chapter of Isaiah about the suffering and death of the Messiah. The Holy Spirit led Philip to ask the man, "Do you understand what you are reading?" (Acts 8:30). This question is the basic interpretive question of biblical study. Three basic rules of biblical interpretation will help answer that question in the affirmative.

Rule # 1—Continuity of the Message. This rule reminds us that the Bible has a unity to it and that we must use the larger teaching of the Scriptures on a subject to help understand the meaning of a particular passage. This is known as the law of non-contradiction. This law of Bible study says that we should use Scripture to interpret Scripture. Although the Bible has a variety of human authors, it has one divine author, the Holy Spirit. Because the Bible is inspired by God, it speaks a consistent message. When dealing with two passages on a subject, the clearer passage should help interpret the less specific passage. Because biblical revelation comes in a progressive and widening manner, the reader should see if other passages, especially New Testament passages, expand the teaching of the one under study. For example, the book of Hebrews gives us insight into the meaning of the sacrificial system of the Old Testament. At the same time, the Old Testament passages describing priesthood and temple practices provide the context for understanding the imagery of Hebrews. To interpret either segment of Scripture, some awareness of the other is important.

Rule #2—Context of the Material. It has been said that "a text without a context is just a pretext." There is a great deal of truth to that statement. One of the dangers that Bible students must avoid in the interpretation of the Bible is "Scripture twisting." Scripture twisting is taking a text out of its context in order to make it say something we want it to say. One sad example of this problem is found in a mission agency that used a verse from Matthew as its theme verse. On a plaque hung prominently above the door of the organization was this quote of Scripture: "All of these things I will give to you if you fall down and worship me" (Matt. 4:9). Although the passage has an evangelistic ring to it we had better check the context. This is a quote not from God, but from Satan. The context is the temptation of Christ. Clearly, this extreme example makes the point that context is everything in the task of interpretation of Scripture.

When applying the rule of context it is important to remember that not only is the immediate context important, that is, the paragraphs before and after the text, but the historic and cultural context must also be considered. For example, again in Hebrews we read, "Let us not give up meeting together, as some are in the habit of doing, but let us encourage one another—and all the more as you see the Day approaching" (Heb. 10:25). Many a preacher has used this verse to encourage a congregation to be in the morning service at church on Sunday rather than on the golf course. Although it is not good for anyone to become habitually absent from the Sunday service, the passage is about a persecuted people. The author of Hebrews is warning them concerning the temptation they feel to avoid contact with other believers in order to avoid persecution. His point is that they need the encouragement such contact provides despite the inherent risk. In this case, historic context helps fill in the picture for the reader.

Rule #3—Customary Meaning. Probably most significant of all of the rules for interpreting the Bible is what has become known as literal interpretation. Many confuse and misunderstand literal interpretation to mean interpretation of every word in an absolute sense without allowance for figures of speech or literary genres. In fact, this is not what conservative Bible scholars mean by literal interpretation. Literal interpretation simply means that we interpret the Bible as one interprets any other form of literature, giving it its natural, normal, and customary meaning. We do not seek to read special hidden meanings into the text or to "demythologize" the accounts of Scripture because of a bias against the authority and historicity of the Bible. Instead, we regard the statements of Scripture as revealed truth written in human words by inspiration of the Spirit of God.

The conservative holds that the key to understanding the meaning of the text is found in the normal approach to language. In this way we take the Bible literally. This does not mean, of course, that we fail to recognize poetic expression like that found in Habakkuk 3:10, which reads, "the mountains saw you and writhed. Torrents of water swept by; the deep roared and lifted its waves on high." Nor do we fail to understand that the Bible contains symbolism such as one would find in statements like "The Lord is my shepherd, I shall not be in want" (Ps. 23:1). What it does mean is that when the Bible makes a statement such as "Therefore the Lord himself will give you a sign: The virgin will be with child and will give birth to a son, and will call him Immanuel" (Isa. 7:14), we understand the statement in its normal linguistic sense. A virgin will have a son. This, of course, is biologically impossible. And so the reader is expected to believe that God accomplished a biological impossibility. We do not reject the option of the miraculous and seek some other explanation or meaning for the passage. In fact, those who practice the rule of customary meaning would suggest that it is the very idea of the miraculous nature of the conception of Jesus Christ that is the point in this passage.

The rule of customary meaning simply states that the very words of the Bible are to be taken for what they communicate. We follow a simple principle: When the natural, normal sense of the Scripture makes sense, seek no other sense. By this we do not exclude cultural or historical factors in interpretation. We mean that the Bible is not a book of hidden ideas demanding that the reader reinterpret the words to discover these religious thoughts. The meaning of Scripture is plain in its normal, literal sense.

Generalization: What Is the Big Idea?

Bible teachers have a significant and sometimes challenging task. They must bridge a gap between the world of the Bible and that of modern living. Consider the fact that teachers are at best third parties communicating to those even further removed from the original writer and recipient. They face a gap of culture, history, and language. How can they hope to communicate the truth of Scripture to their students in a way that is relevant and life changing? The key is the stage of study we call "generalization."

The terms might be slightly different—big idea, proposition, central theme, thesis statement, or central principle—but the concept is the same. Effective communication depends upon a single unifying principle or point. Whether we are considering a term paper, a speech, a sermon, or the Word of God, it is essential to identify the author's thematic focus. This is the goal of the generalization stage. At this point in the process of inductive study, the Bible student formulates a single sentence statement of the main point of the text. Until that is accomplished, the teacher is not ready to move on in lesson preparation.

Haddon W. Robinson has provided a great aid to the Bible teacher in regards to identifying and formulating the "big idea." In his book entitled *Expository Preaching,* he suggests that the main idea of a passage be formulated by asking and answering two questions of the text. The first question is, "What is the author talking about?" The answer to this question he calls the "subject" of the passage. The second question is, "What is the author saying about what he is talking about?" This he terms the complement. By answering both questions, the Bible student can begin to formulate a single sentence that entails the major idea or principle being taught in the passage. Robinson terms this idea the "exegetical idea" because it is the idea presented by the biblical author and it is derived from the text exegetically, that is, through a careful inductive approach to study.[4] He explains that this is a mandatory step in understanding and communicating the Word of God as a creative Bible teacher.

> Since each paragraph, section, or subsection of Scripture contains an idea, an exegete does not understand a passage until he can state its subject and complement exactly. While other questions emerge in the struggle to understand the meaning of the biblical writer, the two—What is the author talking about? and What is he saying about what he is talking about?—are fundamental.[5]

At this point an example might help. Let's take John 15:1–8 as a model for formulating the exegetical idea or central principle of the passage.

> I am the true vine, and my Father is the gardener. He cuts off every branch in me that bears no fruit, while every branch that does bear fruit he prunes so that it will be even more fruitful. You are already clean because of the word I have spoken to you. Remain in me, and I will remain in you. No branch can bear fruit by itself; it must remain in the vine. Neither can you bear fruit unless you remain in me. I am the vine; you are the branches. If a man remains in me and I in him, he will bear much fruit; apart from me you can do nothing. If anyone does not remain in me, he is like a branch that is thrown away and withers; such branches are picked up, thrown into the fire and burned. If you remain in me and my words remain in you, ask whatever you wish, and it will be given you. This is to my Father's glory, that you bear much fruit, showing yourselves to be my disciples. (John 15:1–8)

What is the author talking about? The passage presents an analogy. Luke records the words of Jesus in which Jesus Himself draws the analogy between His relationship with His disciples and the relationship between a vine and its branches. *What is He saying about what He is talking about?* He makes the point that as branches are dependent on the vine for their productivity, so too are Christ's followers dependent upon Him. If we were to state the principle of the passage that is transferable to all believers we might say, "Just as each branch must remain connected to the vine to produce fruit, so too must Christ's disciples remain connected to Christ and His words to be productive spiritually." The principle or exegetical idea that comes from the passage and that can be transmitted from culture to culture is clear: Apart from Christ, we cannot be spiritually productive.

Application: What Difference Does It Make?

In the application stage, the Bible student seeks meaningful connections between the passage and contemporary living. In order to achieve this goal, the student of the Bible must follow a few basic guidelines.

Interpretation always precedes application. Application should be rooted in the central principle taught in the text. In fact, application of a passage cannot and should not be made apart from careful interpretation of the passage. The question, "What difference does it make?" is a legitimate one, but we must exercise care here that we do not make a passage say what it does not say. Walton, Bailey, and Williford are again perceptive in their comments regarding application. "The teacher's task in application is to recognize and communicate Scripture's relevance, rather than to make it relevant."[6] Once we understand the principle taught in the passage, we can more easily apply the principle in a way consistent with the Word of God.

Application focuses on biblical answers to common issues. We tend to think of people in Bible times as far different from ourselves. The fact of the matter is that people have always laughed and cried for many of the same reasons. People in all periods of human history have lost loved ones, seen personal calamity, experienced hurt and broken relationships, and sought meaning in life. We deal with the same issues, emotions, questions, and concerns. Human needs are similar across time, geography, and culture. This commonality in our lives gives the Bible its timeless quality in application.

The Bible was written in concrete, rather than abstract, words. Given that fact, the student of the Bible should look for biblical perspectives that give insight to current matters. Consider application points that center around such matters as attitudes, conduct, character, and knowledge of God. Consider also the contexts of human relationships when applying biblical principles—contexts like one's marriage, the family, employment, school, social life, recreation, the church, the community, and the nation. Each of these provides fertile ground for applying biblical answers to life's pressing issues.

The Bible must be applied as God intended. Do you remember what Paul said was the reason God gave Scripture in the first place? "All Scripture is God-breathed and is useful for teaching, rebuking, correcting and training in righteousness, so that the man of God may be thoroughly equipped for every good work" (2 Tim. 3:16–17). Notice the four-fold use of Scripture proposed here. For teaching, for rebuke, for correcting, and for training in righteousness—all of these are points of application. We can ask,

Is there a teaching here to be learned and followed?
Does this passage communicate a rebuke to be heard and heeded?
Is there a correction to be noted?
In what way does this passage train us to be righteous?

Each of these questions can help bring the application of Scripture into a clearer light. Haddon Robinson suggests four additional application questions.

1. What was the communication setting in which God's Word first came? What traits do modern men and women share in common with that original audience? . . . 2. How can we identify with Biblical men and women as they heard God's Word and responded—or failed to respond—in their situation? . . . 3. What further insights have we acquired about God's dealings with His people through additional revelation? . . . 4. When I understand an eternal truth or guiding principle, what specific, practical applications does this have for me and my congregation?[7]

We move now to the final stage in inductive Bible study—implementation.

Implementation: What Must I Change?

The implementation stage of study becomes highly individual and concrete. It is important that as readers of the Bible we do not merely approach the Word of God as information to be learned, but as life changing truth meant to transform us. James warns us,

Do not merely listen to the word, and so deceive yourselves. Do what it says. Anyone who listens to the word but does not do what it says is like a man who looks at his face in a mirror and, after looking at himself, goes away and immediately forgets what he looks like. But the man who looks intently into the perfect law that gives freedom, and continues to do this, not forgetting what he has heard, but doing it—he will be blessed in what he does. (James 1:22–25)

Ultimately, the blessing of reading and studying God's Word is found in living out God's Word. The Bible teaches us about God, and in that knowledge comes implications for our relationship with Him. We cannot study the God of the Bible through the pages of the Bible without response. We must ask ourselves how we need to change. Do we need to change a viewpoint? Maybe it is an attitude that needs adjustment. Are we to change a habit or behavior? Is there some new perspective, attitude, or behavior we should embrace?

The implementation stage of study requires us to take action. As teachers of the Bible we must live its message. We must allow it to change us as we call others to change. Teachers who do not personally apply what they teach lack credibility and can even risk developing the pharisaic, hypocritical attitude that Jesus condemned.

In his book *Taking the Guesswork Out of Applying the Bible*, Jack Kuhatschek says, "As we immerse ourselves in Scripture, our goal is to develop within ourselves the mind and heart of God. We want to be able to think and to respond to every situation the way God himself would."[8]

This, then, is the ultimate implication of Bible study for personal life—godliness.

In the next chapter we will briefly demonstrate how the creative Bible teacher's inductive method actually works. If you're ready to try your hand at Bible study, then let's embark on the first step of lesson preparation—studying the Bible.

NOTES

1. John H. Walton, Laurie Bailey, and Craig Williford, "Bible-Based Curricula and the Crisis of Scriptural Authority," *Christian Education Journal*, Volume XIII, Number 3, 85.
2. Ibid., 88.
3. Haddon W. Robinson, *Biblical Preaching* (Grand Rapids: Baker, 1980), 31–48.
4. Ibid., 79.
5. Ibid., 41.
6. Walton, Bailey, and Williford, "Bible-Based Curricula," 92.
7. Robinson, *Biblical Preaching*, 94–95.
8. Jack Kuhatschek, *Taking the Guesswork Out of Applying the Bible* (Downers Grove, Ill.: InterVarsity, 1990), 24.

Table 1

TOOLS OF BIBLE STUDY

Bible

Several different versions of the Bible are available for use in study. Three basic types of translation methods are used in producing the various versions that are in print. Literal translations attempt to translate as close to the original words and phrasing as possble (e.g., KJV, NASB). Free translations seek to translate ideas from the original and are less concerned about exact words (Living Bible, The Message). Free translations are also known as paraphrases. Dynamic translations attempt to translate words, phrases, and figures of speech in ways that are equivalent to the original language, updating style, grammar, and phraseology (NIV). You might want to read your passage in each type of version, but use a literal or dynamic translation for your actual study.

Bible Dictionary

Bible dictionaries are helpful in providing information about the book you are studying, the culture, the customs, and the geography.

Bible Atlas

A Bible atlas helps to put Bible events into a geographical and historical context. You can find the cities, mountains, rivers, and regions mentioned in the text. Additionally, you can trace Paul's missionary journeys or see changes in the borders of countries in different epochs.

Commentaries

Commentaries provide helpful information on difficult passages. They can also provide insight into the broader message of a book. Use commentaries to enrich your own study rather than replace it.

Concordance

A concordance is an index to Bible passages. By looking up a particular word or phrase, you can find the references where the phrase occurs in the Bible. This is helpful in finding a reference that you may have forgotten or in studying a specific topic.

Software

Several excellent computer programs exist to make your study of the Bible more complete and rapid. Computer software can provide a very fast and more complete means of searching the text in several translations at the same time. Additionally, complete study helps like Bible dictionaries, atlases, and commentaries are available. Another excellent help in Bible study is the Internet. Literally thousands of resources are on "the net" available free or at a small fee for your use. But be careful here. Just because information is on the Internet does not guarantee its truthfulness. For example, we ran a search on Hebrews 10:19-25 and found material from several cult groups. You'll probably want to stay with Christian publishers, churches, and organizations you know and trust. Like all sources of information, you must know the source's credibility on the subject.

Chapter Five

A SAMPLE BIBLE STUDY:
THE CREATIVE BIBLE TEACHER'S
INDUCTIVE METHOD

Imagine that you are taking a ground school course to learn how to fly. In the classroom, you learn the theory of flight. You learn of the forces of gravity, lift, thrust, and drag. You learn how to plot a course and how to use navigational radios. You learn how various maneuvers are to be performed. In essence, you learn what you need to know to fly. But a ground school course on flying isn't flying, is it? No, it is just theory. Until you actually climb into a plane, roll down the runway, pull back on the yoke, and are airborne, you have not applied your knowledge of flight. In a similar way, you now have a ground school knowledge of Bible study. It's time to take your first actual flight. In this chapter we will climb into the cockpit with you and serve as your in-flight instructors. Before you know it you will be soloing!

It's important that we move from the theoretical to the practical at this juncture. To this point we have reviewed the process of inductive Bible study and have provided some examples. But we need to work through a passage together. The passage we have selected is Hebrews 10:19–25. We will use this passage throughout this book to show you how to develop a lesson plan for creative Bible teaching. We will come back to it as our primary example. Let's begin our study by simply reading the passage.

HEBREWS 10:19–25

[19]Therefore, brothers, since we have confidence to enter the Most Holy

Place by the blood of Jesus, [20]by a new and living way opened for us through the curtain, that is, his body, [21]and since we have a great priest over the house of God, [22]let us draw near to God with a sincere heart in full assurance of faith, having our hearts sprinkled to cleanse us from a guilty conscience and having our bodies washed with pure water. [23]Let us hold unswervingly to the hope we profess, for he who promised is faithful. [24]And let us consider how we may spur one another on toward love and good deeds. [25]Let us not give up meeting together, as some are in the habit of doing, but let us encourage one another—and all the more as you see the Day approaching.

In chapter four we presented *The Creative Bible Teacher's Inductive Study Method*. This five-part inductive study method is again depicted in Figure 6. You will recall that our task is to draw out the "exegetical idea" or "central principle" and then apply that principle to Christian living today. By following each stage of the study process, you will develop a solid foundation for teaching Hebrews 10:19–25.

OBSERVATION: WHAT DOES IT SAY?

The first stage in using *the creative Bible teacher's inductive study method* (Figure 6) is *observation*. In this stage we will use the observational questions we referred to in the previous chapter in looking at our passage. The questions are grouped in three categories—setting questions, context questions, and structure questions. Let's take them, one question at a time, and see how each question helps us come to understand our text.

Setting Questions

1. *Who is the author or speaker?*
The writer of Hebrews is not stated in the book, although he was certainly known to his readers. It seems he elects not to divulge his name. Although it is not known who wrote the book many believe it reflects Pauline qualities. The book exhibits the emphases of Paul's theology and was clearly influenced by Paul, if not written by him. Some have suggested that an associate of Paul, such as Barnabas, Silas, Luke, or Apollos, may have written the book.

2. *Why was this book written? What was the occasion of the book?*
The book was apparently written to Jewish believers. Its consistent references to the Old Testament sacrificial system and the priesthood are clues that a Jewish audience is in view. The book is an encouragement to second-generation Christians to remain faithfully committed to Christ. Their leaders were now dead (13:7). They had themselves professed

Figure 6

THE CREATIVE BIBLE
TEACHER'S INDUCTIVE
STUDY METHOD

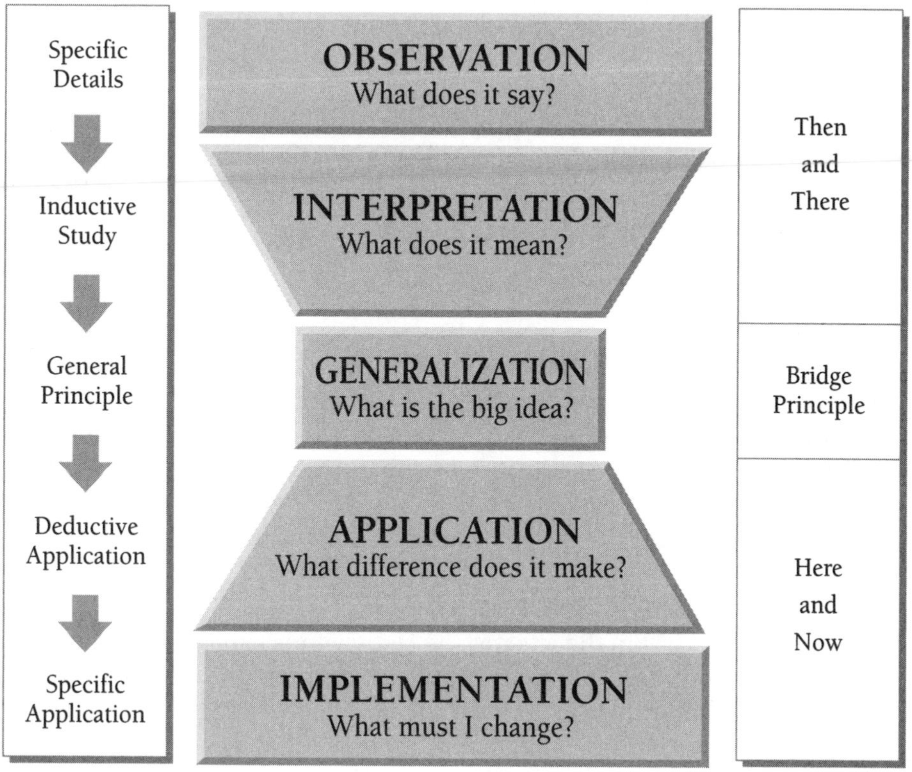

Specific Details	**OBSERVATION** What does it say?	Then and There
Inductive Study	**INTERPRETATION** What does it mean?	
General Principle	**GENERALIZATION** What is the big idea?	Bridge Principle
Deductive Application	**APPLICATION** What difference does it make?	Here and Now
Specific Application	**IMPLEMENTATION** What must I change?	

Christ some time earlier (5:12) with a strong measure of evidence to the genuineness of their faith (10:32–34). But now they had become discouraged and were facing strong opposition for following Christ (12:4). Some were even avoiding meeting together because of the hostility from authorities (10:25). This book was written to encourage a persecuted people.

3. *What historic events surround this book?*

The book was written about A.D. 67 or 68. We know that the temple continued to exist and ceremonial worship rites were still being performed in Jerusalem. This was a very tense time. Only a few short years after the writing of this epistle, the Romans and the Jews faced a bloody conflict. Believers had been awaiting the return of Christ for what seemed to be a very lengthy time. Many may well have been wondering if they had made a mistake in following Jesus.

Context Questions

1. *What literary form is being employed in this passage?*

This book is written as an epistle (letter), but it employs a significant use of analogy and reference to the Old Testament priesthood and tabernacle/temple rites.

2. *What is the overall message of this book, and how does this passage fit into that message?*

The message of Hebrews is *persisting and persevering in the midst of persecution and doubt.* The basis for such perseverance is the uniqueness of Christ and His place above all other angelic or human authorities. This book seeks to show Christ to be the ultimate authority in the universe. This particular passage serves as linkage between the presentation of Christ's greatness and the application of that truth to daily living.

3. *What precedes this passage? What follows it?*

Chapters 1–9 in the letter to the Hebrews present Christ as the superior revelation of God to His people. In chapters 1–5 of this section we see the superiority of Christ over the prophets (chapter 1), the angels (chapters 1–2), Moses (chapter 3), Joshua (chapter 4), and Aaron (chapter 5). In chapters 6–9 Christ is presented as the superior High Priest over a new and better covenant in the true tabernacle. Chapters 10–13 apply the truth of Christ's superior nature to the Christian's life of faith in difficult times. In chapter 10 we learn of the privileges of faith. In chapter 11 we come to understand the examples of visible faith. Chapter 12 deals with the testing of faith, and chapter 13 underscores the outworking of faith. Our passage is the pivotal passage in the book where the author turns from presenting the truth of Christ's superiority to the application of that truth to his readers' lives.

Structural Questions

We turn our attention now to the structure of the text. To do so we will take a somewhat different look at our text. This time we will examine the text by looking at its basic grammatical structure.

Let's proceed now to examine the structural questions as they relate to our text. Some of these questions will pertain to our text; others will not.

> [19]Therefore, brothers, since we have confidence to enter the Most Holy Place by the blood of Jesus, [20]by a new and living way opened for us through the curtain, that is, his body, [21]and since we have a great priest over the house of God, [22]let us draw near to God with a sincere heart in full assurance of faith, having our hearts sprinkled to cleanse us from a guilty conscience and having our bodies washed with pure water. [23]Let us hold unswervingly to the hope we profess, for he who promised is faithful. [24]And let us consider how we may spur one another on toward love and good deeds. [25]Let us not give up meeting together, as some are in the habit of doing, but let us encourage one another—and all the more as you see the Day approaching. (Hebrews 10:19–25)

1. Are there any repeated words? Repeated phrases?

Look at the passage again, and underline any repeated words. (Table 2 aligns various phrases in the text under the phrases they modify or are parallel to.)

Notice in Table 2, the words "since we have" are underlined in verse 19 and again in verse 21. This is to indicate repetition of the phrase. They are aligned because they are parallel phrases linked by the word "and." *What* do we "have"? Also notice the repetition of the words "let us." Three times the author says to his reader "let us _____." Each time he calls the hearer to take a particular action in response to the two "since we have" statements. You have probably underlined these phrases as well. In Table 2, we did not underline the last two occurrences of "let us" in the passage. These we placed in parentheses because they are supplied by the translator and are not in the Greek manuscripts. Most English translations will provide a marginal note informing you of this fact. The translator was seeking to make the text more readable and so supplied the words. In this case, it is probable that they are better understood as phrases that explain how the reader is to "spur one another on toward love and good deeds."

Table 2

HEBREWS 10:19-25

TRUTH

19   Therefore, brothers,
<u>since we have</u> confidence to enter the *Most Holy Place* by the **blood** of Jesus,

20   by *a new and living way* opened for us through the *curtain*, that is, his **body**,

21   and
<u>since we have</u> a great priest over the house of God,

APPLICATION

22   <u>let us draw near to God</u> with a sincere heart in full assurance of faith, having *our hearts sprinkled to cleanse us* from a guilty conscience and having *our bodies washed with pure water*.

23   <u>Let us hold unswervingly to the hope we profess,</u> for he who promised is faithful.

24   And
<u>let us consider how we may spur one another on</u> toward love and good deeds.

25   (Let us) not give up meeting together, as some are in the habit of doing,
but   (let us) encourage one another—and all the more as you see *the Day* approaching.

2. Does the author make any comparisons? Draw any contrasts?

Phrases like "the Most Holy Place" and "a great priest" are clearly comparisons to the Old Testament tabernacle and priesthood. What other words in the passage refer to the priesthood and to the Old Testament priestly rites in the tabernacle? Circle them. The author is using an analogy to explain the work of Christ on behalf of believers.

At this point, you will find it helpful to review the nature of the Levitical priesthood and the tabernacle. A good Bible dictionary would be a useful tool. If you were to trace these phrases to their Old Testament roots, you would discover the Most Holy Place as the place in the tabernacle, and, later, the temple, where God Himself made contact with the priests. The high priest was allowed to enter the Most Holy Place once each year on the Day of Atonement to atone for the sins of God's people. You would also discover an elaborate ceremonial and sacrificial system that was a part of the priestly duties. Your further study will lead you to the fact that the curtain is a reference to the great curtain that extended from floor to ceiling and divided the Most Holy Place from the rest of the tabernacle. It was this curtain that was ripped from top to bottom at the time of Christ's death on the cross.

3. Does the author raise any questions? Provide any answers?

Since we do not see any questions raised by the author in this passage we can proceed to our next observational question.

4. Does the author point out any cause and effect relationships?

This passage indicates that because of the access to God's presence created by the sacrificial atoning work of Christ and His high priestly ministry, the Hebrew believers are, themselves, priests. This access and priestly role of the believer should cause the believer to draw near to God, hold fast to his faith, and spur on other believers.

5. Is there any progression to the passage? In time? action? geography?

This passage uses thematic progression to make its point rather than the use of time, action, or geography. The progression is from truth to application. We have noted this in Table 2 by drawing an arrow between verses 21 and 22. This is where the author shifts from truth to application.

6. Does the passage have a climax?

A climax would generally be found in a narrative passage, so it does not apply to our text.

7. Does the author use any figures of speech?

The author uses several analogies in this passage. An analogy or similitude draws a comparison between the relationship in one situation and that of another. We might put it this way: A is to B, as C is to D. In other words, the relationship of A and B is like the relationship of C and D. We use analogy to help explain difficult relationships by comparing them to other less difficult relationships. In the case of our passage, one analogy is found in the use of the term "curtain" to describe the physical body of Christ. As the curtain provided an access for the priest to enter the Most Holy Place, so too the broken body of Christ provides access for believers to the presence of God.

Other analogies are found in our passage as well. For example, the author speaks of "having our hearts sprinkled to cleanse us" and "having our bodies washed with pure water." These again are analogous to the Old Testament cleansing rites required of the priest who entered the Most Holy Place in the tabernacle. In the same way as the Old Testament priest had to be purified before entering God's presence, so too must the New Testament priest be purified by the work of Christ.

8. Is there a pivotal statement or word?

Integral to our passage are the phrases "since we have" and "let us." Both of these are pivotal in that they indicate the structure and flow of thought in the passage. You will also want to note the use of the word "therefore." It serves as the linkage to the first part of the book of Hebrews. It indicates that our passage is the logical response to what has been taught in the book.

9. What linking words are used? What ideas do they link?

We have already mentioned the use of the words "since we have" and "let us." These words link the truth presented in verses 19–21 with the application of that truth in verses 22–25. We will also want to observe the use of the word "by" in verse 19 and 20. This word shows a causal relationship. The twin uses of the word tell the reader how entrance into the Most Holy Place was gained. (Look at the text of Hebrews 10:19–25 on p. 79 to fill in the blanks here and on the next page.) By what two things was entrance into the Most Holy Place gained? _____ and _____. Additionally, the linking word "and" is used in verses 21, 22, and 24. You will want to observe what is being linked together in these sentences. Finally, the word "but" is used in verse 25. This indicates opposing ideas. In this instance, "let us not give up meeting together" is placed in opposition to _____—the second phrase being the desired action from the author's vantage point.

10. *What verbs are used to describe action in the passage?*

Three verbs stand out in this passage to the observer. These are found in the "let us" phrases of verses 22, 23, and 24. The author calls the reader to _____, _____, and _____. Each of these represents an action that is to be taken in logical response to the truth presented in verses 19–21 regarding the New Testament priesthood.

Now note Table 2, which has moved text to represent its meaning graphically. How is the writer moving his reader through the text?

INTERPRETATION: WHAT DOES IT MEAN?

It is time now to turn to the task of interpreting Hebrews 10:19–25. You will recall from the previous chapter that three rules need to govern our interpretive endeavor. Here is a reminder of these three rules:

Rule # 1—Continuity of Message
Rule # 2—Context of Material
Rule # 3—Customary Meaning

Let's apply each rule to the interpretation of our text.

Rule # 1—Continuity of Message

Hebrews 10:19–25 is a good example of the Bible's unity. The author of Hebrews sees a fulfillment of the Old Testament sacrificial system of atonement and the priestly functions in the New Testament work of Christ. Exodus and Leviticus explain for us the details of the tabernacle, the Levitical priestly duties, and the sacrificial system. It is against this backdrop that we can best interpret the book of Hebrews. As we come to our passage, the author draws some important conclusions.

According to our passage, through the death of Jesus a "new and living way" has been opened. This is in comparison to the old way of death that the priest had to return to, year after year. When Jesus' blood was shed on the cross and when His body was broken as a sacrifice for sin, the veil, or curtain, before the Most Holy Place, or Holy of Holies, was torn from top to bottom. That act indicated that a new way into the presence of God was now open to those who believe. Because of this work of atonement, believers can enter with confidence. The author makes it clear. There is no doubt about it. Believers are acceptable in God's very presence because of the blood of Jesus.

The author reminds the readers that they "have a great priest over the house of God" (21). Believers are not only confident to enter because of the work of Christ in sacrifice for sin, but also, because of the continuing and effective advocacy of Christ, they have a great priest always available. He is constantly aware of the believer's situation. He does not intercede on an annual basis, but moment by moment.

Based upon these two powerful truths regarding Christ, His sacrificial work to make us acceptable priests and His high priestly advocacy, the Hebrew believers are exhorted to take three specific actions: (1) Let us draw near to God with a sincere heart; (2) Let us hold unswervingly to the hope we profess; and (3) Let us consider how we may spur one another on toward love and good deeds. Two suggestions are given as to how this spurring on might occur. First, "let us not give up meeting together, as some are in the habit of doing" (25a). The second suggestion for spurring one another is "let us encourage one another—and all the more as you see the Day approaching" (25b).

Rule # 2—Context of Material

The immediate context helps us to more accurately understand our passage. Chapter 10 is about sacrifice, the final and effective sacrifice of Jesus as compared to the annual and ineffective sacrifice of the Old Testament. In verses 1–4, the author continues a point he has made previously. He indicates that the annually repeated sacrifices were unable to remove sins. If they could remove sin and cleanse the conscience, there would have been no need to repeat them. But these old sacrifices could not fully cleanse from sin because they involved only the death of animals. As a result, the priests and those they represented remained sinners. They continued in their need of an adequate substitutionary sacrifice if their sin was to be removed once and for all. In fact, according to the author of Hebrews, the old sacrifices were but a shadow of the good things to come (1). Animals were inadequate substitutes for humans made in the image of God. That's why the author says, "It is impossible for the blood of bulls and goats to take away sins" (4). But each death of each animal pointed to the continual problem of sin, its seriousness, and the need to finally and completely remove its curse from sinners.

In verses 5–7 the writer quotes Psalm 40:6–8 from the Septuagint, the Greek version of the Old Testament. In words ascribed to Christ, the writer indicates Jesus' willingness to become the final sacrifice for sin. In verses 8–10 the meaning of the quote is expounded. He points out that while God approved animal sacrifices of the past, He was not pleased with them. Instead he indicates that Christ voluntarily did the will of the Father, despite the pain, to become the atoning sacrifice once and for all for sin.

In verses 10–18, he announces,

[10]And by that will, we have been made holy through the sacrifice of the body of Jesus Christ once for all. [11]Day after day every priest stands and performs his religious duties; again and again he offers the same sacrifices, which can never take away sins. [12]But when this priest had offered for all time one sacrifice for sins, he sat down at the right hand of God. [13]Since that time he waits for his enemies to be made his footstool, [14]because by one sacrifice he has made perfect forever those who are being made holy. [15]The Holy Spirit also testifies to us about this. First he says: [16]"This is the covenant I will make with them after that time, says the Lord. I will put my laws in their hearts, and I will write them on their minds." [17]Then he adds: "Their sins and lawless acts I will remember no more." [18]And where these have been forgiven, there is no longer any sacrifice for sin.

Here is his point: By doing the will of God, Jesus in His final sacrifice made all believers holy. Jesus is the complete sacrifice (vv. 11–18). Unlike the priests in the tabernacle who remained standing while fulfilling their ministry, Christ, after having offered Himself for all time, sat down at God's right hand (12). It seems that His sacrifice was so effective that there was nothing left for Him to do except to wait for the final result of His work on the cross; no further sacrifice is needed. The result, verse 17 reminds us, was the total forgiveness of sin. He concludes with a recognition in verse 18 that "where these (sins) have been forgiven, there is no longer any sacrifice for sin."

Rule #3—Customary Meaning

This rule tells us to give our passage its natural, normal, and customary meaning that literature of its kind should be granted. So what is the meaning of all of this? Let's see if we can summarize it briefly. The author begins by presenting the New Testament priesthood in verses 19–21. Here, two facts are in view. First, he stresses the fact that the believer's priesthood is made possible by the sacrificial work of Christ (19–20). Second, he reminds the reader that a great priest continues to intercede over the house of God. These two facts are followed by three calls to respond. The believer is called to respond by drawing near to God, by holding onto the faith he has embraced, and by spurring on others who may be wavering in the faith. The author seems to be giving encouragement to these persecuted, second-generation Christians to stay with Jesus to the very end. Hebrews 10:19–25 is written, then, to second-generation Jewish Christians, who, because of persecution, are tempted to leave the sacrifice of Christ behind.

GENERALIZATION: WHAT IS THE BIG IDEA?

Our study has taught us much about Hebrews 10:19–25. We might even feel we could teach it to others by now, but we must be careful not to miss an essential stage in our inductive process. We must boil this passage down to a single sentence. We do this by identifying a subject (What is the author talking about?) and a complement (What is he saying about what he is talking about?). Let's see what we come up with by answering the subject and complement questions.

Subject: What Is the Author Talking About?

Our subject is the New Testament priesthood. We might state the subject this way: What should happen in every believer's life because they can enter into the presence of God by the sacrificial work of Christ, and because of the high priestly ministry of Christ. That is lengthy, but for now it serves to summarize our subject. We will refine it further in a moment.

Complement: What Is the Author Saying About What He Is Talking About?

What should the believer's response be? According to our passage, believers should draw near, hold fast, and spur on. We could be more elaborate in the statement of the complement, but we know that each short verbal phrase is linked to a longer statement in our text.

Generalization: What Is the Transferable Principle?

How can we bring the answers to these questions into a single sentence that encompasses the major teaching or principle of the passage? We might put it this way: The priesthood of the believer, accomplished by the sacrificial work of Christ, along with Christ's high priestly ministry, calls every Christian to draw near to God, hold fast to his faith, and spur on other believers so that each one might persevere through difficult times and in difficult situations.

We will continue to hone this sentence in later chapters, but this is our transferable (bridge) principle. All believers in all times since the death of Christ are priests who have confident access to God because of the sacrifice of Christ. All believers also have a great priest who continues to intercede for them. As a result, every believer can and should take action on these benefits of the faith. The final result is that Christians are more likely to persevere through persecution and problems. This is not a principle limited to the Hebrew Christians who received this letter. It is transferable to all Christians. Out of this truth can come practical application and teaching.

APPLICATION: WHAT DIFFERENCE DOES IT MAKE?

We said in the last chapter that, in applying the Bible, interpretation always precedes application. As readers and students of the Bible we may feel quite removed from the original recipients of our passage. Two thousand years, thousands of miles of geography, radically different customs and cultures, and even differing languages make understanding and applying the book of Hebrews a challenge. But the gap has been narrowed as we have sought to interpret the passage in its context. By gleaning a bridge principle from the text we can now move on to apply the text to our world. We have fulfilled our first guideline of application.

Our second application guideline was that application focuses on biblical answers to common issues. What common issues does our passage address? Certainly we could begin our application with the matter of drawing near to God in times of difficulty and persecution. Do we run to Jesus to find our strength to face the pressures, temptations, stresses, and difficulties of daily life? Do we recognize our utter need for God in times of hardship, discouragement, trials, and disappointment? All of us have been, or will be, tempted to give up on our faith in Christ and wander from our commitment to Jesus. In a time when standing for Christ as the only way of salvation is considered intolerant and politically incorrect, our passage has a very contemporary ring to it. How easy it would be to "give up meeting together" in an era where faith and religiosity is mocked and considered non-scientific fantasy. In these times, we need each other all the more. These are times when it is essential to hold unswervingly to the faith we have professed. When the media, educators, and culture in general are hostile to the gospel of Christ, the transferable principle of Hebrews 10:19–25 is exceptionally relevant.

Our third guideline concerning application was to apply the Bible as God intended. God's goal in preserving Hebrews 10:19–25 for us was that we might be more adequately equipped for every good work. We must ask four final questions:

1. Is there a teaching here to be learned and followed?
2. Does this passage communicate a rebuke to be heard and heeded?
3. Is there a correction to be noted?
4. In what way does this passage train us to be righteous?

In answering the first question, you will probably detect many lessons in this passage. For example, we are reminded of the once-for-all nature of the work of Christ that allows each believer confidently to enter God's presence. This truth yields an important application. At this very moment, nothing is keeping you from God's presence but your own choices and heart. God invites each of us to freely come to Him. As you consider the text, what other aspects of its teaching do you need to follow?

The second question requires us to consider rebukes that may be offered in the passage. One rebuke we might uncover is a personal failure to meet together with fellow believers. How easy it is to forget that church life is not optional, but essential to Christian living. We can let so many other pressures crowd out the encouragement we could be receiving from other believers. If this is the case in our own walk with Christ, then the rebuke needs to be heeded and our actions need to change.

The third question seeks to ascertain points where our lives need correction. Could it be that we have depended on the wrong means to find God's acceptance? Maybe we have sought God's approval in our works or personal sacrifice. This passage offers a clear corrective to our thinking. We find that it is only by Christ's sacrifice that entrance into God's presence is obtained. It is only when our hearts are sprinkled with the blood of Jesus that our conscience is freed from guilt and our lives are purified. What point in the passage can you apply to your own life as a matter of correction?

The fourth and final question asks us to consider how we might grow in righteousness because of a truth taught. One point of application in this regard might well be our need to spur each other on. Spiritual growth is a group project, not an individual effort. If we are to grow in righteousness, this passage makes plain that we will have to spur one another along and encourage each other to continue to grow. We have suggested one idea. Are there other things to be learned that will allow you to grow in righteousness?

IMPLEMENTATION: WHAT MUST I CHANGE?

The fifth and final stage of the creative Bible teacher's inductive study method is to discover specific implications for change in his personal life and implement those changes. How do you need to change as a teacher from your study of Hebrews 10:19–25? Have you discovered some area in your own life where this passage calls you to change? Why not take a moment before the Lord to seek His power and establish a plan for implementing that change?

YOU'RE AIRBORNE!

Well, congratulations, you've done it! You have worked your way through the study of a Bible passage. To return to the flying analogy that we suggested at the beginning of this chapter, you have just made your first flight into the realm of Bible study and teaching.

Or, to use another image, you have just unearthed scriptural gold. It is a rewarding thing to mine the treasures of Scripture, isn't it! You will discover that, as your skills in Bible study continue to develop, the Bible will take on more of a living and life-changing quality. You will uncover new vistas and insights in your quest for understanding and growth in Christ.

Now, it's possible at this point that you might even feel like you are ready to teach. It is tempting to take study notes in hand and head into the classroom. You might be saying, "But what else is there to be done before teaching this passage?" You have observed, interpreted, and identified a bridge principle. You have discovered several applications and have even seen an implication or two for your own life. What more do you need to do before you are ready to teach the passage?

For starters, you must learn how to enter your students' world. Creative Bible teachers must comprehend both the world of the Bible and the world of their students. From that knowledge they develop a plan to bring the truth of Scripture to students in a timely and creative manner. That is our next step. In the chapters that follow we will learn how to take our study of the Bible and develop a creative Bible teaching lesson. So, let's continue by taking the next step in creative Bible teaching—*focusing the message.*

Figure 7

THE CREATIVE BIBLE
TEACHING MODEL

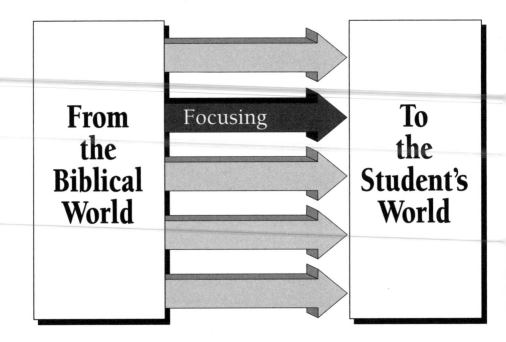

From
the
Biblical
World

Focusing

To
the
Student's
World

FOCUSING THE MESSAGE

Gaining focus and staying focused are critical to many aspects of life. Consider Peter, for example. In Matthew 14 we read of Jesus walking across the water to His disciples' boat. Peter's response was to step out of the boat and walk on the water to Jesus. Verses 30–31 say, "When he [Peter] saw the wind, he was afraid and, beginning to sink, cried out, 'Lord, save me!' Immediately Jesus reached out His hand and caught him. 'You of little faith,' He said, 'why did you doubt?' " Jesus' question was rhetorical in nature and intended for the benefit of Peter. Jesus knew why Peter had doubted: Peter lost faith because he lost focus. He was looking at the wind and the waves and failed to look at Jesus. The result was that he began to sink. Often, as with Peter, when we lose focus, we lose faith. And we begin to sink.

Another meaning of the word "focus" is relevant here. The word can also mean narrowing down something that is too broad to be dealt with all at once. The Internet is a wonderful tool for research and information exchange. The "Web surfer" can find information on almost any topic that can be imagined. But the problem is sorting through the enormous quantity of information. For example, one search of the Internet, using what is known as a search engine, returned more than 500,000 results for the word Bible. *There are greater than one-half million documents or home pages on the Internet with some reference to "Bible." Five hundred thousand documents is an overwhelming number! What was needed was a more focused search.*

By using the words Bible study *we received 20,000 results. That was still too many to be of much use to us, so we became still more focused and entered* inductive Bible study. *This time we uncovered about 100 documents. Although this was a lot of material to go through, it was better than half-a-million items. We focused our search even further. This time we typed in* inductive study of Hebrews. *We received 17 results. Seven or eight documents were exceptionally helpful.*

Focus is important in most aspects of life. Whether you are walking on water or just surfing the Net, taking pictures or driving in your car, perusing this book or performing surgery, a clear focus is essential to the task. If you wear glasses or contacts you know the importance of clear focus. Creative Bible teachers also understand that focus is critical to affecting people with the transforming message of the Bible.

In this section we will help you take the next step in becoming a creative Bible teacher, focusing the message. *As you read the next three chapters you will discover something about learners and learning. You will then understand how you can take that knowledge and use it to bridge the gap between the world of the Bible and the world of your students by focusing the message.*

Chapter Six

FOCUS ON NEEDS:
UNDERSTANDING AND ASSESSING
STUDENT NEEDS

Sometimes the greatest challenge a teacher faces in explaining a concept is bridging the gap between the historic world of an event and the contemporary world of the student. Mary Beth Yoder tells the story of an experience she had outside the Noah Webster home in Dearborn, Michigan's Greenwood Village. As she waited in line to enter the home, a father standing nearby was trying his best to explain the significance of the home's owner and his famous dictionary. After several attempts at bridging the gap between Webster's world and that of his children, the father finally said, "Noah Webster was the grandfather of spell-check!" Yoder comments, "Immediately the kids nodded and smiled, the connection suddenly made clear in their modern world."[1]

There is a very real gap between ourselves and those who lived in the ancient Bible world. It is a gap of time, geography, culture, technology, custom, language, and even worldview. Although these differences do exist, there are still some things we hold in common with the men and women of Bible times. We have a common humanity. We can relate to them and their stories relate to us because we share physical, emotional, social, and spiritual characteristics. It is important for the creative Bible teacher to remember that basic human needs have not changed significantly over the millennia that have passed since the Scriptures were written. J. Daniel Baumann puts the fact of human commonality in this way:

We are very much like the people of the ancient world. It is only in some superficial thoughts, rational beliefs, and mental moods that we are different. In all of the basic heart realities we are the same. We stand before God exactly as people in every age have stood before Him. We have all experienced David's guilt, the doubting of Thomas, Peter's denial, the falling away of Demas, perhaps even the kiss of the betrayer Judas. We are linked across centuries by the realities and ambiguities of the human soul.[2]

As we come to understand the needs of people, especially the people we teach, we can become more effective in teaching the Bible. By knowing our students, we can help our students not only make more direct and specific application of Scripture to their lives, but we can also help them see the very contemporary nature of the message of the Bible.

UNDERSTANDING STUDENT NEEDS

The student is at the heart of the teaching-learning process. The ultimate objective in teaching the Bible is not Bible knowledge, though that is very important; it is *applied* Bible knowledge in the student's everyday life. We have said earlier that Bible content is crucial because of its inspired and revelatory nature. But we must remember, we teach people, not lessons. So we must begin with people.

Jesus said, "The Sabbath was made for man, not man for the Sabbath" (Mark 2:27). His point was that human needs take priority even over religious rites. Jesus focused on people and their genuine personal needs. He tailored His message to those needs. His content, His approach, and His methodology were based on the needs of His audience and on their unique life situations. Take, for example, His response to the rich young ruler who came to Him to inquire concerning the requirements to gain eternal life. Knowing the man's pride and need for humility, Jesus pointed him to the commandments of Scripture. The man's response showed his great pride when he said, "All these I have kept. What do I still lack?" (Matt. 19:20). Jesus called on him to "go, sell your possessions and give to the poor" (v. 21). Jesus understood this man's need and focused His message to that need.

On another occasion, Jesus was with His disciples in the upper room. He was teaching them concerning the Holy Spirit's nature and ministry in believers' lives. Jesus geared His teaching to the needs and readiness of His students when He said, "I have much more to say to you, more than you can now bear" (John 16:12). Jesus recognized the basic educational principle that the student's needs, interests, and readiness determines what is to be taught and how it is to be taught. Whether it was with Nicodemus (John 3), the woman at the well (John 4), the woman caught in adultery (John 8), Thomas in his doubt (John 20), or Peter in his guilt (John 21), Jesus understood human need and adjusted His approach accordingly.

Maslow's Hierarchy of Needs

Abraham Maslow's theory of human needs and motivation is one of the most popular and widely known needs theories.[3] Maslow classified human needs into five categories, each arranged in a hierarchy of ascending importance from low to high (Figure 8). The lowest and most basic level is the physiological level. Here, the needs for food, water, and air drive human behavior. At the safety/security level, the need for a stable life, free from threat, motivates individual behavior. The third level is that of social or belonging needs. At this level, individuals are directed by their need for friendship, affection, interaction, and relationships. The fourth level is the esteem level. Here, the basic need is for personal feelings of achievement and affirmation. A personal sense of worth is sought. Finally, according to Maslow, humans pursue self-actualization needs. By self-actualization Maslow is referring to a sense of satisfaction that one is realizing his personal potential.

It should be noted that Maslow holds a humanistic worldview and that his theory is influenced by his humanistic presuppositions. An example of this can be seen in the fifth level in his hierarchy, which he believes is a level religious people cannot reach. There is scant research evidence for this level. This level seems to come more from Maslow's humanistic orientation than from his observational data. In fact, not only does his fifth level reflect his opposition to organized religion, but his earlier ones allow no place for the supernatural. So Maslow's value is limited by the fact that he does not address issues that Scripture addresses and that areas of his theory are skewed by his philosophy, not research. But to discard everything he says because he doesn't factor in spiritual needs is to dismiss his valuable insight in categorizing physical and emotional needs. Maslow still offers a helpful framework for thinking about human needs. His first four levels parallel studies of human needs and motivation conducted by other behavioral scientists. The great contribution made by Maslow is in the structure or model he creates for considering the importance of human needs and their relationship to one another.

Herzberg's Two-Factor Needs Theory

Researcher Fredrick Herzberg has validated a less complex approach to understanding needs that consists of just two levels. Herzberg theorized that human needs fall into "hygiene" and "motivation" categories

Figure 8

MASLOW'S HIERARCHY OF NEEDS

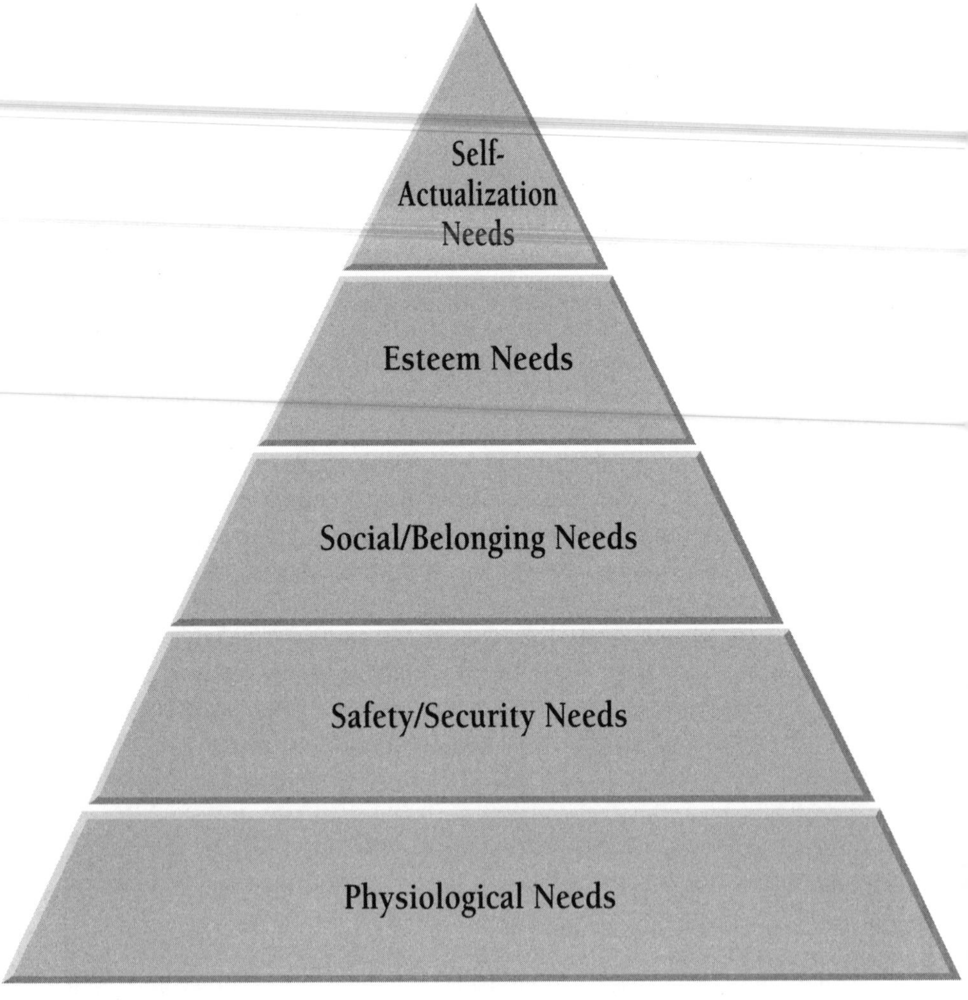

Self-Actualization Needs

Esteem Needs

Social/Belonging Needs

Safety/Security Needs

Physiological Needs

(Figure 9). Hygiene needs are the fundamental needs that human beings face that, if not met, hinder greater effectiveness and success. Hygiene needs correspond with Maslow's first three levels. Unmet hygiene needs tend to demotivate and disengage learners. Motivators are needs that, when met, increase personal effectiveness and further success. These needs correspond with Maslow's esteem and self-actualization categories but are not limited by Maslow's definitions. Motivators may differ between students and therefore, teachers must understand the needs of individual students and the factors that motivate students.

James may have been observing the same human behaviors as Herzberg when he wrote, "If one of you says to him, 'Go, I wish you well; keep warm and well fed,' but does nothing about his physical needs, what good is it? In the same way, faith by itself, if it is not accompanied by action, is dead" (James 2:16–17).

Developmental Approach to Understanding Student Needs

In addition to general needs as seen in the theories of Maslow and Herzberg, creative Bible teachers can turn to general age group characteristics as a means of understanding the student. Because God created humans with a design, it is possible to study human development and recognize common stages and issues in the developmental process. Even Jesus is spoken of as developing in the areas typically addressed by developmental researchers. In Luke 2:52 we read, "And Jesus grew in wisdom and stature, and in favor with God and men." Here we see Jesus developing cognitively (in wisdom), physically (in stature), spiritually (in favor with God), and socially (in favor with men).

Paul also recognized the cognitive side of human development when he wrote, "When I was a child, I talked like a child, I thought like a child, I reasoned like a child. When I became a man, I put childish ways behind me" (1 Cor. 13:11). Although Paul did not identify the various levels of cognitive development that modern researchers have discovered, he observed fundamental differences between the way children process ideas and the way adults process ideas.

Through the workings of maturation, encoded in the genetic structure, God has established a complex design for human growth and development in all persons. It is this common design that makes the study of human development possible and generalizations about various age groups useful. Imagine if people all grew and changed at totally different rates. Some people would not walk until they were thirty while others would be seventeen feet tall by the end of the first year of life. The predictable changes in children, adolescents, and adults are, themselves, arguments for design and a designer.

Figure 9

HERZBERG'S
TWO-FACTOR
THEORY

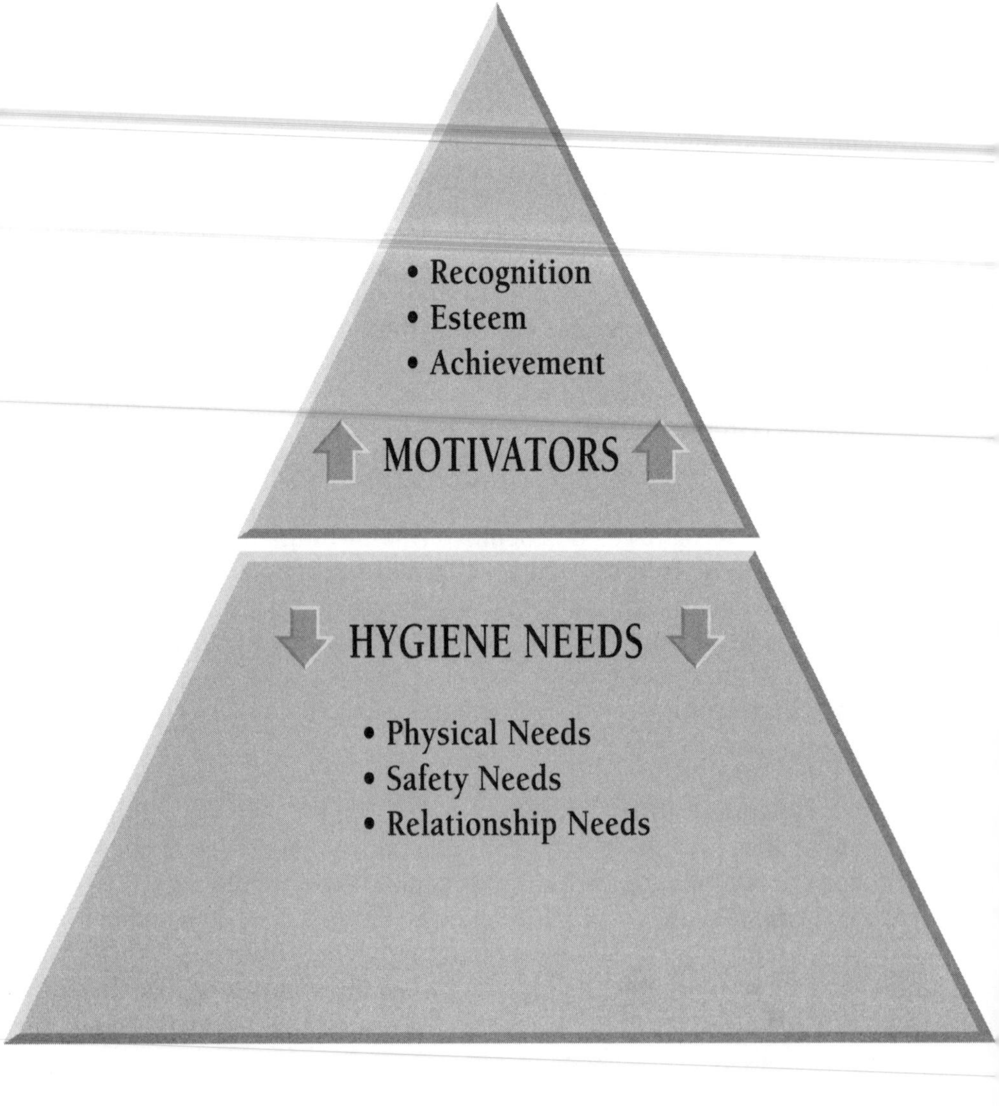

- Recognition
- Esteem
- Achievement

 MOTIVATORS

 HYGIENE NEEDS

- Physical Needs
- Safety Needs
- Relationship Needs

Several excellent books on human development are available to the creative Bible teacher. A knowledge of typical age-group characteristics is invaluable to the teacher who wants to communicate God's Word to students at their level and in a way they can understand. A particularly helpful book is Helen Bee's *The Developing Child*, published by HarperCollins. Although this is a secular book and it reflects an evolutionary bias, the vast majority of its information is presented in a forthright and unbiased manner. It contains exceptionally well written material on human development that teachers will find informative.

For a brief summary of the developmental characteristics and needs of children, youth, and adults, two books, Gangel and Hendricks's book *The Christian Educator's Handbook on Teaching* (Victor) and Clark, Johnson, and Sloat's book *Christian Education: Foundations for the Future* (Moody) provide valuable overviews. Another excellent resource is *Focus on the Family Complete Book of Baby & Child Care*, written by Paul C. Reisser and Melissa Cox (Tyndale). Tables 3–6 provide you with four quick-reference charts to help you think through the needs and developmental characteristics of your students. Later in this book, chapters 15 through 17 will also help you better understand the needs of various age groups and how to teach in light of those needs.

Understanding Spiritual Needs

Ruth Beechick proposes several "spiritual tasks" (Table 7) that she believes should be addressed as students mature.[4] She patterns her spiritual-tasks approach after Robert J. Havinghurst's *Developmental Tasks and Education* (New York: Longmans, 1948).

ASSESSING STUDENT NEEDS

Alex is a twenty-eight-year-old medical professional. His church is a small evangelical fellowship located in one of Chicago's many ethnic neighborhoods. Alex has a group of eleven junior high school students in a Sunday school class he teaches. He also leads a small group Bible study in his home on Thursday evenings. Six to eight high school students attend the study. The students like Alex, and both the Sunday school class and Bible study students have developed a trusting relationship with him. At a recent conference for youth workers Alex came up after a seminar and asked this question, "How does one go about assessing the needs of a class or Bible study group? I want to be relevant in my teaching, but I am unsure where to begin."

We suggested that Alex do a needs assessment with his groups. A needs assessment is a simple process whereby a teacher can become aware of the needs present within his or her class. Many different instruments

Table 3

SUMMARY OF THE DEVELOPMENTAL
CHARACTERISTICS OF PRESCHOOL CHILDREN

Learners tend to:	Therefore, in ministry we:
Physically:	
• Lack small muscle coordination.	• Use supplies and activities designed for large muscle usage.
• Develop from head down. Legs least developed, head most developed.	• Provide appropriately sized chairs, toys in reach, pictures at their level.
• Grow rapidly and are very active while needing periods of rest.	• Alternate activity and rest in programs.
Cognitively:	
• Have short attention spans. As a rule, one minute per year of age.	• Plan several learning activities in an hour period.
• Learn experientially.	• Teach to all senses; use stories, objects, and experience.
• Express curiosity, questioning.	• Use discovery learning, simple answers.
• Have limited time/space awareness and comprehension.	• Refrain from referring to history and chronology. Emphasize the present.
Emotionally/Socially:	
• Feel insecure in new situations and with strangers.	• Provide consistent caregivers and teachers.
• Explore and learn by discovery.	• Provide large, safe rooms with open space and many items of interest.
• Need routine and repetition.	• Use a similar pattern to each class.
• Approach life egocentrically and with an inability to take another's perspective.	• Explain things in terms of their limited perspective.
Spiritually/Morally:	
• Explore and formulate a sense of right and wrong and a concept of God.	• Distinguish between right and wrong, talk freely about God.

Table 4

SUMMARY OF THE DEVELOPMENTAL CHARACTERISTICS OF ELEMENTARY SCHOOL CHILDREN

Learners tend to:	Therefore, in ministry we:
Physically:	
• Increasingly coordinate muscle usage.	• Use writing supplies, group games, and coordinated activities as development proceeds.
• Grow steadily and continue high energy level.	• Provide activities, snacks, increasing physical challenges.
Cognitively:	
• Have a growing attention span. (Kindergarten = 5-10 minutes) (Grades 1-3 = 7-15 minutes) (Grades 4-6 = 10-20 minutes)	• Continue to offer a variety of activities appropriate in length to average age group attention span.
• Think concretely.	• Use multiple illustrations and examples.
• Think literally.	• Teach straightforward material without a great deal of symbolism.
• Have a desire for creative learning.	• Provide variety and creativity in activities.
• Have an excellent memory ability.	• Promote Scripture memorization.
Emotionally/Socially:	
• Have growing social skills, friendships with peers—boys with boys, girls with girls.	• Encourage Christian friendships, separate classes for boys and girls if space and personnel allow.
• Have feelings easily hurt.	• Provide empathy and encouragement.
• Need and desire acceptance, have a "gang" instinct.	• Encourage positive peer group, positive group involvement.
• Collect things and are hobbyists.	• Use hobbies as contact points.
Spiritually/Morally:	
• Believe what teachers believe.	• Model and teach the truth of the Word.

Table 5

SUMMARY OF THE DEVELOPMENTAL CHARACTERISTICS OF YOUTH

Learners tend to:	Therefore, in ministry we:
Physically:	
• Grow and change rapidly during early adolescence (puberty).	• Prepare them for adolescent changes and deal with sexuality issues.
• Have high energy, especially in junior high.	• Provide ample outlets for energy through high activity programming.
• Develop adult bodies and reproductive capabilities.	• Teach students a holistic view of human nature and a Christian perspective on the physical aspects of personhood.
Cognitively:	
• Have increased reasoning abilities, abstract thinking skills.	• Help them address significant questions and doubts.
• Have better argumentation and critical thinking skills.	• Use instructional methods that allow students to vocalize their opinions and beliefs.
Emotionally/Socially:	
• Have adventuresome, risk-taking spirits.	• Program some events that allow students to take measured risks.
• Have concern about outward appearance and physical traits.	• Encourage balanced perspective on the inner qualities of godliness.
• Have an interest in and attraction to the opposite sex.	• Provide a biblical perspective on human relationships.
• Seek a sense of personal identity.	• Focus on their identity in Christ.
• Seek greater autonomy.	• Increase freedom and responsibility.
• Fluctuate emotionally.	• Exercise patience and tolerance.
Spiritually/Morally:	
• Re-evaluate and personalize faith.	• Let them explore their faith openly.

Table 6

SUMMARY OF THE DEVELOPMENTAL CHARACTERISTICS OF ADULTS

Learners tend to:	Therefore, in ministry we:
Physically:	
• Physically peak at about age 26.	• Offer social and physical activities.
• Have children from age 20 to 40.	• Deal with child development issues.
• Heal more slowly, encounter greater stress in mid-life years (35-55).	• Provide various forms of help when facing physical needs.
• Experience significant physical decline after age 55.	• Provide continued help when needed as well as biblical perspective.
• Face issues of death after age 60.	• Provide support in grief process.
• Live longer and have a more active life than previous generations.	• Provide active senior adult program.
Cognitively:	
• Emphasize the practical and pragmatic in learning.	• Focus on relevant application and discussion opportunities.
• Prefer student-directed learning.	• Increase student-centered methods.
• Gain in knowledge and practical wisdom with age.	• Use their growing wisdom to guide younger adults.
Emotionally/Socially:	
• Have differing needs based on age, marital status, age of children, and health.	• Build ministry around life transitional periods when people are most open to ministry efforts.
• Have needs that parallel life "transitions" or "change events."	• Seek to be sensitive to people in various life transitions.
• Focus on marriage and family concerns.	• Develop marriage and family classes and study groups.
• Need a close friendship cluster.	• Emphasize small groups.
Spiritually/Morally:	
• Become more fixed in belief system.	• Evangelize youth; disciple adults.

Table 7

SPIRITUAL DEVELOPMENTAL TASKS

I. **Preschool Years**
   A. Experiencing love, security, discipline, joy, and worship.
   B. Beginning to develop awareness and concepts of God, Jesus, and other basic Christian realities.
   C. Developing attitudes toward God, Jesus, church, self, and the Bible.
   D. Beginning to develop concepts of right and wrong.

II. **Elementary School Years**
   A. Receiving and acknowledging Jesus Christ as Savior and Lord.
   B. Growing awareness of Christian love and responsibility in relationships with others.
   C. Continuing to build concepts of basic Christian realities.
   D. Learning basic Bible teachings adequate for personal faith and everyday living.
      1. Prayer in daily life.
      2. The Bible in daily life.
      3. Christian friendships.
      4. Group worship.
      5. Responsibility for serving God.
      6. Basic knowledge of God, Jesus, Holy Spirit, creation, angelic beings, heaven, hell, sin, salvation, Bible history, and literature.
   E. Developing healthy attitudes toward self.

III. **Adolescence**
   A. Learning to show Christian love in everyday life.
   B. Continuing to develop healthy attitudes toward self.
   C. Developing Bible knowledge and intellectual skills adequate for meeting intellectual assaults on faith.
   D. Achieving strength of Christian character for meeting anti-Christian social pressures.
   E. Accepting responsibility for Christian service in accordance with growing abilities.
   F. Learning to make life decisions on the basis of eternal Christian values.
   G. Increasing self-discipline to "seek those things which are above."

IV. **Maturity**
   A. Accepting responsibility for one's own continued growth and learning.
   B. Accepting biblical responsibilities toward God and toward others.
   C. Living a unified, purposeful life centered upon God.

exist to assess needs, but we believe that a simple, four-fold study of the group is sufficient for most Bible teachers. Table 8 presents the *Creative Bible Teacher's Student Needs Assessment Instrument* that we recommended to Alex. Notice how Alex completed his needs assessment assignment. By thinking in terms of his students, Alex is less likely to simply teach content. He will teach students because he is focusing on assessing and addressing student needs.

Components of a Needs Assessment Survey

How exactly does one go about doing a needs assessment study? Table 8 suggests a four-fold approach to needs assessment. First, begin by listing some of the physical, cognitive, psycho-social (emotional and social), and spiritual needs you have observed in the group. Be specific so that you can gear your lessons around the needs of your students. Second, describe the group. In what kind of ministry situation will you be teaching? How large is the group? What are the social and cultural characteristics of the group? What is the spiritual maturity level of the group? Answers to questions like these will help you as you prepare. You will get ideas for how to make the teaching of the text and the application of the lesson as appropriate as possible. Third, list some of the specific characteristics of group members you have observed. What are their interests? What abilities do they possess? What limitations have you observed? Do you know of any obvious or expressed needs that your students bring to class? Finally, make a list of some ways you can build ministry contact with the group. For example, if the group is involved in sports, illustrations from the world of sports will strengthen your teaching with the group.

Sources for Needs Information

Do you see each member of your class as individual persons, or do you see them as a collective, a class, a group only? How well do you know and understand your students? Do you know their names, interests, concerns, and needs? As a creative Bible teacher it will be important for you to gain this kind of knowledge about your students. But how does one come to know these facts? Where does the teacher find information to effectively ascertain student needs? Here are a few suggestions.

The first and most reliable source of information on student needs are students themselves. If possible, spend some individual time with each student. Ask about interests. Get to know each student as an individual outside of class. Some of the needs assessment information can be discovered simply by observing your students. Recreational activities with students serve multiple purposes. They provide fellowship for

THE CREATIVE BIBLE TEACHER'S
STUDENT NEEDS ASSESSMENT INSTRUMENT

Target Group: _High School Bible Study - Northwest Side Gospel Church_

Assessment Date: _9/5/97_   Assessed By: _Alex Smith_

1. **General Age Group Characteristics**   Age Level: _14-17 Years Old_

    Gender: ☐ Males Only   ☐ Females Only   ☒ Mixed Group

Physical:	Cognitive:	Psychosocial:	Spiritual:
All have completed puberty	All are showing signs of abstract thinking ability	All need acceptance Strong need for a sense of belonging	Minimal knowledge of Scripture
Very energetic and athletic group	Group likes to debate and discuss current events and issues	Some of the students in the youth group are very attracted to gangs	All have accepted Christ as personal Savior
Two students are star athletes on high school baseball team	Some of the students have expressed doubts about their faith	All are seeking a close friendship group	All need to learn to stand up for faith with friends
One student is an accomplished figure skater		Guidance in personal relationships needed, particularly with opposite sex	Greater knowledge of Bible doctrine needed
	Two of the students are very poor readers and lack academic skills	Many have strained relationships with their families	Need help with personal Bible study and devotions

2. **Characteristics of the Ministry Setting**

✓   Kind of Group (Indicate the agency and type of ministry in which the teaching is to take place):

> Small group Bible study. Group is made up of key leaders from church youth group. Meets at the youth sponsor's home once each week. Very relaxed setting.

✓   Size of Group (Indicate the number of students who are anticipated or attend regularly):

> Six to ten in attendance, four boys and six girls (Jeff, Tom, Mike, Larry , Linda, Melissa, Lisa, Katie, Shawna, Breanna)

THE CREATIVE BIBLE TEACHER'S
STUDENT NEEDS ASSESSMENT INSTRUMENT

2.   **Characteristics of the Ministry Setting** (Continued)

✓   Social-cultural Characteristics of Group (Type of community, ethnicity, types of employment, economic level, community size, etc.):

    Ethnically diverse group. Northwest side of Chicago, blue collar community, middle income. Some racial tension in local high school. Strong gang influence in high school and widespread drug use. Students attend one of Chicago's better schools where educational quality is above average. Students who have taken a stand for their faith have faced significant persecution.

✓   Spiritual Maturity Level of Students:

    Most mature students in the youth group. All need to grow spiritually and are involved in the Bible study for that reason. A couple of the teens are new Christians. Two (Mike and Melissa) are dating each other. Two students are Sunday school teachers in the first and second grade classes.

3.   **Specific Group Characteristics**

✓   Interests:

    Sports, music, skating, journalism, dating

✓   Abilities :

    Five skilled athletes, one musically gifted, one writes for school newspaper

✓   Limitations:

    One student limited physically because of being wheelchair bound, all have a limited knowledge of Scripture, and two have almost no Bible training. Two are very poor students and are very poor readers.

✓   Observed Needs:

    All are under great pressure as they try to stand for Christ at their high school. Very small number of believers at school; students need constant encouragement to remain faithful to Christ. Some are facing significant temptations and doubts. Acceptance by a group is the single greatest felt need among the students.

4.   Points of Ministry Contact

    Sports, music, drama, gangs, persecution

students and an opportunity for teachers to get to know individuals in a more relaxed setting than in the classroom. During these times teachers can observe some student needs firsthand.

A second source of information about student needs can come from an informal interview process. The teacher can tell two or three students that he or she wants to learn more about the group and its needs. By taking the students out for a hamburger and soft drink or coffee and pie, the teacher can ask his "informants" to help him organize the class. We have found students very receptive to teachers who value student input. Whether working with children, youth, or adults, teachers who simply ask the question, "How can we make our class better?" will find that students will provide some workable ideas for both methodology and content revision. Teachers must be open to change or this approach can be counterproductive. It doesn't take students long to figure out that the teacher really did not want their input, even though it was sought. Be sure to implement some of your informants' ideas and thank them for their suggestions.

A third source of information on student needs and interests can be a simple questionnaire. Distribute a questionnaire in class or at your Bible study. Let students have time to write their answers out or talk about them if they prefer. Adult learners are often very willing to list needs and ways the class could address those needs if led to discuss these in an open and non-threatening way. One idea that has worked well is to give a needs survey to small groups and let them talk together about what should be written. The groups then either turn in a written survey or discuss their results with the entire class.

Your Turn

Now it's time for you to try your hand at needs assessment. At the end of this chapter you will find Table 9. These have been included so that you can conduct your own needs assessment with your class. Before you continue reading the next chapter, photocopy the pages and complete them for your teaching setting. If you are not presently teaching a class or Bible study group, do an assessment of a group in which you are a member. Keep in mind that the goal of this exercise is to begin thinking in terms of the student, his or her needs, and the world that the student lives in from day to day. Armed with this information, you will be better able to develop a creative Bible teaching lesson plan that bridges the gap between the world of the student and the world of the Bible. By understanding your students you will also avoid the common pitfall of Bible teachers—teaching lessons rather than teaching students. Creative

Bible teachers are student aware. They know that the content counts, but it is students that they teach.

Teaching Students, Not Lessons

Nancy Langley was facing some major problems and difficult times. Her eldest son was in jail for selling drugs, and her middle son had just run away. Her husband, Stan, was not a believer. Nancy attended church by herself and was a regular in John Mathews's adult Sunday school class. She attended the class because John was known for his in-depth Bible teaching. Most often the class was a lecture, but one morning John opened the class for discussion. The class had been dealing with Romans 8:28, "And we know that in all things God works for the good of those who love him, who have been called according to his purpose." John asked, "So, class, how have you seen God work for good in your life through difficult situations?"

Nancy spoke up and told her struggles. She expressed that at the moment she wasn't so sure God was working for her good. She told of her doubts and pain. After a few minutes, John interrupted Nancy and said, "Nancy, I don't think we can solve your problems here today. We really need to move on in our study if we are going to finish Romans by the end of the quarter. Maybe we can talk after class?" Nancy nodded, the class ended, and Nancy slipped out without a word. She has not returned since that lesson.

John may have been right that Nancy's needs were going to slow the progress he hoped to make in Romans. He may have also been correct in wanting to talk with Nancy in private about her situation. But it was clear to Nancy, and to almost everyone else in class that day, that John was teaching his lesson, not people. John felt that Nancy's needs were crowding out his planned material. To John, teaching was communicating content.

Some teachers focus on the content they desire to cover in the class as the primary factor in teaching. Creative Bible teachers do not. They recognize the necessity of teaching the truth of the Bible and the importance of strong content, but they also know that they teach students, not lessons. Student needs and student learning are a priority. Creative Bible teachers see themselves as a link between the content and the student. By knowing and caring for their students, they are able to connect the content in meaningful ways with students' lives. Needs assessment helps teachers do this.

THE CREATIVE BIBLE TEACHER'S
STUDENT NEEDS ASSESSMENT INSTRUMENT

Target Group: _____

Assessment Date: _____ Assessed By: _____

1. **General Age Group Characteristics**   Age Level: _____
   Gender: ☐ Males Only   ☐ Females Only   ☐ Mixed Group

Physical:	Cognitive:	Psychosocial:	Spiritual:

2. **Characteristics of the Ministry Setting**

✓ Kind of Group (Indicate the agency and type of ministry in which the teaching is to take place):

✓ Size of Group (Indicate the number of students who are anticipated or attend regularly):

THE CREATIVE BIBLE TEACHER'S
STUDENT NEEDS ASSESSMENT INSTRUMENT

2.   **Characteristics of the Ministry Setting** (Continued)

✓   Social-cultural Characteristics of Group (type of community, ethnicity, types of employment, economic level, community size, etc.):

✓   Spiritual Maturity Level of Students:

3.   **Specific Group Characteristics**

✓   Interests:

✓   Abilities:

✓   Limitations:

✓   Observed Needs:

4.   **Points of Ministry Contact**

NOTES

1. Contributed by Mary Beth Yoder, in "Virtual Hilarity," *Reader's Digest* (August 1997): 25.
2. J. Daniel Baumann, *An Introduction to Contemporary Preaching* (Grand Rapids: Baker, 1972), 100.
3. Abraham Maslow, *Motivation and Personality* (New York: Harper and Row, 1970).
4. Ruth Beechick, *Teaching Juniors: Both Heart and Head* (Denver: Accent Books, 1981), 24–25.

Chapter Seven

FOCUS ON LEARNING:
TRUTH INTO LIFE

Education is based upon an assumption that what is learned in the classroom can and should be applied outside the classroom. By definition, learning requires that the student be able to meaningfully transfer a concept from one setting to another. But the transfer of truth from situation to situation is not automatic. Effective teachers know this. They know that there is a difference between parroting answers and transferring those facts into life scenarios.

A fourth grade teacher had just completed a unit in science that dealt with rock types, rock strata, and the composition of the earth. She had taught the children about the molten core of the earth and its intense heat. Now it was the day before the exam and time for review. She glanced at the textbook and asked, "Suppose you dug a hole in the ground hundreds of feet deep, so deep that you were nearing the center of the earth. Would the hole be colder at the top or at the bottom?" None of the children responded. She thought to herself, *I'm sure they know the answer. I must not have asked that question quite right. Let me try again.* Taking the book in hand she asked, "What condition would one find at the interior core of the earth?" Almost every hand shot up. The immediate answer she received was "igneous fusion." Clearly, the term was absent of meaning for the children. They had memorized "igneous fusion" but had no comprehension of what it meant.

Learning is complex. From the moment a child enters this world, he or she perceives data, organizes it, interprets it, and makes choices based upon it. Children are born with an innate, God-given ability to learn. They are made to learn. As children grow to become adolescents and eventually adults, they change. They change not only in the physical sense, but also intellectually, socially, and spiritually. Those changes constitute and are driven by learning. Creative Bible teachers are committed to teaching in ways that produce life change. They want their students to learn, not in a sterile factoid way, but in a transferable life-related way. By focusing on learning, creative Bible teachers aim for transformation of the student's life.

The teacher's idea of what learning means colors how the teacher teaches, whether the teacher focuses primarily on facts or on application. Too often we equate knowing what the Bible says with knowing God. The person who can quote the most Scripture in prayer meeting isn't necessarily the most spiritual. He does not necessarily have the closest walk with God. And it's the walk with God that counts.

We all know this is true. Yet too often this knowledge fails to change the way we teach! The Sunday school teacher who concentrates all hour on content is teaching *as if* mastering content is what counts, *as if* life with God is the intellectual exercise the heretics of Paul's day taught.

When a Sunday school teacher merely teaches the Bible as content, he implies that to know about God and to know God are the same. Far too many young people leave our churches, rejecting the hypocrisy expressed by one high schooler: "All they want me to do is to say the holy words." Those who teach like this are tragically "without understanding."

But there is an equal and opposite error. It's the idea that a person can know God personally apart from the truth He has revealed in Scripture. Sometimes that error is seen in the lives of those who would argue most convincingly that they are "applying" Scripture, when in reality they are living by a list of rules that have little or nothing to do with a response to God or to the revealed truth of Scripture. What seems to be moral, Christian living can instead be an attempt to prove one's holiness to God or to others. This too is an error the Christian teacher can unconsciously encourage. There is a profound relationship between knowing about God and knowing God, but it's a relationship over which many stumble. Information about God and from God, applied to and responded to in daily life, leads to a growing knowledge *of* God. There is a specific route leading from knowledge about God to knowledge of God. For a spiritually productive ministry, the Bible teacher must understand this route and guide his students along it. That route starts with looking at the Bible text and analyzing its implications, then results in personal response to Scripture and to God.

Creative Bible teachers understand this principle of learning: *Learning most powerfully transfers and transforms when the material taught has meaning to the student's life and experience.* In an effort at understanding and applying this learning principle in the ministry of teaching, let's look at the matter of meaning and how meaning affects learning.

MEANINGFULNESS AND THE TRANSFER OF LEARNING

The Importance of Meaningful Material

Which list of words is easier to remember? Which has more meaning?

1. dog, elephant, rabbit, mouse, whale, horse
2. mouse, rabbit, dog, horse, elephant, whale

In all likelihood you selected the second list as the one more easily remembered. It is the more meaningful listing. The first list is random; the second has order. It moves from smallest to largest. This illustrates a basic principle of learning and, therefore, of teaching—*order and structure give meaning to information and ideas.* An effective teacher understands that for students to learn a concept, some sense of structure or order is important. Random ideas simply are not retained and transferred to life as well as ordered concepts.

Let's consider another example of the importance of meaning to learning. Examine the next two lists of words. Again, which is easier to recall? Which has more meaning?

1. young, black, airplane, happy, suitcase, the, in, gentleman, the, placed, the
2. the, happy, young, gentleman, placed, the, black, suitcase, in, the, airplane

Again, it is easy to see that the second set of words has more meaning to the reader. Although it is possible to memorize the first list word-for-word, the second list is much easier to retain. Why? Because it has structure, and structure gives meaning to the reader. In the second case we are dealing with an idea rather than a random list. Ideas have structure, sequence, and order.

Consider one more example of the importance of meaning to learning. Suppose you were asked to remember the following letter sequence: OTTFFSSENTETTFF. Would you find it difficult? You could review the list over and over until you get it "letter-perfect." But what if we give the sequence meaning: What if you knew that each letter is the first

letter of the words one, two, three, etc., through fifteen? Would you now
be able to more easily retain and recite this sequence? By giving meaning to the letter sequence, learning is made more effective.

Educators have understood this principle for years—*meaningfulness
is important to learners.* The significant challenge for the teacher is in applying this principle to the classroom setting. Here, then, is the task of
the creative Bible teacher. *The task of the creative Bible teacher is to make
the biblical material meaningful to the contemporary learner.*

Making Truth Meaningful

Ed Collins and his wife, Gail, teach the kindergarten Sunday
school class at their church. Last Sunday they were teaching the concept
of God's care for His children to the class. They used Psalm 23:1 (KJV) as
their memory verse. "The Lord is my shepherd, I shall not want." Over
and over they worked with the children to memorize it. Using the verse,
they taught the children that God cares for them like a shepherd cares
for his sheep. At craft time they made cardboard sheep, glued them on
to craft sticks, covered them with cotton. All through the craft time they
talked with the children about the shepherd and sheep and how wonderful it is that God is our shepherd. Ed and Gail did an excellent job
teaching their class and they really felt they had communicated with the
children. But at the very end of class, when they were reviewing the
memory verse with the children a final time, they became aware of how
challenging teaching can actually be. Michael spoke up. "Teacher, if the
Lord is my shepherd and He is so good, why wouldn't I want Him?" Obviously there was a breakdown in learning because there was a failure to
communicate meaningfully.

On occasion the debate arises as to which Bible version children
should use to memorize Scripture. Frankly, without attention to meaning, it probably doesn't matter which version is used because learning
will not effectively occur. The principle of meaningful learning should
point the teacher to a version that has meaning for the children doing
the memorizing. But the teacher should also define terms, discuss the
verse, and ensure that the meaning is clear. Remember, the job of the
teacher is to make the learning material meaningful to the learner. To
simply memorize a verse without seeking understanding falls short of
effective teaching and sufficient learning. One publisher of children's
club materials still requires students to memorize all of their memory
verses from the King James Version. Although the King James Bible is
poetic and reliable, it lacks meaning for many readers. That fact draws
many to modern language translations as preferable for teaching. Teachers who are interested in student learning will not say, "This is my pre-

ferred translation; that is why I use it to teach." Rather, they will say, "This translation is most meaningful to my students; that's why I use it to teach."

Beyond the selection of a translation of the Bible, how does a creative Bible teacher make material meaningful? What can a teacher do to enable the student to perceive the material in a way that has meaning and thus is more readily understood and applied? Research in teaching and learning theory points to three specific things that will give learning material meaningfulness.

Order and structure. As we have already pointed out, material that is organized and structured in a way students can understand will be more readily learned and transferred to new situations. Many teachers make the mistake of teaching concepts as isolated facts. Often the goal is to slowly build to a general structure from the various facts. But what actually happens is that the student does not remember the material because it was meaningless to him or her at the time it was taught. If a student cannot see how one step leads to the next, or if it is unclear where the class is heading, the class becomes frustrating, retention becomes poor, and soon the student is lost. The result is a bored, restless student, disinterested in the subject.

Just such an experience happened in a course called "Educational Foundations" that is required of students at a major Bible college. A structure was used to link the concepts taught in the class to a system called the "Frankena Model." Although the model is useful to seasoned Christian educators and graduate level students, it proved to be too complex and confusing for first year undergraduate students. As a result, what had been considered to be a positive course experience in the past became quite negative to students. Students began to express a negative attitude toward the material and the course. Many indicated that they were uncertain how everything fit together. Some became bored and restless. Others said they thought the material had little value to their ministry training. In response, the team of professors who taught the course redesigned it around a less complex structure, one with which the students were already familiar. The result was a reversal of attitudes of most students. The new structure made sense to students. Even though the same material was presented, by reordering it and sequencing it using the new structure, learning objectives were achieved.

Comprehensible vocabulary. Meaningful understanding of material requires a vocabulary that the student can understand. Even very intelligent people can be stymied in their learning when the vocabulary being used is unfamiliar or highly technical. Take Jenny for instance. Jenny types legal materials in her home for a law firm in her town. She did all of her work on a typewriter until her boss told her he wanted a copy of everything she produced on a computer disk as well as on paper. So Jenny took the plunge. At forty-two, learning to use a computer for the first time was a challenge. One problem was the terminology. Words like *gigabyte, hard drive, RAM, modem, protocol, server,* and *download* all were unfamiliar to her and seemed like a foreign language. Her transition to computers was difficult not because she lacked the ability, but because the vocabulary had little meaning to her. Then she made a trip to a local bookstore. The manager suggested the "For Dummies" series. He showed her titles like *Computers for Dummies, WordPerfect for Dummies,* and *The Internet for Dummies.* He said that the books were designed to help people like her, who felt like dummies because of the technical nature of the jargon, comprehend computers in everyday terms. Jenny bought two books and used them to transition nicely to comfortable use of the computer. Now she will tell you that she doesn't know how she did her work before she had her computer.

By using familiar terms and being careful to explain and illustrate new terms, teachers can encourage meaningful understanding of new material. Sometimes our use of terms can be inconsistent and can result in faulty ideas on the part of students. For example, we most often use the word *church* to mean the church building. We say to our children, "Don't run in church." What we really mean is, "Don't run in the church building." The difference might sound like splitting hairs, but it is significant if we want to teach children that the New Testament meaning of the word *church* is *the gathering of God's redeemed people.* In the first case we are talking about a building; in the second case we mean people. The building concept is not a biblical concept. Rather, the use of the term to describe a building has developed over time. Now, if we want to help students understand the nature of the church, we will have to adjust our vocabulary accordingly.

One congregation decided to shift its vocabulary usage with regard to the word *church.* Its members believed that most Christians had a faulty understanding of the church because of the poor usage of the term. In that church, the word *church* is reserved only for reference to the people of God, believers in Jesus Christ. All other uses of the term are modified to avoid misunderstanding. For example, when the building is being referred to, the term *church building* is used. This is done consistently in all publications and all classes. It is an intentional effort to teach a correct biblical idea.

Another term that is often used but seldom defined is "ask Jesus into your heart." Although the term is never used in Scripture, it is perhaps the primary term used today in explaining salvation, especially to children. We're so used to hearing it we assume it has deep meaning. But if children have been urged to ask Jesus into their heart, but have not been told of sin, the cross, or forgiveness, has the gospel been presented? It's important that the gospel be given clearly rather than in code words that we understand but those we teach may not. "Ask Jesus to forgive your sins" or "believe that Jesus died for you" are more precise than "be saved" or "become a Christian."

Linkage to life experience. Probably the most effective way to give meaning to the material we teach is to relate it to students' life experiences. The closer an idea or concept can be linked to something a student has already experienced or is currently experiencing, the more likely it is that the student will meaningfully understand and learn the material.

For example, a student growing up in an urban environment will have a far different range of life experiences than a child raised in a suburban or a rural setting. Which child will most readily understand the phrase, "I am the true vine, and my Father is the gardener" (John 15:1)? All the students may have experienced vines and gardening. The urban child might immediately envision Chicago's Wrigley Field where vines cover the outfield walls. The suburban child might picture a vine that is primarily decorative that climbs a trellis alongside a wall at his house. The rural child might picture a vineyard where grapes, watermelon, or pumpkins are grown. The phrase has a somewhat different meaning to the students because of differing prior experiences with vines. Teachers must be aware of how their students give meaning to the concepts they are teaching. By selecting stories, illustrations, and models closest to the student's experience, the teacher can encourage more effective learning.

Because the experience of the students is important in helping to make material taught in class meaningful to them, teachers must know something of the students' world. The creative Bible teacher must become aware of the social-economic background of the children, their family situations, and their interests. This is where the material we discussed in the last chapter becomes consequential. Needs assessment and a study of students' interests will give the teacher the connection points for teaching new concepts.

Bill Hart teaches a group of third grade students at Hope Baptist Church in an urban setting. Most of the children come from low income families, and many are from single-parent homes. In this week's Sunday school curriculum is a story that Bill is supposed to use to aid the students in applying the lesson. The story is about a father who comes home from work in the evening wearing a white shirt and tie, briefcase in hand, to a house in the suburbs with a two-car garage. The father is frustrated that his children have left toys and bikes out on the driveway. Although the story is well written and actually fits with the lesson theme, Bill knows it will not work with his students. There is nothing wrong with white shirts, ties, briefcases, and two-car garages, but, for Bill's third graders, they simply are not part of their experience. In fact, fathers aren't part of the experience for many of the children in his class. Bill must re-think the story and make it fit his student's world or substitute an entire-ly different story that will be relevant and will teach the same idea. By knowing his students Bill can make the material meaningful.

Remember Alex from chapter 6? Alex is conducting a small group Bible study with six to eight teens in his home each week. He did a needs assessment with his study group to better understand how to teach his students. The students he is working with attend a city of Chicago high school, have been Christians for varying lengths of time, and are potential leaders in the church youth group. Alex is teaching through the book of Hebrews with his students and is seeking ways to make the study meaningful for his students. He believes that the con-cept of persecution is the key to relevant learning of Hebrews 10:19–25. Since both the original readers of the passage and his own students have the experience of persecution in common, Alex will focus on this com-mon experience in teaching the passage. Alex knows that some of his students are struggling in their stand for Christ. They are tempted to hide their faith in Christ or even dump it altogether because of the diffi-culties that they face. This is a linkage that he believes will make teach-ing the Hebrews passage meaningful for his students. His assumption is that if he can make it more meaningful, they will more readily transfer the concepts taught in the passage to their everyday life.

THE LEVELS OF LEARNING TRANSFER

Those who teach the Bible ought to understand the kind of learn-ing they are aiming for. And they ought to realize that there are several levels at which learning can take place. Each level represents a stage of greater transfer from sterile fact to life-changing experience with biblical truth. Figure 10 depicts the five levels of learning transfer. Let's look at these five levels and their significance for those who teach the Bible.

The Rote Level

Carpe diem. Look at that phrase again: *Carpe diem.* Now, close your eyes and repeat it from memory: *Carpe diem.*

You may not realize it, but you've learned something! What? "Carpe diem." You have learned a meaningless phrase that, neverthe-less, you can repeat from memory.

Figure 10

LEVELS OF LEARNING TRANSFER

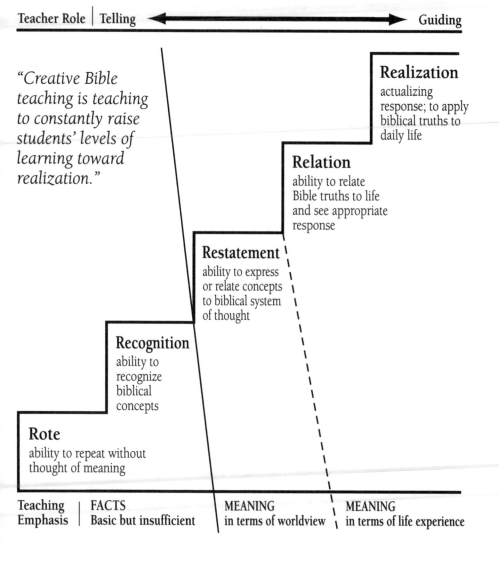

Teacher Role | Telling ⬅➡ Guiding

"Creative Bible teaching is teaching to constantly raise students' levels of learning toward realization."

Realization
actualizing response; to apply biblical truths to daily life

Relation
ability to relate Bible truths to life and see appropriate response

Restatement
ability to express or relate concepts to biblical system of thought

Recognition
ability to recognize biblical concepts

Rote
ability to repeat without thought of meaning

Teaching | FACTS
Emphasis | Basic but insufficient

MEANING
in terms of worldview

MEANING
in terms of life experience

This is rote learning: *to repeat something from memory, without thought of the meaning.* Unfortunately, much learning in our churches is on this level. Each Sunday we sing hymns and praise songs, often so familiar that our mouths form the words while our minds think other thoughts. We sometimes repeat the Lord's Prayer or the Apostles' Creed in the same way. At club meeting, in Sunday school, and even in Christian school classes in Bible, we drill students and help them learn their memory verses—by rote.

Although rote memory has its place in learning—such as when learning dates of historic events, the books of the Bible, the alphabet, multiplication tables, and state capitals—such learning is, by the definition above, meaningless. It is interesting that we often judge individuals as "well educated" by their ability to recall such esoteric information from rote memory. But such recall requires no real understanding, creativity, or intellectual analysis. Rote memory is simply the storing of data, not meaningful learning. Storing data is necessary, but it's limited in its usefulness if what is learned is not understood or applied. Learning the books of the Bible makes Bible study easier and helps students develop a skeleton for understanding the Bible, but it doesn't make one a growing Christian.

Some are aware of the dangers of rote learning—like the youth leader who led a Sunday school class for high school students. The topic was "Deepening Your Faith." As a matter of introduction and in an effort to involve students, the teacher asked, "So, what is faith?" Immediately one student's hand shot up. "'Faith is the substance of things hoped for, the evidence of things not seen,' Hebrews 11:1." "Hey great!" the teacher said, and nodded. "Now, what does that actually mean?" Clearly surprised, the teen stumbled. "Why, it means the substance of things hoped for. And, er, the evidence of things not seen." But, unwilling to accept a rote answer, the teacher pressed the student further. "Yes. But what does that mean?" Finally the teen shrugged. "I don't know," he said. "I just learned that verse a couple years ago to get to go to camp." Although such learning may be necessary to begin the learning process, clearly the Bible, taught and learned by rote, is unlikely to change lives!

The Recognition Level

Go back to *Carpe diem.* As you repeated it a moment ago, it seemed meaningless. But suppose you are told that *Carpe diem* in Latin means "Seize the day!" You've moved up the ladder of learning. The phrase is now invested with at least some meaning. To discover if you really had learned on this level, a teacher might give you a simple test: True or False? *Carpe diem* means "Seize the day!" Or perhaps a multiple choice question: *Carpe diem* means (a) God is good, (b) The day is gone, (c) Seize the day, (d) Night is near.

It's not difficult to teach or learn on this level. In fact, this is how much teaching is done in our schools. The tightrope walker _____ on the tightrope. (a) balanced, (b) baked, (c) bubbled, (d) barked. This is a typical question found in a children's reader to test reading comprehension. It is doubtful that it actually tests comprehension. Rather, it simply tests recognition, that is, the ability to recognize the right answer, not the ability to comprehend that answer. All that is required in this kind of learning is the ability to recognize something that has been said or read. This is often what happens in our Sunday schools.

Let's drop in on Karen Laine's class. She has just taught her first and second grade girls a series of lessons on the gospel. Now she wants to make sure they have learned the vital truths. So she is questioning them, one by one.

"Ann, can a person get to heaven by always obeying parents and being kind to friends?" "No," says Ann, shaking her head. (Good!) "Ah, Jan, can a person get to heaven by coming to church and reading the Bible and praying every day?" Jan too thinks and shakes her head. "No." (Wonderful!) "Now, Mary, can a person get to heaven by believing on the Lord Jesus Christ as his Savior from sin because He died on the cross to take the penalty for our sins?" Mary nods. "Yes." (Terrific!)

Has Karen Laine taught? Have her girls learned? It would seem to Karen that they know a person doesn't get to heaven by good works or religious behavior. And it seems they understand that one only goes to heaven by "believing in the Lord Jesus Christ as their Savior from sin because He died on the cross to take the penalty for their sin." But do they know what that means, or do they simply recognize that to be the "right" answer? What have the girls learned? *All her teaching and testing have required is the ability to recognize the things she has said in class!* She still does not know what that means to her students.

There is evidence that this is the level at which many Sunday school students learn Bible truths. A Michigan State University survey of religiously oriented college students showed that 74 percent of the group tested agreed with the statement "Christ died for the sins of humanity." Yet on the same survey, only 38 percent agreed that "faith in Christ is necessary for salvation." They recognized and agreed with the most familiar idea. But they did not grasp its meaning! They could not see the relationship between this truth and the lostness of all apart from Christ.

Tragically, the ability to recognize a truth as from the Bible, or as something a Sunday school teacher or parent has said, does not imply either a personal response or an integration of the truth recognized with the learner's total understanding of the Bible and life. It's important to recognize biblical concepts, of course, and to recognize their meanings as they have been taught. This kind of learning has an important place in the process of transfer of learning from facts to life, but this is never sufficient. This kind of learning simply does not lead to transformation. It should lead to further learning. As creative Bible teachers we cannot stop with or be satisfied with the recognition level.

The Restatement Level

While Karen Laine was testing her first and second grade students at the recognition level, over in the third and fourth grade boys' class Mark Ransom was shooting for something more. He too had just completed a series on the gospel and wanted to test his boys' understanding. So he drew on an experience he had had that week with a neighborhood boy.

"Guys," he began, "I was talking with Tom this week, a boy who lives in the house next door, and he told me that today he's being confirmed in his church. He said that the bishop was going to anoint him with the Holy Spirit, and that with the Holy Spirit to help him, he was sure he could be good enough to get to heaven. If Tom told you that, what would you say that might help him understand how to get to heaven?" And then Mark stopped and waited.

What he was shooting for is no easy kind of learning. It's no multiple-choice type, where the answer is laid out for the student to recognize. It demands a grasp of content in terms of relationship to other ideas, and an ability to express the whole without clues, because the ideas have been mastered. Although even this level of Bible learning is not sufficient, it is necessary.

The restatement level is the level at which the student can meaningfully understand a truth and creatively analyze that truth in relationship to other truths. For example, by rote memory one could learn a list of composers' names and the compositions they produced. One could go a step further and be able to recognize who produced a particular piece when the composition is played. But to be able to compare and contrast composers' styles and messages is quite different. This level demands understanding and meaningful learning.

The Bible is God's Word, communicating true information about Himself, about us, about our world. It expresses the fundamental realities on which we have to base our lives. Thus, its teachings must be understood. We must know what the Bible teaches, not merely as something we recognize—"Oh yes, that's in the Bible, isn't it?"—but as a

mastered system that controls our patterns of thought and our philosophy of life. This kind of mastery comes only when Bible truths are
learned on the restatement level. Only when we have the ability to take
a Bible truth, relate it to other ideas and values, and express that truth in
our own words, have we begun to learn meaningfully. Even children can
be led to this kind of learning of the Bible truths that are important for
them.

Notice in Figure 10 that it is at the restatement level where learning begins to have meaning for the student. Students must understand
what they have learned in order to restate it in their own words. They
must go beyond simply parroting to actually explaining. This is an important and pivotal step in the transfer of learning to life.

Learning characterized by this ability is significantly different from
the teaching that takes place in most of our Sunday schools. Too many
of us are satisfied to check and see if our students recognize the truths
we've taught. Too few of us consciously seek to help students achieve
mastery of the teachings of God's Word.

The Relation Level

Although it's vital to understand the Bible as content, this in itself
is not enough. The Word of God is more than information; it is a point
of contact with God Himself. The crucial issue in bringing us beyond information about God to personal experience with God is that of response. To discern the appropriate response to a Bible truth, we must
see the relationship between that truth and our lives.

This level of learning presupposes the restatement process. When a
person thinks through a biblical teaching and expresses it in his or her
own words, that insight into its meaning for life is most likely to come.
It is when Mark Ransom's boys are trying to formulate and express their
understanding of the gospel that one of them is most likely to suddenly
see a truth. "Say, this means I have to put my trust in Christ as Savior."
"Then my dad isn't a Christian." "So that's why we talk so much about
missionaries. That's why we give and pray."

When a learner discovers such a relationship for himself, when in
a flash of insight the parts fit together and he sees meaning in terms of
life, then the pathway to personal response stands open.

There is much that a teacher can do to lead his students to meaningful involvement with God's Word and, thus, provide opportunities
for the Holy Spirit to point out to each student personally the response
He wants him to make. It's only when the teacher consciously teaches
for learning in terms that lead to appropriate response that his teaching
is in harmony with the nature of God's Word. The Bible, taught in har-

mony with its nature, transforms. Learning on any lesser level is inadequate. When the student can see relationship between the concepts he or she has learned in class and everyday life, the possibility of the student actually making the transfer of learning to life is enhanced.

The Realization Level

This is the goal of all Bible teaching: realizing, in the sense of making real in experience. Here is truth, applied in life. It's one thing to understand what response to God's Word is appropriate; to actually make that response is another. This is the difference between being a hearer of the Word who merely deludes himself into thinking he is righteous and a doer of the Word who actually lives out its teachings.

It's in the sense of "response made" that the Bible often uses the word *know*. In 1 Corinthians 6, Paul asks five times, "Do you not know . . . ?" In each case he asks this about concepts they had heard from him and that were familiar. He asks because their lives were out of harmony with the truth they had heard. In the biblical sense they did not know these truths, for they were not living them.

This is the level of learning for which every Bible teacher vaguely hopes, but for which he must consciously teach. For, humanly speaking, learning that changes life is a product of a particular kind of teaching. This is not teaching for rote, to produce the ability to repeat without thought of meaning. Not teaching for recognition, the ability to recognize biblical ideas. Not even teaching for restatement, the ability to understand Bible content as part of a system. The Bible teacher must teach in such a way that his students, understanding the truth of God, discover and are led to make an appropriate life response to the God who speaks to them through His Word. Only when God's work is learned in this way can God's Word transform.

The realization level completes the process of transfer of learning from the classroom to life. Transfer is the clearest indicator of life-change teaching. In all aspects of education, people take classroom teaching and use it to modify daily living. Take, for example, the physician who transfers techniques he has learned in medical school to his practice of medicine. Or the engineering student who takes his knowledge of aerodynamics and designs aircraft. All of us who read this book are examples of transfer of learning. We have taken the principles taught in elementary school from special textbooks that helped us to learn to read and are applying them now as adults to reading this book. Transfer occurs in our Sunday school classes as well. But the question that remains is, How can we promote the transfer of our classroom teaching to practice in the students' lives? In many ways, that is what we will deal with in the third section of this book. For now, let us suggest a few ideas that will help your students move up the transfer of learning steps.

TEACHING CREATIVELY FOR THE TRANSFER OF LEARNING

Teacher: All right, boys and girls, what's fuzzy, has a bushy tail, and gathers nuts in the fall?

Johnny: Sure sounds like a squirrel to me, but I know the answer must be Jesus.

Many times our teaching does not promote thinking. It merely promotes rote memory or recognition levels of learning transfer. Without much mental effort, students come to expect the answers to be predictable, fill-in-the-blank type responses. Little real thinking is needed in the non-creative classroom. Creative Bible teachers approach their task in a different manner than non-creative teachers. They seek more student learning at the highest levels of learning transfer.

Realizing that students may learn at various levels, we can now more closely define creative teaching as *consciously and effectively focusing on activities that raise the students' learning level*. The weaknesses in our Sunday schools can often be traced to a failure to understand learning on the higher levels and a resultant failure to help students learn significantly. What, in practice, distinguishes creative Bible teaching from non-creative teaching? Let's look briefly at three areas of contrast.

Focus on Facts vs. Focus on Meaning

Drop around a Sunday school department during the last five or ten minutes of class, and you can quickly separate the creative and non-creative teachers. In most classes you'll hear climaxes like these: "Now, Johnny, will you review the lesson for us? The rest of you raise your hands if he leaves anything out." Or, "Jean, how many fish were there in the great draught of fishes?" Or, "Our time is almost up, and we still haven't quite finished our lesson. So be quiet and let me tell. . . . " These comments—and the teachers who make them—focus on biblical facts. During the last moments an illustration or exhortation may be thrown in, but the hour has been spent mastering facts rather than meaning. When teaching has this focus, the students develop only the ability to repeat or recognize Bible truths. Learning has stalled on the lower levels.

Yet now and then you will overhear probing questions that force attention to meaning. "How might Christ say that if He were talking to people like us?" "What would John be like if he were a teen going to your high school?" "Is it always right to separate ourselves from unbelievers? What would it mean if all Christians cut themselves off from unsaved friends?" And then you hear students talking, discussing, testing their ideas, exploring until the meaning of God's words becomes clear and relevant to contemporary life.

Teaching for meaning isn't easy. Normally, the creative teacher knows and uses a variety of methods. He knows how to cover content quickly and clearly. He knows how to stimulate his students to test and relate truth. But the dividing line is not the use or nonuse of methods. The dividing line is focus. The creative teacher finds time for a thorough exploration of the meaning of the truth taught. And learning in his class moves on up to the higher levels, where appropriate response to God's Word can be seen and made.

Student Passivity vs. Student Activity

Kelly teaches elementary schoolchildren at a church in Dallas. When she teaches she puts on a fantastic demonstration. She typically has a class of eighteen first and second grade children, crammed in a little quonset hut out behind the church, all seated uncomfortably on adult-sized folding chairs. Yet she holds these children spellbound for forty-five minutes! She has outstanding storytelling ability, and she uses two flannelboards, a chalkboard, puppets, cutout figures, and visualized verses and songs. If the boys and girls were given a test over the content she teaches, they could pass with perfect scores. She is an accomplished teacher and an imaginative one—but not a creative one in the sense in which we are using the term. Her pupils listen and learn, but only on the first two levels. Creative Bible teachers seek restatement, relation, and realization levels of learning. Kelly is good at what she does. She even uses a great variety of methods, but something in her teaching is missing—life change.

To move up even to the restatement level of learning, students must be led beyond listening. They must personally think through the meaning of Bible truths. They must toss the ideas around in their own minds to formulate and express them in their own words. For this kind of learning, the students have to participate, to express their own ideas and their own insights. Creative teachers do the things that Kelly does, but they do more. The creative teacher makes sure that his students take an active part in exploring meaning.

This is vital. You can tell a class what a Bible truth means. But then the meaning becomes just another piece of information to recognize. For meaning to be conveyed to the student, he needs to discover for himself the relationship of a truth to his life. And this discovery requires an active student. It demands a student's thinking, integrating, relating, reasoning. Listen in on the creative teacher, and this is what you'll hear: his students actively exploring meaning.

Teacher as Teller vs. Teacher as Guide

When the focus of the lesson is on facts that the students can learn without participating, the teacher serves as a teller. He communicates information, and class activities center on himself. Sometimes non-creative teachers use a variety of methods. Yet the methods of a non-creative teacher have two characteristics: They are designed merely to communicate content, and they are primarily teacher activities. Creative teachers are focused on the students and their learning. Student-centered activities that engage student thinking are the key.

The creative teacher has a different concept of his role. His responsibility is to stimulate his students to discover meaning and to see the response to God's voice that God requires of them personally. He feels that student activities are more important than teacher-focused ones. The class does not center on him; it centers on them. The creative teacher serves as a guide to learning and strives constantly to structure situations that will stimulate his students to discover meaning. The methods he uses are also set apart by two characteristics: They are chosen to focus attention on meaning, and they create student involvement in this process of discovery.

Jesus was a creative teacher. Through the use of parables, questions, and thought-provoking content, He challenged thinking. Go through Matthew's gospel some time and note Jesus' use of questions. You will find that your Bible will be highlighted with verses that read: "Why do you worry about clothes?" (6:28), "Why do you look at the speck of sawdust in your brother's eye and pay no attention to the plank in your own eye?" (7:3), "Which is easier: to say, 'Your sins are forgiven' or to say, 'Get up and walk'?" (9:5), "Why did you doubt?" (14:31), "What do you think about the Christ?" (22:42). Through questions, Jesus pushed His learners to think and to advance on the learning transfer steps to higher levels.

This, then, is creative Bible teaching. It is teaching the Bible in ways that cause learning on the significant levels of restatement, relation, and realization. To cause this kind of learning the Bible teacher must (1) focus on the meaning of the Bible truth taught, (2) involve his students in active search for meaning, and (3) stimulate and guide his students in this discovery process.

Chapter Eight

FOCUS ON RESULTS:
TEACHING FOR LIFE CHANGE

When Randy Johnson teaches he gets results. Randy is a Little League baseball coach who knows how to take an average team and make it into a winner. Last season, Randy was asked to coach an expansion team in his community's eleven- and twelve-year-old "bronco" league. The team struggled during most of the season, but when the playoffs came around Randy had them ready. He had taught a team with little natural talent and minimal skill development to be ballplayers. They took second place—far from the cellar finish everyone expected. When asked how he teaches the game to his players, Randy replied, "Well, first you must know what you want them to learn. Second, you must also know how you want them to change because of what they have learned. Once you know what you are seeking to accomplish you can make a plan to get there. The problem with a lot of coaches is that they are not focused on the results they want to achieve with each player. You've got to know what you hope to change and develop in a player."

Randy is right! If we answer those two basic questions—What do I want the student to learn? and How do I want the student to change?—we can plan our teaching in such a way as to achieve the results we desire. Whether we teach baseball or the Bible, a clear sense of direction and a target for our teaching is mandatory to success. In this chapter you will discover how to focus your lesson on results and life change by asking and answering these fundamental teaching questions.

DEVELOPING THE TEACHING IDEA:
WHAT DO I WANT STUDENTS TO LEARN?

The typical Bible teacher concentrates on communicating clearly and accurately just what the Bible teaches. He or she may add a word of exhortation or an illustration or two, but the focus is nevertheless on the Bible as information. This is commendable and is the teacher's first responsibility, but it is not enough. The creative Bible teacher, whether in a Sunday school, a Christian school classroom, or the pulpit, does not neglect the Bible as information. But he goes beyond information. *Creative Bible teachers focus on helping learners bridge the gaps between the world of the Bible and the world of the student.* It is not easy to bridge the gap between the truth and culture of the Bible and the life and response of the student. But bridging the gap is necessary, and it can be done. Here is how to take the next step in the process of creative Bible teaching.

Begin with the Bridge Principle

You will recall from chapters 4 and 5 that the fruit of effective Bible study is found in the discovery of the "bridge principle." The bridge principle, also called the exegetical idea or big idea of the passage, is the central truth that the author of the scriptural passage intended to communicate to the original recipients or hearers of the text. In chapter 5 we used Hebrews 10:19–25 as our example study passage. We concluded that the bridge principle of the passage might be stated as follows. *The priesthood of the believer, accomplished by the sacrificial work of Christ, along with Christ's high priestly ministry, calls every Christian to draw near to God, hold fast to his faith, and spur on other believers so that each one might persevere through difficult times and difficult situations.* Although this sentence summarizes the central idea or the passage as the author communicated it to his original readers, it is not yet an effective teaching idea for the contemporary setting.

Consider the Student

The creative Bible teacher must take the bridge principle and relate its meaning and implications to the modern-day student. By clearly understanding the transferable concept, the teacher can seek links to the student's experience and needs. This is where the needs assessment that we did in chapter 6 becomes relevant. By understanding the passage (the bridge principle) and by knowing the student's needs, creative Bible teachers can develop what we might call the "pedagogical idea." The word *pedagogy* literally means "the teaching of children," but it has come to refer to teaching people of any age. The pedagogical idea or teaching idea restates or revises the bridge principle or exegetical idea in light of the student audience.

Remember Alex? He was the twenty-eight-year-old medical professional who works with youth in the city of Chicago. Alex did a needs assessment with his group. His needs assessment indicated that his students face a great deal of persecution when they stand up for Christ with their peers. Alex determined that that fact was a linking point he can use to make the teaching of Hebrews relevant to his students. Now, Alex must ask the question: "What do I want my students to learn?" His answer will constitute the pedagogical, or teaching idea, for his class or series of classes.

State the Pedagogical Idea

Here is the pedagogical or teaching idea that Alex stated for his study with his group of urban teens. *In times of persecution, students who follow Jesus must learn to draw on their most powerful resources—God and one another.* Notice how he took the central concept of the passage and related it to the level and needs of his group. Alex is dealing with high school students who face real persecution for following Jesus. Alex is aware of this and has designed his pedagogical idea to reflect the needs of his students.

The pedagogical idea, or teaching idea, summarizes the major concept of the lesson that the creative Bible teacher desires to communicate to students. It is rooted in the exegetical idea or general principle of the passage. In essence, the teacher writes the pedagogical idea in order to contemporize the message of the passage. Table 10 on page 134 depicts the relationship between the exegetical idea and the pedagogical idea.

The pedagogical idea answers the question, "What do I want students to learn from this lesson?" Creative Bible teachers understand that they cannot teach everything a passage teaches in a single lesson. Therefore, they must select the message they plan to communicate that bridges the gap between the biblical world and the students' world.

DEVELOPING LESSON AIMS: HOW DO I WANT THE STUDENT TO CHANGE?

Creative Bible teachers seek transformation. The apostle Paul expressed this goal of Bible teaching in these words: "The goal of this command is love, which comes from a pure heart and a good conscience and a sincere faith" (1 Tim. 1:5). You'll find this idea stated in different ways throughout the New Testament. In Ephesians Paul calls it being "filled to the measure of all the fullness of God" (3:19) and being "mature, attaining to the whole measure of the fullness of Christ" (4:13).

Table 10

Exegetical Idea	Pedagogical Idea

What it is...

• The truth that the author of the passage intended the original hearers or readers to understand	• The truth that the teacher of the class wants the students to understand from the passage

Also known as...

• The Bridge Principle	• The Teaching Idea
• The Central Idea	
• The Big Idea	

Answers the question(s)...

• What is the author talking about?	• What do I want the student to learn from this lesson?
• What is the author saying about what he is talking about?	

Focuses on...

• The world of the Bible	• The world of the student

An example from Hebrews 10:19-25

• The priesthood of the believer, accomplished by the sacrificial work of Christ, along with Christ's high priestly ministry, calls every Christian to draw near to God, hold fast to his faith, and spur on other believers so that each one might persevere through difficult times and difficult situations.	• In times of persecution, students who follow Jesus must learn to draw on their most powerful resources—God and one another.

The writer to the Hebrews speaks of the mature, who "by constant use have trained themselves to distinguish good from evil" (5:14), and urges believers to "go on to maturity" (6:1). These transformed persons that Paul speaks of in Romans (12:2) he also describes in Galatians as led by and living in the Spirit, full of the fruit of "love, joy, peace, patience, kindness, goodness, faithfulness, gentleness and self-control" (5:22–23). In each case, the idea is the same. When God's Word is allowed to impact God's people, they are transformed from the inside out. Life change is not optional; it is the focus of learning for the creative Bible teacher.

The question that the teacher must answer is: *"How do I want my students to change as a result of this lesson?"* Certainly, the most immediate answer to this question is that we want our students to be like Christ. We want them to be transformed. The trouble is, transformation is a big aim—too big. We all want this, but the idea of transformation or Christian maturity doesn't give us sufficiently helpful guidelines for constructing a specific lesson. To say, "I want this lesson to bring my students to maturity" may be commendable, but it really isn't meaningful. It is far too general. One lesson simply won't do it. You can see why when you break down the idea of maturity. What's involved? Many, many things— like one's relationship with God: prayer, Bible study, worship, meditation, praise, confession, honesty. And then there's relationship with our family: love, patience, guidance, discipline *and* receiving discipline, forgiveness. And how about relationships with non-Christians, and its cluster of concern: witness, separation, exemplary living, consideration, suffering, and so many others. And we can go on and on.

Certainly no single class, no series of lessons, no year of lessons, will bring a student to absolute maturity in Christ or complete transformation. So, while the big aim of transformation is always there, our *teaching aim* has to be more specific.

Kinds of Learning

University of Chicago professor Benjamin Bloom developed what is known as a "taxonomy of learning."[1] The word *taxonomy* means "classifications or kinds." For example, one could develop a taxonomy of college students in a number of different ways. We could speak of freshmen, sophomores, juniors, or seniors. Each is a distinct category that we could describe and discuss. We could develop a different taxonomy of students based upon their majors in college—mathematics, chemistry, elementary education, biology, sociology, and so on. We could classify students as commuting and resident or as married and single. We create taxonomies to aid in discussing and understanding a subject. By creating categories or classifications, differences and similarities between classifications can be identified and explained.

Bloom developed a taxonomy of learning that had three classifications. He called these classifications "domains" of learning. Each domain is a category that describes a type of learning that human beings can achieve. The first domain he identified was the *cognitive,* or thinking, domain. The second was the *affective,* or emotive, domain. And the third he called the *pyscho-motor,* or behavioral, domain. It is important to understand something of what is meant by each domain category because these domains provide a target for potential change in the life and learning of the student.

In Acts 2 we read of Peter's Pentecost sermon. Peter told his listeners of the plan of God for salvation fulfilled in Jesus Christ's death and resurrection. As a result of his message his audience was transformed. By hearing the Word of God taught with the power of God's Holy Spirit, lives were changed. In a remarkable verse recorded by Luke in Acts 2:37 we read, "When the people heard this, they were cut to the heart and said to Peter and the other apostles, 'Brothers, what shall we do?'"

Notice that each of Bloom's domains of learning was affected by Peter's teaching ministry. First, the listeners *heard* his message. Peter's teaching provided content that had to be mentally processed and considered by his audience. Peter taught in such a way as to motivate cognitive learning. His students had to understand his message. They had to change their thinking. Teaching that touches the cognitive domain encourages the acquisition of information and the processing of that information in meaningful ways. Second, we read that they were "cut to the heart." This phrase refers to a change in attitudes and values. Peter's listeners were *emotionally affected* by his teaching. Not only did Peter teach to the head, but his message also focused on heart level learning—the affective domain. Finally, we read that in response to what was taught, the learners in Acts 2:37 asked, "Brothers, what shall we do?" Not only did Peter's teaching affect learning on the cognitive and affective domains, but it also motivated a behavioral response. So we have in this verse all three kinds of potential learning—cognitive, affective, and behavioral. Figure 11 helps us visually capture and explain these three learning domains.

The first area of learning and life change is cognitive. Here the focus is on the processes of thinking and knowing. The purpose is to communicate biblical information and help the students to comprehend that information. Clearly, the teaching target is the head. Second, creative Bible teachers seek to change students affectively. In this domain, teachers seek to change students' values and attitudes. The goal is to

Figure 11

BLOOM'S THREE DOMAINS OF LEARNING

ACTS 2:37

COGNITIVE

Thinking and Knowing

Cognition

"Head"

When the people heard this,

AFFECTIVE

Values and Attitudes

Conviction

"Heart"

they were cut to the heart...

BEHAVIORAL

Actions and Skills

Competence

"Hands"

and said to Peter and the other apostles, "Brothers, what shall we do?"

bring the students to a point where they develop new convictions and beliefs. Here the teaching target is the heart. Third, creative Bible teachers seek to address the behavioral domain. They want to change the students' actions or impart skills. The purpose is one of developing competent Christians who not only know the Word, but do the Word as well. The target in this case is the hands. All three are essential—head, heart, and hands. Creative Bible teachers aim at all three domains.

What Is an Aim?

A lesson aim is a statement developed by the teacher to describe the kind of learning and life change that is desired or expected in the life of the student as a result of completing a lesson, unit, or course of study. Teachers develop aims to describe changes that grow out of learning. Aims describe the targets of teaching. By defining the goal or target, teachers use aims to design and evaluate their teaching plan and effectiveness. Like archers, teachers must have targets. The better defined the target, the more likely it is that the teacher will accurately hit it. Therefore, effective teachers carefully write lesson aims for their teaching sessions. Let's look at the various kinds of aims we could write to help focus our Bible teaching.

Kinds of Aims

If there are three kinds of learning, it stands to reason that there are three kinds of aims that creative Bible teachers can write for their lesson plans, each related to one of the learning domains. Christian educators suggest that Bible teachers focus on one or more of these types of aims in their weekly teaching ministry. One is the *content aim,* in which his purpose is to communicate biblical information. Then there's the *inspiration aim,* in which his purpose is to inspire, touch the emotions, change or challenge an attitude, affect a personal value choice, or engender commitment to an ideal or belief. Finally there is the *action aim,* in which his purpose is to move to action or impart a skill. Each of these aims has a valid but different place in Christian teaching.

If our goal is the Christlike maturity of the student, *which kind of aim leads to transformation?* Can they be separated, or do they all work together? In 1 Corinthians 2:15 Paul claims that the spiritual man "makes judgments about all things." The Greek verb here, *anakrinō,* speaks of a capacity to discern. The believer, in virtue of his salvation and relationship with God, has the capacity for spiritual discernment of "all things." He can look at life the way God does. He can see the implications of God's truth for life situations and can respond in harmony with God's will. But this is only a capacity—one that is not developed in all believers.

The development from capacity to ability is intimately related to maturity. Hebrews 5:14 says that mature believers "distinguish good from evil." The word *discern* is from the same root (*krinō*) as the word *appraises* of 1 Corinthians. It's set apart by a prefix (*dia*), which indicates that what is a capacity in all believers has become an ability in the mature.

Now, how did the mature move from capacity to ability? How did they become mature? Because of practice they have their senses trained to "distinguish good from evil." *These are people who have seen the implications of truth and responded appropriately.*

This is the educational significance of Hebrews 5:14. Growth comes by experience, by using our capacity to understand and to respond. For the teacher whose goal is spiritual growth, this means that his teaching aim will be to produce response. For it is those living responsively to God who grow and mature. As all three aims are essential, all three must be emphasized in our teaching ministry.

The content aim. We suggested a moment ago that content and inspiration aims are valid ones for the Bible teacher. In Bible college and seminary, students learn much about the Bible as content. They are trained in theology, which is a systematization of the information contained in Scripture. In such classes they do not go deeply into implications of those truths. Yet this training is essential. Why? Because the Bible should be mastered as content. With a framework of understanding of the whole, tremendous light is thrown on every passage. Without such a framework, it's possible to misinterpret a passage or verse. Bible students, all Bible students, need to come to know, contemplate, and understand the content of the Bible. Without changing the student's knowledge base and thinking categories, changes in attitude and behavior are generally just superficial.

Certainly somewhere in the Christian education of our children, youth, and adults, the church should provide for teaching the Word as a whole, as a system of truth. Such teaching is an important framework for more meaningful personal Bible study. Students must get the big picture and comprehend the story line of the Bible. To do that students must be taught the content of the Bible.

The inspiration aim. This actually is a type of response aim. After all, to some truths of Scripture the appropriate response is emotional. It's one of praise or an expression of love for God. No response to God can be a cold, emotionless performance of actions that are distasteful to us. If a response is truly to God, love must be the underlying motive (cf. 1 Cor. 13). Anything less is not response to God but response to law. And response to God's Word as law leads only to the frustration of our hopes and of God's purposes for us.

Inspiration aims are some of the most difficult to achieve, yet it is essential that teachers target the heart in their teaching efforts. Jesus focused much of His ministry on inspirational (affective) learning. We could open to any of the Gospels and find Jesus challenging people's values and attitudes. A very pointed example of Jesus aiming for the heart of the learner is found in Matthew 13. Notice what Jesus has to say to His disciples:

> [13]This is why I speak to them in parables: Though seeing, they do not see; though hearing, they do not hear or understand. [14]In them is fulfilled the prophecy of Isaiah: "You will be ever hearing but never understanding; you will be ever seeing but never perceiving. [15]For this people's heart has become calloused; they hardly hear with their ears, and they have closed their eyes. Otherwise they might see with their eyes, hear with their ears, understand with their hearts and turn, and I would heal them." (Matt. 13:13–15)

Here Jesus explains to His disciples His reasons for speaking in parables. His point is that parables cut to the heart. If one's attitude is open and receptive, the message is perceived; but if the attitude is calloused, the response is one of rejection. Jesus recognized that content alone would not change His learners. Rather, He had to teach in a way that the heart or affective aspect of the learners would be challenged.

The action aim. For spiritual growth and Christian maturity to occur, creative Bible teachers must aim at a behavioral and skill response in the learner. It is necessary for learners to hear and understand biblical content. Therefore, content aims have an essential place in Bible teaching. It is also necessary that the student is inspired to believe and value the truth that is taught. For this reason teachers should include affective aims. But ultimately, the blessing comes not through just hearing the Word of God or even in a deep heartfelt conviction as to its importance and validity. The blessing comes in obeying or doing what it says. James is clear on this point.

> [22]Do not merely listen to the word, and so deceive yourselves. Do what it says. [23]Anyone who listens to the word but does not do what it says is like a man who looks at his face in a mirror [24]and, after looking at himself, goes away and immediately forgets what he looks like. [25]But the man who looks intently into the perfect law that gives freedom, and continues to do this, not forgetting what he has heard, but doing it—he will be blessed in what he does. (James 1:22–25)

Action aims are framed in terms of behavioral response or skill development. When the teacher builds his lesson, he must think in terms of the learner response he hopes to achieve. A survey of evangelical Sunday school lessons shows that this principle is often overlooked by editors and writers. Look, for instance, at these aims, drawn at random from materials of several independent and denominational publishers.

1. To teach that Christ is a powerful Person who can change our lives for good.
2. To help primaries realize that God loves them and cares for them in difficult situations.
3. To communicate to high schoolers the length and depth and breadth of the love of Christ, and to help each understand that this love is made available to him today through trust in Christ.
4. To convince each pupil of the importance of looking to Christ for help when in need.
5. To help each student discover why the present ministry of Christ as our High Priest is important to him.
6. To explain clearly and compellingly the necessity of accepting Christ as personal Savior.
7. To help students dispel any fears that they may have which might prevent them from dedicating their lives to Christ for His service.
8. To discuss the implications of the gospel for our growing tense national racial situation.
9. To help young teens understand that church membership is an important spiritual responsibility and a vital part in a developing Christian life.

Notice that all of the aims are written in terms of what the teacher hopes to accomplish with the student. But notice also that none of the aims actually speaks to what the student will do or how the student will change as a result of the learning experience. When teachers only construct aims that emphasize "to know that," then the teacher is led to think of his job as one of teaching the Bible only for information. Some aims lead the teacher to think in terms of implications (see 5–9). But none of the aims quoted directs the teacher where he must go if his students are to grow, to respond. It's important, then, for teachers using curriculum, as well as for those who are not using teaching aids, to write objectives that require action on the part of the student.

Remember, you must understand your goal clearly enough to state it if you hope to build a lesson that will achieve it. So let's consider together how we might construct lesson aims that assist us in lesson planning.

Building a Lesson Aim

Study and understand the passage. This comes first. Any response we seek to evoke must be appropriate to the true meaning of the passage. That is why we spent a great deal of time in the first step of lesson preparation on developing the exegetical idea. It is important that you carefully study the passage.

We could cite an example at this point to remind us of the importance of including this essential lesson preparation step. You may recall that Christ said to one man, "Go, sell everything you have and give to the poor, and you will have treasure in heaven. Then come, follow me" (Mark 10:21). Is the appropriate response for us to sell all we have? Not when the context is understood. Not when we see Christ's purpose, which was to forcefully point out to this law-abiding young man that he had unknowingly violated the first and great commandment. He did not love God with his whole heart. He loved his wealth—so much that he chose it and rejected the invitation of Christ, his God.

Rightly understood, the appropriate response to this passage is a careful and honest self-evaluation. Has someone or something displaced God in my affections? Only when I examine my life and decisively reject any idol have I made an appropriate response.

So "What does this passage teach?" is the first question that must be asked in building a lesson aim. The response at which we aim must be appropriate to the Word.

Understand implications for the learner. This is particularly important when you teach children or youth, or adults whose life situation is different from your own. Sunday school curriculum writers often try to select passages that present truth relevant to each age group. This is one advantage of a graded curriculum. With this curriculum plan a lesson can be geared directly to the characteristics and needs of each age grouping.

This is an important concept, this choosing passages that are relevant to the learners' present lives and experiences. Of course, there are areas in which the teacher will need to move beyond the learners' present experiences. We can teach children doctrinal concepts they might not find "relevant," such as the inspiration of Scripture, the Trinity, the nature of the church, or the Second Coming. Some fundamentals of Christian living, such as what the Bible teaches about the permanence and sacred nature of marriage, should be addressed before the learner is old enough to care very much about the subject. But generally, lessons should deal with subjects that help the student know how he should respond to God today. In Proverbs 22:6, the familiar command to train up a child in the way he should go, the Hebrew clearly indicates that such training involves teaching the truth needed, in ways it can be used, at each developing stage of life. How clear this should be. If spiritual growth comes through response, we must teach truth to which the learner can respond.

To guide this response the teacher needs to know as much of the life and patterns of life of his students as possible. Read up on the characteristics of the age group you teach. Observe the students, visit their homes, talk with them. The better you understand their lives, the better you can tailor your lessons to lead them to response. Again, the needs assessment that we conducted earlier helps us in this aspect of writing lesson aims. Here too is where a well-considered pedagogical idea is crucial to effective lesson design.

Assuming that you have written your exegetical idea and pedagogical idea, you are ready to write lesson aims for your teaching session. Here is how a lesson aim is typically written.

Writing a Lesson Aim

When you understand the passage and see its relevance to the lives of your pupils, you're ready to state your aim. Usually four criteria are suggested for constructing aims:

1. short enough to be remembered
2. clear enough to be meaningful
3. specific enough to be achieved
4. written in terms of the student

Let's see how Alex developed lesson aims for his group of urban teenagers who attend his weekly Bible study. You will recall that Alex is planning to lead a study on Hebrews 10:19–25. Alex developed his exegetical idea and his pedagogical idea. Now he is ready to try his hand at writing some lesson aims. His lesson aims will describe how he wants his students to change as a result of the class. Alex could focus in any of the three domains of learning—cognitive, affective, or behavioral—by writing content, inspirational, or action aims. He has decided to write one of each type of aim. He used a simple structure to help in the writing of his lesson aims. Here is how he formatted his aims.

Students will _____ the _____ by _____.
          (learning verb)   (learning concept)   (learning response)

This structure helps to keep his aims short, clear, specific, and written in terms of what the student will learn rather than what the teacher will teach. Here are the aims Alex developed for his lesson.

Content Aim (Cognitive): Students will discover the three primary life implications that grow out of the priestly work of Christ by doing an inductive study of Hebrews 10:19–25.

Inspirational Aim (Affective): Students will commit themselves to the practice of encouraging one another in times of persecution and difficulty by agreeing to meet together for prayer before school twice each week.

Action Aim (Behavioral): Students will draw upon three vital means of survival in the midst of persecution and difficulties—prayer, perseverance, and people—by meeting together each week to "spur each other on."

Notice that the first objective focuses on content to be learned or discovered. Although the content is important to Christian living, this aim does not call students to actually live out the message of the passage. The change being called for in the students is a change in their knowledge and understanding of Christ's priestly work. The second aim appears to be behavioral but actually is not. It focuses on commitment to an ideal or action. This step is important, but still action itself is not necessary to fulfill the aim. A commitment to an action is different from taking the action. But commitment is necessary if action is to follow, so Alex is wise in including an inspirational aim in his lesson plan. Notice how Alex framed his third aim statement. This aim is an action aim because it requires the student to take action if the aim is to be achieved. Alex will know that the aim is accomplished when the students actually begin to meet together to encourage each other. This aim pushes the lesson beyond the classroom to real life. It is much more difficult to achieve, but it does result in students who "do the Word" rather than simply "hear the Word."

The danger here, as Alex realized, is that teachers will try to play the role of the Holy Spirit in their students' lives. Is it possible that the student might apply Scripture to his life, yet not be moved to act on the specific application the teacher lines up? Clearly it is. Spelled out applications cannot be seen as the only way to apply truth in a particular passage. Mass applications are not necessarily the best sort, but for practical reasons the teacher often must make them and then hope the students' response is truly a response to God's Word rather than just to the teacher who taught the lesson and guided the application.

Haddon Robinson[2] provides a helpful chart of verbs that can be used in writing lesson aims. Table 11 on page 146 reproduces this chart for you. Columns one and two deal with content aim verbs, column three deals with inspirational aim verbs, and column four deals with action aim verbs.

Relating the Truth

By this time you might be a bit confused. All this talk about exegetical ideas and pedagogical ideas and lesson aims sounds like a lot to understand. It might be helpful just to remind ourselves what we are trying to accomplish here. We are trying to relate the truth of Scripture written in a specific cultural setting some two thousand or more years ago to people who live in a modern world dramatically removed from that biblical setting. We are trying to be teachers who are able to bridge the gap between the biblical world and the students' world. Truthfully, that is a very challenging task. It takes more than just opening the Bible and jointly telling our mental musings about a passage. It takes dedicated study and an effort to focus the results of that study on the students we teach in such a way as to see lives changed. Although it is a challenging task, it is far from an impossible one. By following some basic lesson preparation guidelines, with practice we can become effective and creative Bible teachers. Table 12 on page 147 will summarize what we have learned to this point regarding lesson preparation. Review it as we move to the third step in our study of creative Bible teaching—structuring the lesson.

Christa McAullife, "the teacher in space" who died in the Challenger explosion on January 28, 1986, was interviewed the night before her tragic death. She was asked what motivated her to teach. She said, "I touch the future, I teach." Christa was right. Teachers do touch the future by affecting students in the present with the truths of the past. In a very real way, as a teacher of the Bible, you touch the future of God's people.

NOTES

1. Benjamin S. Bloom, et. al. *Taxonomy of Educational Objectives: Handbook I* (New York: MacKay, 1956).
2. Haddon Robinson, *Biblical Preaching* (Grand Rapids: Baker, 1980), 111.

Table 11

VERBS FOR USE IN LESSON AIMS

If the goal is:	Knowledge	Insight	Attitude	Skill
Then the verb can be:	list	discriminate between	determine to	interpret
	state	differentiate between	develop	apply
	enumerate	compare	have confidence in	internalize
	recite	contrast	appreciate	produce
	recall	classify	be convinced of	use
	write	select	be sensitive to	practice
	identify	choose	be enthusiastic about	study
	memorize	separate	desire to	solve
	know	evaluate	sympathize with	experience
	trace	examine	view	explain
	delineate	comprehend	plan	communicate
	become aware of	reflect on	feel satisfied about	assist in
	become familiar with	think through	commit to	pray about
	define	discern		
	describe	understand		
	recognize	discover		

Table 12

Exegetical Idea	Pedagogical Idea	Lesson Aim
What it is...		
• The truth that the author of the passage intended the original hearers or readers to understand.	• The truth that the teacher of the class wants the students to understand from the passage.	• A statement that describes the kind of learning and life change desired or expected in the life of the student as a result of completing a lesson, unit, or course of study.
Also known as...		
• The Bridge Principle • The Central Idea • The Big Idea	• The Teaching Idea	• Instructional Objectives
Answers the question(s)...		
• What is the author talking about? • What is the author saying about what he is talking about?	• What do I want the student to learn from this lesson?	• How do I want my students to change as a result of this lesson?
Focuses on...		
• The world of the Bible	• The world of the student	• The life of the student
An example from Hebrews 10:19-25		
• The priesthood of the believer, accomplished by the sacrificial work of Christ, along with Christ's high priestly ministry, calls every Christian to draw near to God, hold fast to his faith, and spur on other believers so that each one might persevere through difficult times and difficult situations.	• In times of persecution, students who follow Jesus must learn to draw on their most powerful resources—God and one another.	**Content Aim (Cognitive):** Students will discover the three primary life implications that grow out of the priestly work of Christ by doing an inductive study of Hebrews 10:19-25. **Inspirational Aim (Affective):** Students will commit themselves to the practice of encouraging one another in times of persecution and difficulty by agreeing to meet together for prayer before school twice each week. **Action Aim (Behavioral):** Students will draw upon three vital means of survival in the midst of persecution and difficulties—prayer, perseverance, and people—by meeting together each week to "spur each other on."

Figure 12

THE CREATIVE BIBLE
TEACHING MODEL

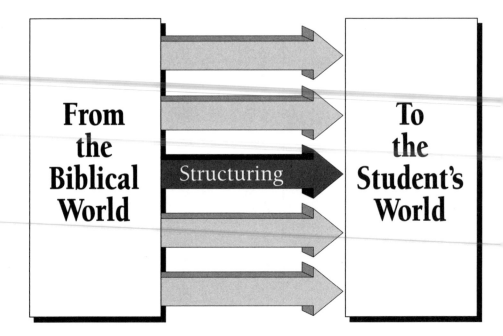

From
the
Biblical
World

Structuring

To
the
Student's
World

STRUCTURING THE LESSON

Teaching a Bible lesson is something like taking a flight in an airplane. After rolling back from the terminal, your plane taxis to the runway. Brakes are set. The engines are throttled up to the correct RPM level for take-off. Then the plane begins to roll. Rapidly gaining speed, the plane is airborne. Before long the plane reaches its cruising altitude and you enjoy the flight. As you travel, the pilot follows a flight plan that takes you over cornfields, lakes, mountains, and rivers. You watch the in-flight movie and enjoy a meal. As you near your destination, the plane begins its descent. You stow your tray table as instructed and raise your seat to the full upright position. You tuck the book you have been reading into your carry-on bag and buckle your seatbelt. After a few more turns, your plane is lined up with the runway. Minutes later the plane's wheels touch the concrete with a squeal and soon you are again rolling up to the gate. You deplane and depart.

Like your airplane flight, your lesson needs a powerful take-off. We call the first aspect of the teaching session the Hook. In this section we will explain what we mean by the Hook, but for now let's simply see it as the beginning, the introduction to the lesson. Like the take-off in an airplane flight, the Hook gets the class airborne. Once the class is underway, it moves to a second phase of the creative Bible teaching process, the Book.

The Book is a bit like level flight. It is designed to take the student into the world of the Bible and back again. The Book, like the plane's cross-country flight, requires planning and some navigating by a skilled pilot-teacher to bring the class ultimately to the destination of effective learning and application.

Eventually, your teaching session turns from the Book to the Look. The Look is the phase in teaching in which general applications are discovered by the class. This is like the maneuvering a plane must make before it can touch down. By carefully turning to align with the runway, the pilot prepares the plane for landing. Similarly, the creative Bible teacher must help the student explore potential application points by preparing the student's heart for the final landing—personal application.

Then it's time for the final and most important part of the flight, the landing. Let's face it. You can have a rough take-off and a bumpy flight, and you can have turbulence on your approach, but the ultimate measure of a flight is the quality of the landing. A bad landing can ruin an otherwise perfect flight. Serving the same function as the landing of a great jet, the Took is the last section of the creative Bible lesson. The Took is the touchdown. It is the lesson's final destination—the heart and life of the student.

This section introduces you to the third step in the creative Bible teaching process—structuring the lesson, using these four elements. Here you will discover how to plan the flight. So let's get this bird off the ground, shall we?

Chapter Nine

THE PATTERN:
HBLT APPROACH

Imagine boarding an airplane you know was designed without a plan. Or how about zooming up an elevator to the sixty-seventh floor of a urban skyscraper that was built without architectural drawings and plans. Frightening thought! Because of the risk to life and limb, haphazard approaches to airplane design or structural engineering are unwise. But even in the lesser things of life, planning seems to be a wise action that prudent people undertake. Whether we are making a dress or making investments, a well-thought-out plan is essential. Most human endeavors require planning. As a general principle, things done right are done with a plan. Generals need battle plans, coaches need game plans, and teachers need lesson plans. This chapter is about lesson planning. It is about doing things right when it comes to teaching the Bible.

Spontaneity has its place. Certainly it is a welcome aspect of a relationship between a husband and wife. When he brings home flowers just because he saw a person selling them on the street corner, that's a good kind of spontaneity. Or when the family pulls off at John's Rock Museum on its way through the Black Hills just out of curiosity and it turns out to be a highlight of the family vacation, that's another good kind of spontaneity. When a student in your adult Sunday school class tells openly and spontaneously her personal story of a life struggle that fittingly illustrates a point made in class, and as a result people open up and discussion becomes more meaningful—that too is a good kind of spontaneity. But ironically, in teaching the Bible, planning must be done for spontaneity to be meaningful. Otherwise "spontaneity" is more likely to be small talk. The wise teacher knows when to set aside his agenda and even his theme, but he also has a theme that can bring students back to look at the passage when the discussion turns to topics more suited for casual conversations outside class. He is open to teachable moments, but his class does not wander aimlessly in the name of spontaneity.

It is interesting how some equate spontaneity with the leading of the Holy Spirit. Planning is looked at as a human characteristic that hinders the work of God in a group. It is believed that God works in a spontaneous, unpredictable way. Some believe that worship services and teaching sessions should be free-flowing and unplanned. They believe that God leads in spontaneous ways that cannot occur when an order of service or a lesson plan is followed. They come to class and simply trust God to lead them and the class concerning what to say and what applications to make. But spontaneity is not God's way of working in the vast majority of situations. Remember what Paul said in response to the Corinthian church, whose spontaneous approach to worship had gotten out of hand. He said, "For God is not a God of disorder but of peace. . . . everything should be done in a fitting and orderly way" (1 Cor. 14: 33, 40).

It is God's nature to plan. In fact, we take personal encouragement in the midst of our life struggles from this truth. We rest on the fact that God is not haphazard. He has a sovereign plan for our lives. God designed His world by very exacting plans. He orders events by a master plan. And we as human beings made in His image have an innate tendency to make plans as well. We plan our days. We plan events. We plan travel. We plan our work. We plan our homes. We plan our lives. We plan worship services. We even try to plan our families. Should we not develop plans for teaching the Word of God as well?

A PLAN FOR TEACHING

There are numerous ways one could plan a classroom experience. We are going to look at one with you in this book. We call it the HBLT approach. That stands for Hook, Book, Look, and Took. Don't worry, we already know it's a bit corny, but that's why you will never forget it! It is an easy-to-remember approach to lesson preparation that, when followed, opens up the student to learning biblical truth and to making meaningful application of the truth in his or her life.

It is not a new approach. In fact, when Paul addressed the philosophers at the Areopagus on Athens's Mars Hill, his approach to teaching paralleled the lesson planning approach we'll present here. So pause now and read the account from Acts 17. What steps did Paul follow in teaching his audience?

> While Paul was waiting for them in Athens, he was greatly distressed to see that the city was full of idols. . . . Paul then stood up in the meeting of the Areopagus and said: "Men of Athens! I see that in every way you are very religious. For as I walked around and looked carefully at your objects of worship, I even found an altar with this inscription: TO AN UNKNOWN GOD. Now what you worship as something unknown I am going to proclaim to you.
>
> "The God who made the world and everything in it is the Lord of heaven and earth and does not live in temples built by hands. And he is not served by human hands, as if he needed anything, because he himself gives all men life and breath and everything else. From one man he made every nation of men, that they should inhabit the whole earth; and he determined the times set for them and the exact places where they should live. God did this so that men would seek him and perhaps reach out for him and find him, though he is not far from each one of us. 'For in him we live and move and have our being.' As some of your own poets have said, 'We are his offspring.'
>
> "Therefore since we are God's offspring, we should not think that the divine being is like gold or silver or stone—an image made by man's design and skill. In the past God overlooked such ignorance, but now he commands all people everywhere to repent. For he has set a day when he will judge the world with justice by the man he has appointed. He has given proof of this to all men by raising him from the dead." . . .
>
> A few men became followers of Paul and believed. Among them was Dionysius, a member of the Areopagus, also a woman named Damaris, and a number of others. (Acts 17:16, 22–31, 34)

We find Paul in Athens waiting for Silas and Timothy to join him. While he waits for his ministry companions he takes a stroll around the city. He becomes personally distressed by what he observes. It is a city filled with idols. It is a place utterly lost and in need of Christ. So many idols exist that one even bears the inscription: "To an unknown God." How does Paul approach a people that so desperately needs the truth of Christ?

After doing his observational needs assessment, Paul strategizes the best approach with this group. He begins teaching in his students' world. He starts where they live. He tells of his observations and he stimulates their interest. In particular, his statement "now what you worship as something unknown I am going to proclaim to you" is designed to stimulate curiosity while giving direction to his teaching. Surely his listeners' ears must have perked up at that point. He had them hooked! They were ready to listen to more.

His next step was to explore the truth with them. He told them that all persons are created by God and that each one longs for a relationship with Him. He also declared the truth that the resurrected Jesus Christ provides the means for that relationship.

After gaining attention and presenting his message, Paul helped his hearers identify a general implication for all persons. He said, "In the past God overlooked such ignorance, but now he commands all people everywhere to repent. For he has set a day when he will judge the world with justice by the man he has appointed."

Finally, it was time to respond. Paul's teaching ministry moved from general implications to personal application. We are not told exactly how Paul brought learners to this response. Possibly it was without prompting from Paul at all. But some did believe, and, of course, others did not. Application can go either way when we teach biblical truth. Some may respond by rejection. There are no guarantees that all will respond as we would like. The important point is that all are brought to the place of a response. The lesson must lead to the point of action, which indeed Paul's did.

THE FOUR ELEMENTS OF YOUR LESSON

Your teaching aim has been developed from a study of the passage to be taught. It spells out in a flexible way the response for which you are teaching. You have a clear idea where you want to go. Now it's time to design a lesson that will get there. Creative Bible teaching lesson plans are composed of four basic sections—the Hook, the Book, the Look, and the Took.

It's best to avoid thinking of these as mechanical steps. They're more like four parts of a continuous, systematic but exciting process. In class the students probably won't even notice passage from one part of the process to another. No part is marked by routine; each is full of opportunity for flexibility and interaction. Yet each of these parts in the process has its own—and essential—role. Let's look at the four in sequence.

The Hook

You have prepared the class. You've been gripped by the truth you're to teach. You've seen it work in your life. When you come to class, you're excited about the lesson. But your students aren't. They haven't had your experiences, and they aren't thinking about your lesson. They have their own problems. One adult may be worrying about a late income tax return. Another is thinking about the iron left out: *Now, did I turn it off, or didn't I?* Others are contemplating significant personal matters like lost jobs, broken relationships, or sick and dying loved ones. A teen may be replaying last night's game or nursing the tragedy of a rejected date. A child may be still fuming over a fight with her sister and the fact that she was punished and her sister wasn't. All differ, but each comes to class operating on his or her own wavelength. You must seek to entice them away from their private thoughts and share in this time of learning. And so you use the hook. Fishermen use it to get the fish out of the lake into the boat. You use it to bring your students into the Word of life.

There are several qualities of a good hook:

1. *It gets attention.*

"When Princes Diana lost her life, it seems the whole world felt her loss. Many people say she had finally found happiness after years of searching. Team up with a person near you, and in two minutes come up with a list of what most people think makes them happy," asked Pete Carson of his senior adult Sunday school class. Here's something everyone can do, a way in which all can take part. He has their attention. The hook is in. But getting attention isn't the only task of a good hook.

2. *It surfaces a need.*

All of us have needs in our lives. Many of these are right at the surface of our conscious lives; others are more hidden from view and less obvious to us or others. Maybe we are experiencing tension with a coworker or neighbor. Possibly the need is in the form of financial stress or chronic illness. Some have need for friendships and a sense of belonging. Others may face family problems and failing marriages. Then there is the need for encouragement or mutual support in Christian parenting. We want to be godly husbands and wives, mothers and fathers. Children face needs related to family, friends, or school. They have needs that include encouragement, attention, recognition, and acceptance. Adolescents face needs requiring understanding, decision-making guidance, building healthy relationships with the opposite sex, and developing a sense of identity.

When we design the hook, we should have the needs of our group in view. The needs assessment we did earlier should guide us in devising a hook that surfaces needs in the group in a non-threatening, thought-provoking manner. When students sense that the class is related to their needs, they are far more likely to participate in the activities of the class and in the learning process. This can be difficult because frequently students' perceived needs and their true needs differ. The teacher must work to open students' minds and hearts to the spiritual needs Scripture addresses.

3. *It sets a goal.*

We might call this the "direction step." The Hook must provide something to answer the question, "Why should I listen to this?" This is a fair question. If this lesson is going to be about something important to me, I want to pay attention. If it's an irrelevant recounting of dusty data, I do not. Students make that decision quickly. In just the first few words you speak, students tune in or tune out. That's why a hook must set direction for the class. The teacher must give students a reason for listening.

After Pete's students listed their ideas of typical sources of happiness, he showed that the writer of Philippians spoke of joy at a time when his life was far removed from anything we associate with happiness. He then made this statement: "Our goal today is to discover what gave Paul joy, when he had nothing that most people think makes them happy." By this statement he told his class why they should pay attention. All of us want joy. To discover its source the class would listen. He had earned the right to teach. When your students have no reason for learning, no reason that is important to them, you'll find it hard to hold them. But set a goal they want to reach, and they'll be with you. Sometimes students set their goals too low—most of us would prefer to avoid suffering rather than finding purpose in it, for example—so helping them see Scripture through the mind of Christ and set worthy learning goals is part of the teacher's task.

4. *One more thing.*

The hook should lead naturally into the Bible study. When Pete turned to Philippians, the class was under way. A good hook is one of the secrets of effective Bible teaching. When you capture interest, set a goal, and lead your students into the Word, you have a good start on a creative class.

The Book

In the Book section the teacher seeks to clarify the meaning of the passage being studied. In this part of the teaching-learning process, the teacher helps his students get—and understand—the biblical information. Many methods are available for this purpose. The teacher can use a participatory one, such as buzz groups and small group reports. Or he can use a teacher-centered method. A good lecture is the fastest way to cover content and make points. Or one can use charts, visuals, and so forth. Whatever the method, the purpose in this part of the lesson remains constant: to give biblical information and help students understand it.

Pete decided to have the class divide into small groups. He gave each group a set of questions to consider that helped explore the meaning of the passage. He gave one volunteer member of each group a blank overhead transparency along with a marker to record their findings. Each group was to review several references to joy in Philippians. Then the groups reconvened to share the result of their study. After the groups reported back, Pete summarized the comments and said, "Great, now let's put the message of Philippians into a single sentence." After a few tries the class had a single sentence that described the theme of Philippians. Pete had led the class in meaningfully and purposefully exploring the text. As a result, the class had a much better understanding of the overall message of the book. Not only had Pete laid the foundation for the next several classes on this book, but he had set the stage for an investigation of the implications of biblical joy in the lives of his students.

The Look

When the students understand what the Bible says, it's time to move to implications. Their knowledge must be tempered with "spiritual wisdom and understanding" (Col. 1:9). So the next step the teacher must plan for in the lesson preparation process involves guiding the class to discover and grasp the relationship of the truth just studied to daily living.

In the Book section of the class, Pete's students discovered that the sources of Christian joy are getting out the gospel, sacrificing self for others, and the Lord Himself. They learned this through the use of small group inquiry methods. In essence, they gained a head knowledge understanding of the passage. What they discovered together was true information about the nature of Christian joy. But they had not yet identified the implications of that information for Christian living. Pete had to lead the group a step further. Through the Look section, Pete guided the class in dealing with the essential question necessary to reveal life implications. He asked, "But what does this mean for the pattern of our daily lives?" This is the issue explored in the Look section of the teaching plan. Let's see how the Look section unfolded in Pete's class.

Pete recognized that his senior adult class was comprised of Christians with a wide range of life experiences to draw upon. He decided that he would tap that wealth of experience in the group by using a combination of a case study and probing questions to encourage the discovery of implications from the group's study of Philippians. Pete distributed a case study. Here is the case the class was to discuss.

Bob and Peg Short are a retired couple living in the Midwest. Bob has been retired from his job with a major airline for nearly eight years. He has just turned seventy-three and is in moderately good health. But Bob faces a debilitating condition that will worsen in the next two to three years to the point where Peg will not be able to care for him alone. So, with reluctance, they decided to move into a life-care retirement community. Both were unhappy with the decision to move but felt that it was the best thing to do in their situation. They dreaded giving up their home and moving into the cramped apartment, and they wondered if they could ever be happy there.

Pete asked the class to consider how the principles they had just learned together might apply to this couple's lives. After much discussion and telling of personal stories related to the case study, the class concluded that Bob and Peg should look at the move as a commissioning to a new mission field. They suggested that they would have opportunities to tell of their faith, minister to others, and deepen their dependence on Christ. In the process of discussing Bob and Peg's case, the students were exploring practical ways that the material covered in class could be related to daily living. Pete summarized their ideas on the overhead. The result—the class had gone the next step in the study of the Bible—they had identified implications for daily life.

The Took

But, like a vaccination, the Word of God is of no effect until we can say it "took." Response is required. Normally, response to teaching will take place outside of class, in weekday life. "Faith by itself, if it is not accompanied by action," the Bible says, "is dead" (James 2:17). For spiritual growth and reality in Christian experience, faith demands response in all the varied situations of human life.

In the Look section of the lesson the teacher encourages such response. The teacher leads the class members to pinpoint personal areas in which they could respond and helps them plan specific ways they *will* respond. Often we leave church full of good intentions. We'll be more loving that week, more dedicated. But because the resolution is vague, because we haven't gone beyond the generalization and implementation phase of learning to actually plan *how* we'll change, no change takes place. The creative Bible teacher knows this. The goal is transformed lives—change. Therefore, creative Bible teachers help students respond by leading them to see God's will and by helping them decide and plan to do it.

Pete did this by distributing postcards to his class. He asked everyone to write their name and address on one side of the card. On the other side he asked them to write down how they would apply the passage in the week ahead. He reminded the group of the implications they had discovered and then gave them time to think and write. He collected the

THE PATTERN: HBLT APPROACH

cards. On Monday he dropped them in the mail so that everyone would have a reminder that arrived in their mailbox later in the week. The next Sunday, the class discussed how they did applying the class on joy to their own life situations.

A TRIP THROUGH TIME

Another way to understand the Hook, Book, Look, Took approach is to picture it as a teacher-led trip through time. Movement of the lesson proceeds from the present (Hook) to the past (Book), back to the present (Look), and into the future (Took). Figure 13 depicts the lesson structure in this way. The teacher's role is one of travel agent and tour guide. As travel agent, the teacher plans the journey. As tour guide, the teacher then leads the trip. But, always, the students are in view. They are the ones doing the traveling. They are full participants in the travel experience. Travel agents and tour guides have a purpose—to enable others to make the journey.

Values of Lesson Structure

The ability to handle lesson structure is invaluable to the Bible teacher. The process we've described and the key words (Hook, Book, Look, Took) suggested to characterize its parts are tools for the teacher. These are practical tools with which to develop structuring ability. How can these tools be used?

As a guide to method choice. When you understand the purpose of each part of the teaching process, it's easy to select methods. Most books on methods are rather confusing. They talk of role play, of buzz groups, of brainstorming, of dozens of other techniques, and give rules for their successful use. But what should determine your choice of method is function, the job a method is to do in class.

This is how you should understand methodology. A method is simply an activity designed to hook students, to communicate information and meaning, to lead to insight, or to encourage response. The next section of this book talks about activities suited to these purposes for various age groups. But the main thing is this. *If you understand what you are trying to accomplish, you can select or invent an activity to accomplish it.* Master the parts of the lesson process, and method skill will follow.

To simplify lesson planning. Breaking down the process of creative Bible teaching into four parts simplifies lesson planning. It's easy for a teacher who understands the parts of the lesson to build a lesson or to find and correct weaknesses in printed lesson material. Planning is enhanced when some sort of template is followed. That is the advantage of the Hook, Book, Look, Took format.

Figure 13

HOOK, BOOK, LOOK, TOOK: A BRIDGE THROUGH TIME

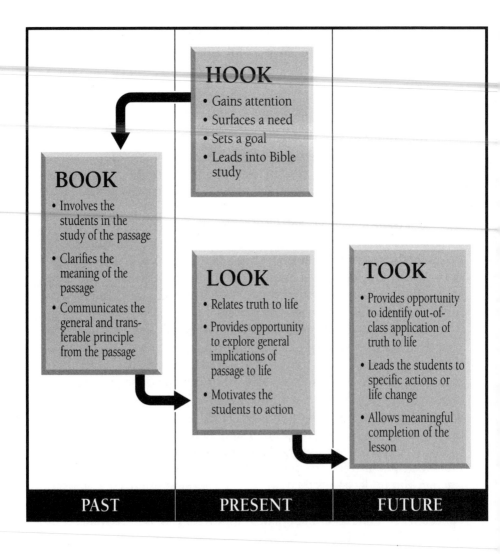

HOOK
- Gains attention
- Surfaces a need
- Sets a goal
- Leads into Bible study

BOOK
- Involves the students in the study of the passage
- Clarifies the meaning of the passage
- Communicates the general and transferable principle from the passage

LOOK
- Relates truth to life
- Provides opportunity to explore general implications of passage to life
- Motivates the students to action

TOOK
- Provides opportunity to identify out-of-class application of truth to life
- Leads the students to specific actions or life change
- Allows meaningful completion of the lesson

PAST   PRESENT   FUTURE

One More Example

Models are a way many of us learn best. We have to see how something is done, and then we can follow the pattern ourselves. So let's consider one more lesson planning example. We'll see how Alex, the youth worker who leads an urban group of adolescents in a weekly Bible study, planned his lesson on Hebrews 10:19–25. Table 13 is a copy of Alex's lesson plan that shows how he designed the study. You will notice that he has identified his exegetical idea, pedagogical idea, and lesson aims on his lesson plan worksheet. Following this, his worksheet is divided into four sections where he has written his Hook, Book, Look, and Took plans. Through the lesson, Alex hopes to lead his group to establish a group covenant involving a commitment to meet regularly for prayer and mutual support.

NOW YOU TRY IT

Table 14 is a lesson planning worksheet designed to assist you in putting together your own lesson plan. It brings together all of what you have learned to this point in this book. It shows how you can use your understanding of the lesson preparation process to develop a teaching plan. At the top of the worksheet is a place to record the date, the location, and a filing reference for the plan. Use these for future reference. Next is a box to summarize information about the target group. Draw this information from your needs assessment study. Below that are places to indicate the passage being studied and any cross references you plan to use. Continuing down the worksheet you will find boxes to write out the exegetical idea, pedagogical idea, and lesson aims that we discussed in previous chapters. Following these is space for your Hook, Book, Look, and Took. Notice that the Book section is divided vertically so that you can include both your content outline and the methods you plan to use to teach that content. Finally, there is a place to record any evaluative insights you might have after you teach the class. These will help you if you ever teach the material again.

Look over Table 14. Use it to prepare your next teaching session. Review chapters 1 through 9 if you need to. Make sure that your Hook gets attention, sets a goal, and leads into the Bible. Plan the Book to communicate both information and meaning. Check the Look to be sure you guide your students to implications. Finally, construct a Took that will aid and encourage response. The next chapter will give you further help with the application side of teaching, but you already have the tools you need to plan your class!

LESSON PLANNING WORKSHEET

Date: 9/15/97   **Location:** Northwest Side Gospel Center   **File Under:** Hebrews

Target Group: High School Bible Study Group, Urban Church

> All are under great pressure as they try to stand for Christ at their high school. With a very small number of believers at school, students need constant encouragement to remain faithful to Christ. Some are facing significant temptations and doubts. Acceptance by a group is a great need among the students.

| **Passage:** Hebrews 10:19-25 | **Cross-references:** Exodus 25-31; Leviticus 1-27 |

Exegetical Idea:

> The priesthood of the believer, accomplished by the sacrificial work of Christ, along with Christ's high priestly ministry, calls every Christian to draw near to God, hold fast to his faith, and spur on other believers so that each one might persevere through difficult times and difficult situations.

Pedagogical Idea:

> In times of persecution, students who follow Jesus must learn to draw on their most powerful resources—God and one another.

Lesson AIM(s)

Cognitive (Head):

> Students will discover the three primary life implications that grow out of the priestly work of Christ by doing an inductive study of Hebrews 10:19-25.

Affective (Heart):

> Students will commit themselves to the practice of encouraging one another in times of persecution and difficulty by agreeing to meet together for prayer before school twice each week.

Behavioral (Hands):

> Students will draw upon three vital means of survival in the midst of persecution and difficulties—prayer, perseverance, and people—by meeting together each week to "spur each other on."

Hook:

> 1. Video Clip—Use clip from the film *The Hiding Place* to show the persecution of Christians who hid Jews from Hitler's SS troops.
> 2. Question—Do you think you would have hidden the Jews? What risk was there in doing so?
> 3. Question—Does persecution of Christians still happen today?
> 4. Question—Have you or anyone you know ever been persecuted for being a Christian?

Transition: Our study today deals with a group of Christians who were persecuted for following Christ. Our passage provides some advice for persecuted Christians.

LESSON PLANNING WORKSHEET (Continued)

Book: Content Outline	Methodology
1. Background to Text	Mini lecture: Teacher provides background regarding the persecution being experienced by the Christians in the first century.
2. Truth—The New Testament Priesthood (Hebrews 10:19-22)	Student Report: Student reports back result of research on priesthood. Group discusses role of priests. Teacher will point out the fact of Jesus' high priestly role as discussed in earlier studies. Note that each believer is a priest as well. Discuss reasons this is a significant change from Old Testament priesthood.
3. Application—Three vital means of survival for persecuted Christians (Hebrews 10:22-25) a) Prayer b) Perseverance c) People	Discussion: Students are led through each of the three implications suggested by the author of Hebrews regarding the priestly ministry of Christ and the priestly role of the believer. Q1: As a result of Christ's work on our behalf and our own access to God, what actions are we to take as Christians? Q2: How do these actions benefit people under persecution?

Look:

1. Brainstorming: Students will consider together all possible ways they can think of to apply the lesson. They will take five minutes to make a brainstorming list of applications. If the idea of a regular small group meeting before school comes up, key in on it. Otherwise, tell a story of a group that decided to meet at their school each week for mutual support.

2. Goal Setting: With guidance, the group will write a goal for supporting each other through persecution and challenges to their faith. The leader will stress the importance of believers not giving up meeting together.

3. Group Commitment: Together the group will design a commitment. It will spell out the things the group will all commit themselves to doing in order to encourage each other in times of persecution.

Took:

Commitment signing ceremony: Each person will receive a photocopy of the group commitment in the mail this week as a reminder.

Group prayer: Time focused on supporting one another in persecution and in times of doubt.

Evaluation:

Table 14a

LESSON PLANNING WORKSHEET

Date: Location: File Under:

Target Group:

Passage:	**Cross-references:**

Exegetical Idea:

Pedagogical Idea:

Lesson AIM(s)
Cognitive (Head):

Affective (Heart):

Behavioral (Hands):

Hook:

Table 14b

LESSON PLANNING WORKSHEET (Continued)

Book: Content Outline   Methodology

Look:

Took:

Evaluation:

Chapter Ten

THE PROCESS:
ENGAGING STUDENT RESPONSE

N ed Phillips is a small group leader working with six high school boys in his church youth ministry. His role is to get to know each of the boys personally, build a relationship with them, and serve as the discussion leader in the small group session that follows a large group teaching time led by the youth pastor. About thirty-five students attend the large group session. Usually, the youth pastor skillfully presents a "youth talk" that captivates the students. He is a superb speaker and storyteller.

Ned's job is to "debrief" the students and help them to make personal application from the youth pastor's talk. Ned finds his task an enormous challenge. It seems that the students can remember and even explain what the youth pastor was addressing, but they have a hard time applying the truth in a specific way to their own lives. For example, last Sunday the message was on John the Baptist. The point of the message was that John was willing to go against the flow and stand up for Christ despite the persecution and ridicule it might bring. When Ned asked the students to relate the passage to their own lives, they simply could not do it. John the Baptist seemed so removed from their world that they could not make a direct application. One student said, "If you want to be popular, stay away from locusts, honey, and out-of-style clothes." Clearly he missed the point. Ned was frustrated. How could he make the Bible message relevant to a junior high boy two thousand years removed from its culture and content?

167

THE DIFFICULTY OF ENGAGING STUDENT RESPONSE

The most difficult task of the Bible teacher is to help students see truth in terms of their own lives. This is particularly difficult because *the teacher himself may not know the implications of a passage for his students.* What do we mean by this? Let's say you teach a class of second grade students. You teach them, but you don't live the life of an eight year old. You may be a thirty-five-year-old stockbroker, a fifty-year-old mechanic, or a twenty-year-old college student. You don't think as they think or feel as they feel. You don't have her problems, or his parents, or any of their personalities. The culture of childhood is much different than it was when you were their age, even if you can remember being that age. You may teach high schoolers, but your life is fantastically removed from theirs. Although you may come close to understanding your students, you know that teens today don't think or understand in the same patterns as adults. You may even teach adults, but you do not live another adult's life. Although God's truth is relevant to everyone, and although you can see specific implications of that truth for *your* life, you will not see all its implications for another.

Because each human being is a unique personality, living a life that is distinct, no one outside can determine with assurance all the implications of a truth for another. And certainly no one dares claim to know *the* response another must make, a response that God alone has the right to direct.

Approaches to Application

Nearly everyone who teaches the Bible believes that the Word should be put to use. All teach with a purpose, with some thought that the Bible is relevant to life. And most try to make it relevant. They attempt to apply what they teach.

The problem is how to make an application that works. The purpose of application is to make truth usable, to get it into the experience, into the life, of the learner. Yet many Bible teachers make applications that do not show up later in the lives of their students. The techniques they use simply do not work.

Content is not enough. Sometimes we meet a teacher who says, "I teach the Word. It's the Holy Spirit's job to make it relevant." Not many of us would agree. If the Holy Spirit uses us to teach the Bible, He may want to use us to relate it too! Yet even teachers who disagree with this statement, and some curriculum writers, plan lessons as if content *were* enough.

A peculiar picture of people and learning underlies this approach.

The student is looked at almost like a computer. The teacher enters data (the biblical information) into the student's hard drive (the student's mind) where it is stored for later retrieval and processing. Whenever a situation arises in which the truth is needed, the student's mind is automatically supposed to sort through the data, and *whirrrr!* the truth is there, ready to be used.

But human beings don't operate that way. Minds don't automatically sort content and relate it to experiences. Content, taught as information, is filed away all right. *But without training, the student is unlikely to see its relationship to his life.*

If you doubt this, test yourself. Write down what you know about the present ministry of Christ in heaven. Now, jot down what this truth means to you personally. Write down how you *use* it. Difficult? Yet there's hardly a more relevant doctrine to Christian experience in the Word of God. But the chances are that unless you've been taught the doctrine *with a view to its meaning for life,* you can't apply it. And if you don't understand what it means for your life, you cannot possibly use it!

The idea that filling the mind with information will allow individuals to develop the ability to use that information has been thoroughly tested. And the tests show that this idea simply is not true. What can we say, then, about the Bible teacher who covers only content and expects lives to change?

One senior high Sunday school lesson from a major curriculum publisher serves as an example. It's a lesson on the apostle Paul's commitment to preaching the gospel to the lost in any and all situations. It concludes by attempting in a *single sentence* to apply the lesson to teen lives: "Let's pray to the Lord to help us be as evangelistic as Paul." To close your lesson with a prayer or an exhortation to "use what we've studied today" is not to apply it—not so the truth is likely to affect the life.

Generalization is better. A better teacher, realizing that he must get beyond content, may move to generalization. Take the youth pastor's message about John the Baptist mentioned at the beginning of this chapter. The content was clearly organized. One section looked at John in the wilderness, pointing out his way of life, his clothing and diet. In it the youth pastor stressed the idea that John did not find material comforts important. In another section he looked at John's sermons to the crowds. The youth pastor pointed out John's blunt honesty. He told the students that John never simply told people what they wanted to hear. John spoke God's message plainly, and no possible threat to his popularity could stay him. In the third section the youth pastor looked at John after his disciples had left him to follow Jesus. At this point he underscored John's attitude: "He must increase, but I must decrease." John put Christ first.

Ned, who is a good teacher and unwilling to leave his class with only information, asked, "What qualities of character set John apart from others—qualities that are important for Christians today?" With this question he would lead his high schoolers to generalize. He led them from facts to principles. This leading of students from facts to principles is important in effective application. *But it, too, falls short.* To achieve response, Ned must help his students see how to use the principles in their lives.

Illustrations help in application. One way we can see a principle in operation is through an illustration. But this has its problems. Let's say that you've been teaching a class of seven year olds. In your lesson you've shown that being honest is one way to please the Lord. Your class expresses a desire to please the Lord and is willing to be "honest." But you want to help them see that honesty means more than "don't steal." So, to bring this down on their own level, you use an illustration.

> Katie found a jump rope on the playground. It had bright red handles and a colored rope, and she ran all the way home to show her mother. It was just like the one she had always wanted. But her mother didn't seem too happy. "Katie," her mother asked, "is it really *yours?*" "Oh yes, Mom," Katie said. "I found it." Her mother still didn't look happy. She talked about the girl who had lost it and how she must feel. And she asked Katie if it was really honest to have someone else's rope, even though she didn't steal it. Katie went into her room and thought and thought. When she came out, she looked happy. "Mom," she said, "I'm going to take the rope back and give it to the teacher. If no one claims it, I can have it in two weeks." She smiled and said, "I really do want to be honest, to please the Lord Jesus."

The next day one of your class members finds a doll on the playground and takes it home. If it had been a jump rope, she'd have taken it to the teacher. Think about that. Do you see why? The illustration idea rests on the theory of "transfer by identical elements." You verbally create a "real" situation, as much like an actual experience as possible. The hope is that when the learner finds himself in a similar situation, he'll remember and use the truth taught.

The difficulty is that elements of situations are seldom identical. To a literal-minded child, just the shift of one factor (a jump rope to a doll) may change the situation enough so that the relationship of the one to the other isn't noticed. This happens with adults as well as children. A pastor cites as an illustration of failure to "do that which is honest in the sight of all men" by telling a story of a Christian business-man's unwillingness to honor a commitment. But the illustration doesn't make you think of the vacation you're planning, even though you know it means late payment of some bills. And it doesn't make you think of the paper and pencils you bring home to your children from the office. The principle is the same, the illustration is a good one, but it is not sim-ilar enough to your experiences to help you relate the truth to yourself.

The Problem of Self-Guided Lesson Application

The problem with these self-guided approaches to application—content only, generalizations, and illustrations—is that they assume that if one knows what is right or if one knows the biblical truth to be lived, practice will follow. When teachers see their task as getting stu-dents to *know* the truth or even to *know how to apply the truth,* they can only hope that students will take the next step and practice the truth in a specific way in their own lives. Creative Bible teachers want to go a step further. They want to change lives. They want results. Although they can't make students apply the passage, they can go further in making ap-plication more concrete.

Findley Edge, in his now classic book *Teaching for Results,*[1] identi-fies six reasons that self-guided application of Bible lessons tend to fail. These can be summarized as follows.

1. *The problem of meaning*—The students may not understand the meaning or significance of the passage, so they are unable to make application in their personal life.
2. *The problem of relationship*—An individual may not see the rela-tionship between a particular life situation in which he finds himself and any spiritual teaching.
3. *The problem of prejudice*—Prejudice sometimes makes us unwill-ing to apply Christian ideals. . . . When prejudice and spiritual truth come into conflict, people often hold spiritual truths in their minds while their lives are guided by prejudice.
4. *The problem of information*—Often an individual has insufficient information to understand how the Christian ideal would oper-ate in many normal relationships of life.
5. *The problem of personal and social pressure*—The individual may be unable or unwilling to make his own specific application be-cause of pressures from society or from within his own life. Be-ing human, we are all subject to the weaknesses of the flesh.
6. *The problem of complex situations*—There is no clear distinction between right and wrong in many of the complex situations of

life. The Christian does not face much difficulty in making decisions when the issues involved are either black or white. But the
Christian does have difficulty in making decisions when the issues are gray.

Given these potential obstacles to application and response to the
teaching of the Bible, Edge concludes with these words:

> The conclusion seems inescapable that teachers must become more spe-
> cific in their teaching. Generalized teaching is the basic reason for the
> teacher's failure to secure more carry-over from his teaching. If we are go-
> ing to teach for results, we must make teaching personal. The assumption
> that the teacher can teach general principles and leave the class members
> entirely unguided to make their own application seems not to be a valid
> or safe assumption. There are too many things against his making these
> applications, especially when it would involve change in his life.[2]

A Better Way

Content proclamation, generalized application, even excellent illustrations are not enough. None is really effective. None does a really
good job of opening up students' lives to the illuminating ministry of
the Holy Spirit. Of the three, generalization *plus* illustration is best. The
high schoolers studying John's life may see one of his qualities as
"speaking up for God even when it's unpopular." The teacher may illustrate this and tell of a high school student who witnessed to teammates
on a trip even though he knew they might laugh at him. This may hit
one or more members of the class squarely, especially if the teacher
knows his class well and chooses the illustration because he knows it is
a problem area. But this is unlikely to touch all the class members. And
it will not help any develop the ability to relate the principle to new life
situations they'll face that week. For truly effective application, we must
look elsewhere.

ENGAGING STUDENT RESPONSE
THROUGH GUIDED SELF-APPLICATION

In the introduction to this chapter we noted the relationship of individuality to application. Each student needs to see God's truth as it relates to his unique life. Each has different areas in which a lesson truth
will apply, as well as some areas shared in common with his classmates.
The creative Bible teacher wants to expose a number of these areas, in
order that the Holy Spirit might direct each student individually to the
specific response(s) He wants him or her to make. Application, then,

must be flexible enough to include all, yet individualized to touch the life of each.

Prerequisites of Effective Application

Truth must be related to the individual's life. Some teachers try to hit all their class members with a shotgun burst of illustrations. This is better than using only one or two, but it still falls short. The reason goes back to the uniqueness of each individual life. Every person lives in his own peculiar situation, in a whole complex of relationships and personality that make his life uniquely his. Thus, each individual has special opportunities to use a Bible truth in his own special areas of need.

It's true that we all share certain experiences. We have basic things in common. But because of our individuality we are tested at different points. One of us may see a neighbor child cut through our flower bed and, in a friendly way, ask him not to do it again. Another may love his flowers so passionately that he struggles to resist strangling the child! One person may keep calm when someone is disagreeable, whereas another may become upset and angry, or even hurt. We each need God's strength, His calming grace. But we need it in different situations, at different points in our experience.

This clarifies the task of the creative Bible teacher. It's not to simply illustrate truth used in "life." It's to help each student discover how truth studied may be used in *his* life. And these situations, these personal points of need to which a word from God applies, must be discovered by each of us for himself.

Relevant areas must be explored. This seems to be the best way to help students to self-discovery. And such a course demands class participation. The search for relationship of truth to life must be an active thing. Each of the learners must be involved. And participation stimulates thinking. It initiates the search.

When several people tell their ideas, new ideas are born. One application leads to another as students have opportunity to discover together the specific and personal implications of a passage. This is what happens when a whole class seeks together to put flesh on a Bible truth. New channels of thinking are opened for all. And as the group goes on to explore the areas exposed, the Lord gives each individual flashing insights into the meaning of the Word to his life and his needs.

In a process like this the teacher has to protect the class members. Each one, whether he realizes it or not, risks exposing his weaknesses and sins. The things they suggest reveal where sin might reside. Lisa Williamson has a class of students who have not yet established trust and openness, and she is effective at motivating student interaction about application while still protecting her students. After teaching a lesson on the example of Paul in 1 Thessalonians she doesn't ask, "If you were living like Paul, how would your life be different?" She feels that this is an invitation to open confession of sin, an invitation few are ready to accept in her class setting. Instead she asks, "If someone in our church were to live like Paul, how might you expect them to behave?" This is close enough to make the situation real, yet distant enough to permit objectivity. No one feels personally threatened. Later the truth will become personal. The teacher suggests that each person plan to respond. But for open participation she sets up a situation in which each can express himself freely, without threat.

Results of Guided Self-Application

The kind of application just described—a shared search for life implications of a Bible truth, in which each pools his insights and experience—produces results. The primary result is that class members discover uses for the truth in their own lives. Only when use is known can a response be made. But there are other results too.

A sensitized life. A person who sees a variety of life implications for a truth is likely to see more. After each class its members step back into life. None knows what new situations will arise that week, what new experiences wait. But if, in the class, a student has developed awareness of a wide range of situations to which a particular truth relates, he or she is likely to recognize new opportunities for response when they arise.

An independent ability to grow. An eleven-year-old boy told his teacher, "You're the teacher. You're supposed to talk. I'm just supposed to sit here." Already he had developed an approach to the Bible that said, "I listen. I'm not involved."

But for the Word of God to produce growth, we must be involved. We must be involved in actively searching for implications, in actively responding to every word from God. Students in a class using guided self-application are being trained to study the Word of God for growth. They are learning how to learn.

This should be one of the major goals of the Bible teacher: not to keep the learners dependent on him, but to equip them to study the Word independently and to study it in such a way that they grow. Such study requires understanding Bible content, recognizing the implications of that content, and specifically applying that content to daily life.

The Process of Guided Self-Application

Last chapter we looked at the Hook, Book, Look, and Took lesson structure. Application takes place in the last two steps, in which the student is guided to discover the relation of the truth studied to his or her life and is encouraged to make a response. When we look at these steps in detail, the elements of the process become clear and take on a distinctive pattern.

The pattern described. Stated simply, the pattern is this: Generalization / Implications / Personal Application / Decision to Act. This pattern is shown in Table 15.

In generalization, discussed earlier in this chapter, the pedagogical idea is discovered. Using a variety of methods, the creative Bible teacher guides students in study of the biblical passage. This is the function of the Book section of the lesson, as we discussed in the last chapter. When the principle of the passage is clearly defined, the teacher then leads the class beyond the generalizations to implications by transitioning from Book to Look in the lesson plan. Rather than just giving illustrations, creative Bible teachers encourage their students to give illustrations themselves. Creative Bible teachers use methods that guide their class to think through the ways the biblical principle might be worked out in their lives. By the use of open-ended stories, life situation dramas, thought-provoking questions, case studies, and other participatory methods, the class session is designed to stimulate or guide students to think concretely in a new area or to think more deeply about an idea already understood. Here is a brief example of how one teacher encouraged his students to think about the implications of the gospel on Christian living.

> Teacher: Let's suppose that everyone in our church were living out the implications of the gospel in their daily lives. I don't mean that they never have a problem or are never sorrowful. What I mean is that they truly lived as if Jesus Christ had utter control of their lives. In fact, let's suppose that our lives became so distinct in this regard that a local TV station plans to send a cameraman over to follow our church members around for a week to tape a special news segment. What would they videotape?

The class proceeds to discuss what qualities might be expected in the lives of committed Christians. By using this short scenario, the teacher has given students opportunity to discuss the implications of the gospel in general terms.

The next step in engaging student response is to bring the students to the point of identifying a specific application in their own lives. This is the role of the Took section of the lesson plan where students finally discover a specific way they can change by taking action on the principle taught in class. In practice, decisions and responses will normally be made outside of class. During the week when situations arise, each individual will be faced anew with the opportunity to respond. But through

Table 15

PETE CARSON'S SENIOR ADULT CLASS ON PHILIPPIANS
(An Example of the Process of Application in Creative Bible Teaching)

Generalization	Implications	Personal Application	Decision To Act
Joy in sacrificially serving others	• by listening to their concerns and problems • by visiting the sick • by helping those who are shut-ins • by putting others' needs ahead of ours • by cleaning someone's apartment or home • by shopping for a shut-in • by baby-sitting for young couple who need time together • by serving in the educational ministry of the church.	I need to make time for those who are lonely and unable to fellowship with other believers. Possibly I could visit someone from our class who can no longer make it to church and have a devotional time with them each week.	Visit George and Esther at Senior Village Retirement Community each week to read Scripture and pray with them.

the creative process in class you will have equipped your students with eyes opened to new meanings for God's truth, with new sensitivity to its relevance in their lives.

The process illustrated. Remember the youth pastor's lesson on John the Baptist that we described at the beginning of this chapter? Ned's task was to lead a follow-up discussion with his Sunday school class of teens after the youth pastor's session. If you were Ned, how might you lead that session using the guided self-application process? How might you teach it? Well, let's spin out the scenario as it might develop.

You've covered the content by reviewing the youth pastor's message to the point where the principle is clear. After some discussion, your teens suggest two qualities John had that they agree other Christians should share: he was unconcerned about personal popularity, and he didn't place great importance on material things.

Now in various ways you lead your students to see how these qualities would show up in life today. What pressures of popularity exist in the high school world? You think together of times when the desires of the crowd and of God pull different ways. You write their ideas down on an overhead projector transparency or dry erase marker board (see Table 16). Moving on, you talk together of ways their friends put a premium on things. These too you record. This is the implication stage. It is general rather than specific application.

As your class suggests various applications, you notice that the idea of "geeks" comes up several times. These are the kids who don't fit in, those who aren't in the "in" crowd. Often they are the kids without sharp clothes, at least a year behind the fashions; the ones without much athletic ability, without the looks, the right labels on their clothes or wealth that identifies them as "acceptable." They include the computer "nerds," the socially uncomfortable, the intellectually challenged. So you now guide your class to think together about this group. How would a person like John relate to these kids? What would his attitude be? His actions? What does count about a person, if not his money or clothes or appearance? Which is really important: meeting another's needs or making sure of your standing in your group? What is the risk that a student will face if he reaches out to these kinds of individuals?

You close the class by reminding the students of John's greatest quality, the one that is basic to all the the others: John put Christ first. And you ask, "If you really want to put Christ first in your life, how might you do it this week? How might you follow Him, rather than the crowd, or see people and things from His viewpoint?"

The results? Kurt expresses his decision to try to bring a new friend into his group at school. Matt, the football player, tells of his determina-

Table 16

APPLY A LESSON ON JOHN THE BAPTIST
(An Example of the Guided Self-Application Process)

Generalization	Implications	Personal Application	Decision To Act
Christians should seek to please God even if it makes them unpopular and should not place undue importance on material things.	• Accept people who are different	• We can bring a new friend into our social group at school.	• Kurt: Going to invite Tom to go to a football game with him on Saturday.
	• Avoid lifestyle choices that may not please God		
	• Be friends with a geeky person	• We can have lunch with a kid at school no one likes.	• Alisa: Going to invite Ann to sit with her at lunch tomorrow.
	• Do not swear or do something that displeases God just to fit in		
	• Be willing to take a stand for Christ publicly	• We can speak up and tell people of our relationship with Christ.	• Matt: Going to share Christ with Jeff and Scott and invite them to youth group next week.
	• Do not judge people by the things they have or do not have		
	• Be concerned more with the inner person than simply developing the outer person	• We can stop judging people by their clothes.	• Jan: Going to go out with Chris even though his clothes are unstylish.
	• Be friendly to new people who visit the youth group meetings		

tion to speak up and tell of his relationship with Christ with a couple of friends on the team. Alisa decides to have lunch with a kid at school no one likes. Jan, the popular socialite in the group, says that she will accept a date from Chris, a Christian boy at her school, even though his clothes are embarrassingly unstylish.

Well, you think as you leave class, *serious or funny, they do respond.* Kurt in his honest and earnest way, Matt in his courageous stand, Alisa in her willingness to reach out to the unlovely, and even Jan in her fluttery and somewhat superficial way. And you thank God. Because you realize that while you were the "teacher," it was God who taught their hearts.

NOTES
1. Findley B. Edge, *Teaching for Results* (Nashville: Broadman, 1956), 130–35.
2. Ibid., 135.

Chapter Eleven

THE MEANS:
METHODS MAKE
A DIFFERENCE

After the two-hour bus trip, the members of the high school youth group were glad to arrive at Camp Freedom. They looked forward to their annual fall kick-off retreat. The camp had superb facilities, including an indoor pool. It was located on a private lake surrounded by a pine forest and nestled in the rolling hills of Tennessee. The food was better than average camp cooking, and the youth leaders had a reputation for planning a great retreat.

Many of the teenagers were less than excited when the first activity of the weekend was a game of Monopoly in groups of four. "This looks like a totally boring retreat," commented one freshman guy. Most of the students shared his opinion. Bob, the youth pastor, said, "Trust me and just play the game. In an hour we will call time and everyone will tally up their money."

Play progressed for exactly one hour, then Bob called a halt to the game. The kids all counted their money. Some had already amassed great wealth, whereas others were near bankruptcy. Then an auction took place. One of the youth sponsors took the role of auctioneer. Everything at the camp went on the block: the game room, the pool, the dining hall, the lake, the canoes, the sports equipment, even the restrooms. The bidding began slowly, then the students got going. Students bought each of the available items. Some students could not buy anything.

"For the next twenty-four hours we are going to have a mini-economy here," the youth pastor explained. "If you want something you will have to buy it, rent it, or trade for it." And so it went. Students would pay for their meals with the money they had accumulated in the game. They had to pay to go swimming, use the restrooms, or play in the gym. Everything had a price tag. Some students had to become employed in order to live. The dining hall "owner" hired students to carry dishes to the kitchen. The pool owner had to hire students to collect fees from patrons. Some made others' beds just to get enough money to buy a meal. In one case a fight nearly erupted as the wealthy restroom owner was "mugged" and robbed of some of his money.

Ten students were told in advance of the activity that, regardless of what happened during the event, they were to seek to live out their Christian value system. On Saturday evening the mini-economy was called to an end. After everyone had enjoyed a terrific evening meal, the group met for a debriefing session. The youth pastor led the group in a discussion about "the haves" and "the have-nots." They discussed the good and bad sides of competition. Then the youth pastor asked, "How many of you feel you faithfully lived out your Christian values throughout this event?" Only a few hands went up. What followed was a powerful teaching time on the role of Christians in culture. Even the ten who were asked to keep their faith values in view during the activity admitted the difficulty of remaining Christlike when being cheated or mistreated.

The retreat was a powerful teaching time. In an experiential way, students learned a number of biblical truths. The rest of the teaching time on Saturday night and Sunday morning was linked to principles for Christian living in a non-Christian world.

Bob had used a method of teaching known as a simulation game to engage student learning. He had discovered that methods and method selection are an important aspect of creative Bible teaching. Bob followed the Hook, Book, Look, Took structure that weekend to plan an entire retreat experience. In this chapter, we will look at how you can select methods that will affect your students and accomplish your goals.

SUPPORTING THE BRIDGE

Teaching the Bible is like building a bridge from the modern world to the biblical world, and back again. This two-directional span enables students to explore the meaning of the ancient texts of Scripture and their application for contemporary living. But this bridge through time demands structural supports. Figure 14 depicts some of the supports that undergird a creative Bible class or lesson. Some of the supports to Bible teaching include illustrations, examples, stories, analogies, explanations, models, quotes, drawings, and classroom teaching methodologies.

Figure 14

A BRIDGE
THROUGH TIME

THE LESSON

ILLUSTRATIONS
STORIES
EXAMPLES
MODELS
DRAWINGS
ANALOGIES
METHODS

WHAT IS A TEACHING METHOD?

In simplest terms, a method is a learning activity. Methods are selected for the purpose of engaging students in the learning process. It stands to reason, then, that the key issue in the selection and use of a teaching method is student learning. In chapter 8, we discovered that learning can occur in three domains—the cognitive (head), the affective (heart), and the behavioral (hands). Methods are the means by which teachers engage learning in these domains. Some methods are more effective in stimulating cognitive learning, whereas others seem to reach the affective level with greater success. Still other methods affect the behavioral domain with greater force. Teachers will want to match the appropriate methods to the domain of learning they are seeking to address. With this awareness, it can be said that a method is a learning activity that stimulates or engages student learning in a particular learning domain.

Categories of Methods

Cognitive methods. One way we could categorize the methods available to creative Bible teachers is by learning domains. Let's consider the cognitive domain. What methods are most effective in stimulating thinking? Well, that depends on what level of learning transfer we are hoping to achieve (see figure 10 in chapter 7). At the rote memory level, methods that emphasize memory recall are desirable. Songs, puzzles, simple games, acrostics, and other memory aids are useful. But the teacher must understand that these methods only enable the student to recall information. To recall a verse from memory by use of a Scripture song is not the same as understanding the meaning of the Scripture. At higher levels of learning, such as at the recognition, restatement, relation, and realization levels, methodology must become more student centered. The role of the teacher shifts from telling to guiding and, therefore, the method must shift from teacher centered to student centered.

Cognitive methods can include brainstorming, small group discussion, case study analysis, debates, forums, interviews, neighbor nudging (a brief discussion in groups of two), panel discussions, question and answer, provocative questions, open-ended stories (stories the group gets to complete), parables, skits, role plays, and lecture. Notice that different methods demand different levels of student involvement. Generally, the greater the involvement, the higher the level of learning that is achieved. Involvement is not necessarily in the form of activity, however. Students can become involved in a well-delivered lecture that stimulates higher levels of thinking. Some methods basically provide information.

Others force students to think through the information or solve a problem with the information (e.g., case study). These are only a few of the options teachers have available. In a moment, we will examine a set of criteria for identifying which method is best suited to your class.

Affective methods. A second category of methods includes those that are most readily suited to the affective domain of learning. Remember, the affective domain deals with human emotions, values, attitudes, convictions, and motivations. Methods that help a teacher tap into this area of student learning tend to require the use of story. For example, Jesus used parables to deal with the matter of His learners' value system. His parabolic stories taught thought-provoking lessons. In many cases, the lesson required His listeners to do some personal soul-searching to fully understand the story. Take the parable of the famous "Good Samaritan." This parable of robbery and religious piousness is designed to evoke a reaction among Jesus' listeners. It was the hated Samaritan who helped the man in need; the self-absorbed religious leaders had not responded. Jesus told the parable to make some uncomfortable enough to evaluate their values and the genuineness of their faith. What was Jesus' learning target? The affective domain.

Probably the most potent methods for teaching in the affective domain are those that involve *modeling* the truth. It has been said that "more is caught than taught." Jesus used modeling to teach servanthood by washing His disciples' feet. His goal was not to teach more information about servanthood, but to demonstrate the nature of a servant. And it was a moving moment for the disciples. He had broken through to the affective domain of learning.

Affective methods include such learning activities as case studies, stories, dramas, skits, testimonies, mission trips, work days, trips to nursing homes and prisons, creative writing, debates, and discussions. Any method that goes beyond simply filling the head to affecting the heart is appropriately categorized an affective methodology.

Behavioral methods. The third category of methods are best linked to the behavioral domain. These methods help the student change a behavior, develop a new desirable behavior, learn a skill, or enhance an already existing skill. Typically, these methods require a form of repetition and reinforcement to succeed, because learning takes place gradually over time. Most habits and behavioral patterns do not change instantly. They require practice. Because behaviors are ingrained over time, teachers must provide a means by which the student can mark progress and find a measure of personal satisfaction and encouragement with each success.

Consider, for example, a teacher who is trying to encourage personal devotions among a group of high school students. In all likelihood, the teacher will have to demonstrate the behavior or skill that she wants to instill in the students. Then, some means of accountability and reinforcement should be used to encourage student successes. In time, doing devotions becomes a matter of habit, and the reinforcements become more intrinsic than extrinsic. At this point, the reinforcement becomes unnecessary in that the new behavior has become habitual. But no amount of telling the students, "You must do your devotions" will help. Behaviors are not changed that way, nor are skills developed on command. Some form of reinforcement is essential to encourage the continuance of new behavior. Wise teachers will move beyond telling to guiding and supporting desired results. This support or reinforcement may come in many forms, ranging from appropriate rewards to verbal recognition.

Behavioral methods include examples, workshops, experiments, rewards, programmed learning, apprenticeships, accountability partners, role-plays, star charts, public recognition, practice sessions, and support groups.

Criteria for Choosing Teaching Methods

How does one select the best method for the teaching situation? We would suggest that each potential teaching method be filtered though a four question grid. Figure 15 depicts this grid.

Learner. The first question that must be considered has to do with the learner's age and ability. By asking "Who are my learners?" teachers can filter out methods that are too difficult or too simple for their learners' capabilities. Methods must be on the learners' level. A method that expects kindergarten children to read is destined to fail. To select a method that requires junior high or middle school students to analyze a deep theological issue may well be asking too much. On the other hand, some methods would make adults feel a bit silly. High school students may be insulted by a method that undershoots their abilities. So we begin with the learner and limit the method selection based on the age group we are teaching.

Lesson aim. The second question that must be considered when selecting a method is "What is the lesson aim?" Sometimes a method appeals to us not because it fits our goals, but because we like the method itself. If our goal is to engage students in a discussion of the high priestly role of Christ, it does little good to simply lecture. Although a lecture may be necessary to begin the lesson, some time must be given to student ideas and insights. Our method selection must reflect our purpose in teaching the lesson. Many a teacher has discovered some great stimulation game or other learning activity and used it in teaching a class only to find that it was, at best, only remotely related to the lesson. The class

Figure 15

CRITERIA FOR
METHODS SELECTION

METHODS

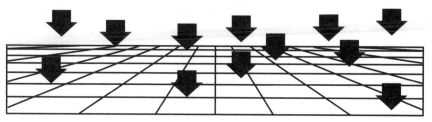

Question #1: Who are my learners?

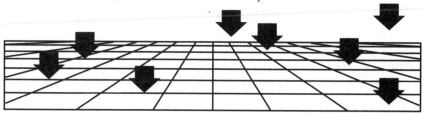

Question #2: What is the lesson aim?

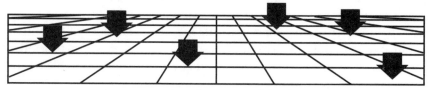

Question #3: What part of the lesson?

Question #4: What resources will I need?

Methods Used in Your Lesson Plan

may well have had a great time with the method, but the learning objectives were not reached. Despite the fact that all may go home having enjoyed the experience, the class was ineffective. Why? Because the method was inappropriate to the lesson aim.

HBLT structure. The third question that creative Bible teachers ask in selecting methods is "In what part of the lesson will this method be used?" This is important because some methods are useful in gaining attention in the Hook section, whereas others work most effectively in communicating information in the Book section. Still others are more useful in the Look section where class participation is essential. Finally, some methods lead well into personal application in the Took section.

Methods used in the Hook should engage student interest. Often these methods focus on the affective domain and evoke an initial response in the student. Telling a moving story can cause the student to become emotionally open to the truth to be presented in the class. The Book section tends to address the cognitive domain, therefore cognitive methods work well. The Look section is designed to move student thinking from the cognitive level to the affective level again. In the Look section, therefore, affective methods are often preferred. Finally, the Took section focuses on change in the learner. Here, behavioral methods have their place.

Resources. The fourth grid that potential methods must be sifted through is "What resources will I need?" Often, despite a wonderful idea, resourcing can become an obstacle. Using a videotape excerpt from a popular television program can be a great way to gain interest in the Hook section of the lesson. But if the video machine is broken or being used by another teacher, or a machine is not available in your church, you'll have to come up with an alternative approach. Sometimes the method you want to use requires resources that are not available or are simply too expensive.

It is equally possible that the resources needed require significant advance preparation. If you hope to use a craft to illustrate or reinforce a truth taught in class, you'll have to plan far enough in advance to have the materials necessary to do the project. A few minutes spent searching for supplies can disrupt the class and learning long enough to lose the teachable moment.

Resource issues also include such factors as class size, room location, room environment, time available, equipment and facilities, and group climate. Teachers may have to reject or modify some methods because of one or more of these variables. Creative Bible teachers must be aware of these factors and variables. Each of these provides challenges unique to your specific situation. All of these variables can be potential resources for effectiveness or potential obstacles to effectiveness. At any rate you, the teacher, must give these resource factors consideration in method selection.

Creative Methods for Creative Bible Teachers

Some methods are like common hand tools in a handyman's toolbox. Every home owner has a hammer, a few screwdrivers, a tape measure, some adjustable wrenches, and maybe a pair of pliers or two. Why? Because these tools are used often. Creative Bible teachers have a set of teaching tools that they must also have at their disposal. These are methods that are used over and over again in Bible teaching. Allow us to suggest a few methods that every Bible teacher should seek to develop and eventually master. We suggest the six foundational methods of creative teaching.

Storytelling. "That reminds me of a story." When the preacher says that in the morning sermon, everyone seems to listen. Many sit up in their seats. Even those who were drifting mentally are drawn to his words. As listeners, they shift into story mode. People love stories. We fill our lives with stories. Television programs, the evening news, movies, videos, newspapers, magazines, and everyday conversations are all dependent upon the ability to tell a story. We all do it. Students may tell a story about why their paper is late and hope they tell it well enough to gain the sympathetic response of the teacher. Coworkers discuss the events of the weekend or a near accident they had on the way to work. Parents tell bedtime stories and want to hear of the events of their children's day. Spouses recount the incident at work or in the supermarket that brought stress or joy to their afternoon. Stories are a part of people's lives. Generally, people are the material from which stories are made.

Creative Bible teachers understand this aspect of human nature. They know that telling a story is part and parcel of teaching. So they collect stories. Maybe it is an article from the morning paper they read on the train or a story from the pages of *Reader's Digest.* Maybe it is a personal story or that of a friend. Whatever the source, creative Bible teachers are always listening for stories that provoke thought or illustrate a point. Those who teach children especially need mastery of this method. Although children can be taught truth in other than story form, most curriculum is laid out as stories, and stories are a basic element of teaching children.

Jesus was a master of the story method. It is estimated that 30 percent of Jesus' recorded teaching ministry is in the form of parables,[1] a kind of story with a teaching theme. Jesus knew people and He knew people are interested in people. It has been said, "Storytellers sow seeds that ripen into knowledge, wisdom, character, and conduct." Jesus' use of story certainly fulfills that quotation.

Why are stories so important to teaching? Because stories relate. Stories entertain. Stories instruct. Stories illustrate. Stories motivate. Stories challenge. Stories model. Stories touch the heart. Stories teach. Stories change listeners. That's why teachers must learn to tell stories as part of their teaching repertoire.

A few words of advice are worth noting. Here is a brief list of suggestions for those who tell stories. This list is primarily geared to those who use stories to illustrate lessons, not to teachers of children, who may use a story as the lesson.

- ◆ Don't tell a story without practice.
- ◆ Do not analyze the story. Let the story speak for itself.
- ◆ Don't make it a sermon. Stories enhance sermons; sermons do not enhance stories.
- ◆ Keep it vivid. Use words that paint mental pictures.
- ◆ Make sure it is appropriate. Age group and context are important considerations.
- ◆ Visualize the story. Rather than memorize, visualize. See the story in your mind's eye.
- ◆ Consider student vocabulary level.
- ◆ Beware of tangents. Tangents tend to confuse.
- ◆ Avoid too many details. Excessive detail also tends to confuse.
- ◆ Don't show and tell. Use props sparingly. Let your words do the communicating.
- ◆ Resist asking for feedback. Let the story simmer in your listeners' minds.
- ◆ Do not illustrate a story. Stories within stories may work in writing but not in teaching.

Provocative questions. "Who do people say I am?" asked Jesus of His disciples in Mark 8:27. After several suggestions, Jesus asked a second question: "Who do *you* say I am?" (Mark 8:29, italics added). Jesus used thought-provoking questions to encourage student learning. The first question had no wrong answer. All His disciples had to do was provide a response consistent with public opinion. The second question pushed His disciples a step further in their thinking. They now had to make a decision regarding Jesus. Through the careful use of questions, Jesus moved His disciples from general implications to personal application.

Questions are an essential part of a teaching strategy. It is important that questions be developed that are open-ended and challenging.

The provocative question is the key to student response. Questions must probe thinking and encourage further dialogue. Closed questions have single word answers that are right or wrong. Usually, they merely provide bits of information and do not allow for further communication. Open questions fuel student involvement.

But good questions do not just happen. One of the common mistakes teachers make is to think that they will be able to compose questions on the fly. It is assumed that good questions will occur to the teacher as the class progresses. Actually, questions that are formulated on the spot are often vague and unproductive. It is best for teachers to write out questions carefully in advance. They should avoid yes/no and short answer questions in favor of questions that motivate thinking. Often good questions will come from the class members themselves. Teachers should resist the urge to answer every question asked. Instead, a simple, "That's a great question! What do the rest of you think?" will go a long way in stimulating learning in the class.

Questions can bring a group or class to the point of seeing and making application in their own lives. "What specific steps could we take to make this a reality in our day-to-day lives?" is an example of an application question. Remember, the key to good application questions is being specific. It is tempting to write general application questions. It is best to ask application questions that lead to specific actions the class members can take in the week ahead to apply the lesson. "What is one thing you could do at your office [or at your school] or in your home with your family that would demonstrate a servant's heart?" is a better question than "How can we apply this to our lives?"

Case studies. Case studies are stories of a kind. They provide students with information about a situation or incident in a person's life. The student is given the essential details of the case and a set of questions to consider. Usually in groups, students interact about the case based upon the questions that were provided. Case studies are an excellent way to generate class interaction and opinions. They can be a means by which implications from the study of a Bible passage are developed. Case studies may be real or invented by the teacher. They are open-ended stories that provide students with an opportunity to consider a truth in light of a real or possible human situation. At first, students may not be comfortable discussing a case situation. They may want more information than is provided or may struggle in understanding the situation. But, once they get used to working with case studies, most students find them stimulating. Experience has shown that case studies bring an exciting, real world dimension to the classroom. The case must be carefully selected to provide students with opportunities to apply a variety of analytical techniques to everyday life issues.

Case studies can be used to raise significant issues in applying a passage. For example, let's say you have just studied the first chapter of James and have discovered some significant principles regarding the role of trials in the life of the believer. Then you introduce the class to a case study in which a family is facing a significant trial—possibly the serious illness of a child. This could set the stage for the group to apply the passage to the scenario you have presented.

In using case studies, a four-step approach to analyzing the case will make the entire discussion process more effective and will also increase the learning benefits. Here are the steps we suggest in using case studies.

1. **Read the Case Thoroughly.** To fully understand what is happening in the case it is necessary to read the case carefully and thoroughly. This may mean reading it more than once before beginning any analysis.

2. **Define the Central Issue.** Define the central issue(s) involved in the case. Occasionally, a case will involve several issues or problems. It is important to identify the most important problems or issues in the case and separate them from the more trivial issues.

3. **Categorize the Issue.** After identifying a major underlying issue, it is often helpful to categorize the issues or problems (e.g., spiritual problem, relational problem, circumstantial problem, medical problem, etc.).

4. **See the Problem Biblically.** Identify how the passage applies to the problem or issues under review. How does this passage relate to this case? Or how is this case related to this passage?

Discussion. The skill of facilitating a discussion is of great value to the creative Bible teacher. The requirements of an effective discussion facilitator are more diverse than commonly perceived, however. Devising questions, keeping the group on the discussion topic, dealing with people who monopolize the conversation, working with difficult personality types, and reaching group consensus are just a few skills that discussion leaders need to develop.

Discussions are appropriate in the process of creative Bible teaching. They provide an avenue for a group to explore the meaning and implications of a passage. Often among adults a wealth of knowledge and experience can be tapped. Although some adults consider discussion a waste of time and others claim it is simply pooling a group's ignorance, the majority of adults will value a well-led discussion opportunity.

Discussion may appear on the surface to be spontaneous. But to succeed, it must be a well-considered and well-planned learning experience. The key to good discussion comes in the use of questions that stimulate thinking and the use of case studies that bring the class close to real human experiences. When these ingredients are involved, discussion becomes a means by which students think together about the application of truth to life.

An excellent resource for those who want to lead classroom discussion well is a book by Terry Powell entitled *You Can Lead a Discussion Group!*[2] In it, Powell shows the reader how to prepare the environment for discussion, develop discussion questions that encourage learner involvement, and deal with problems that a person might face as a discussion leader.

Buzz groups. Buzz group are small groups that have been assigned a passage of Scripture and a list of questions to discuss together. A leader is appointed by the group, and someone else is asked to record the group's conclusions. Then the group is turned loose. The teacher circulates among the groups to see if assigned questions are understood and to be sure that the groups' questions concerning the task are answered. After a period of group work, the buzz groups are reconvened with the rest of the class to report their findings. Sometimes these are used as springboards for the teacher to move into the lesson content. Other times, a larger debate or discussion follows.

Teachers can assign different groups a different set of questions, making them the experts when the groups return to the large group setting. Alternatively, all groups can receive the same questions, and a summary of all findings can be made as the groups report back.

Most creative Bible teachers use buzz groups to engage students in the learning process. Not only does this take the burden off the teacher to communicate all class content, but each student becomes responsible. Teachers can reinforce the importance of every person's contribution by stressing that the teacher's role is one of facilitator rather than instructor. The group can be reminded that they have many experiences, opinions, and understandings that the entire group can benefit from. When a teacher creates that kind of environment, in time, discussions will become fruitful and meaningful tools to group learning.

Lecture. Lecture? Yes, lecture! Lecture, when done well, with adequate illustrations, examples, visuals, stories, and structure is still a good method for creative Bible teaching. The lecture method has fallen on hard times. Educators have rightly pointed out that lectures can hinder student cognitive development. But it is still true that lecture can be an effective method of teaching and changing lives. Lecture is still the most widely used means of teaching and, according to some studies, it may be the most effective means.[3] If we doubt this, consider Jesus' ministry.

If asked, "What was Jesus' preferred method of teaching?" most would probably respond by saying "stories." But a recent inductive analysis of Jesus' teaching conducted by Perry W. H. Shaw indicates otherwise. He concludes that Jesus used lecture in 81 percent of His teaching events as recorded in the gospels.[4] Although lecture was combined with other methods in Jesus' ministry, it was the dominant approach that He employed.

The problem in the use of lecture, it seems, is not the method itself, but the level of ability manifested by those who use it. As William McKeachie puts it, "Effective lectures combine the talents of scholar, writer, producer, comedian, showman, and teacher in ways that contribute to student learning."[5] When a lecture is developed well and is supported by methods that engage student thinking, it is a powerful means to communicate life-changing truth.

THE MASTER TEACHER'S METHODS

Jesus was the consummate example of creative Bible teaching. His repertoire of teaching methodologies is impressive. Robert Joseph Choun lists twenty examples of Jesus' use of varied methodology.[6]

1. Object lessons (John 4:1–42)
2. Points of Contact (John 1:35–51)
3. Aims (John 4:34)
4. Problem-solving (Mark 10:17–22)
5. Conversation (Mark 10:27)
6. Questions—As recorded in the Gospels, Jesus asked more than 100 questions for the purpose of provoking people to think and seek the truth.
7. Answers—Jesus used His answers to move people from where they were to where they needed to be in order to grow spiritually. Jesus encouraged people to discover the truth.
8. Lecture (Matt. 5–7; John 14–17)
9. Parables (John 10:1–21; 15:1–10)
10. Scripture—Jesus quoted extensively from the Old Testament to teach people God's truth.
11. The teachable moment (John 4:5–26)
12. Contrast (Matt. 5:21–22, 33–34, 38–39, 43–44)
13. Concrete and literal examples (Matt. 6:26–34)

14. Symbols (Matt. 26:17–30; John 13:1–20)
15. Large and small groups (Matt. 5–7; John 14–17)
16. Individual teaching opportunities (John 3:1–21; 4:5–26)
17. Modeling (Matt. 15:32; Luke 18:15–17)
18. Motivation (Matt. 16:24–27; 20:21–28; Mark 1:16–18)
19. Impression and expression (Matt. 4:19–20; 7:20)
20. Himself (Matt. 28:19–20)

Creativity in teaching is modeled by Jesus and should be our goal as well. Selecting methods that encourage student involvement and response is a crucial aspect of creative Bible teaching. Once learners have become engaged in the learning process through the use of creative methods, they will be more likely to be open to applying the Word of God outside the classroom. Methods are not an end. They are a means to an end. But means are important. Just as our youth pastor friend at the beginning of this chapter found, the appropriate methodology can open the student to deeper insights and applications of God's Word. Methods are more than time fillers and gimmicks. They are tools for those who would seek to build God's Word into the hearts of God's people.

NOTES
1. Perry W. H. Shaw, "Jesus, Oriental Teacher Par Excellence," *Christian Education Journal*. Deerfield, Ill.: Trinity Evangelical Divinity School. Vol. 1 (Spring 1997): 83–94.
2. Terry Powell, *You Can Lead a Discussion Group!* (Sisters, Ore.: Multnomah, 1996).
3. R. J. Hill, *A Comparative Study of Lecture and Discussion Methods* (New York: Fund for Adult Education, 1960).
4. Shaw, *Jesus, Oriental Teacher*, 83–94.
5. W. J. McKeachie, *Teaching Tips: A Guidebook for the Beginning College Teacher* (Lexington, Ma.: Heath and Company, 1986), 69.
6. Robert Joseph Choun, Jr., "Choosing and Using Creative Methods" in *The Christian Educator's Handbook on Teaching*, ed. Kenneth Gangel and Howard Hendricks (Wheaton, Ill.: Victor, 1988), 166–68.

Chapter Twelve

THE TOOLS:
CHOOSING AND USING
CURRICULUM

Without his tools Steve simply could not work. Steve and his family depend on the tools he uses to earn a living as a carpenter. But Steve, a young father, struggles to make ends meet. To save some money each month he made what proved to be an unwise decision—he carried only liability insurance on his truck. That's why it was devastating to have his tools stolen from his truck. His tools were expensive, and replacing them meant a hardship for a young family with four children. But Steve's church came through as God's people often do for one another. The church decided to have a "tool shower" for Steve. The wife of one of members of the board of elders had the idea. Steve was asked to make a list of the tools that had been stolen. The church secretary sent out invitations to a party for Steve and his family to be held on a Sunday evening at the church building. With the invitations was the list of tools. The secretary also arranged with the local home center to keep a shower registry. Each family in the church was to bring a tool from the list to the party.

Steve was shocked when he received every tool on his list, including some expensive power tools. Only one tool on the entire list went unpurchased—a very costly power miter box saw that Steve used when he built cabinetry or cut ornate trim. But what a wonderful gift everyone had provided! Steve was overwhelmed with emotion and literally wept at the generosity of his church family. The store manager was amazed too. To make the list complete, he decided to donate the power miter box saw. God had indeed provided.

Tools are essential to a carpenter or mechanic. A surgeon would be hampered greatly by a lack of surgical instruments. A dentist would have to go back to a string and a doorknob to do a tooth extraction. One of the unique characteristics of human beings as compared with animals is their ability to create and use tools.

Creative Bible teachers need tools as well. A good study Bible, commentaries, word study books, Bible atlases, and computer research software all serve as tools to the teacher of the Bible. One tool that the lay Bible teacher will certainly want to have is a high quality published curriculum.

Larry taught his first Sunday school class as a newly converted sailor, in a church that "taught the Bible." Curriculum materials? They didn't use them. He doesn't know whether his six first- through third-grade boys suffered from the lack, but he certainly felt like he did. It wasn't the easiest thing for a new Christian to select passages for eight year olds, to know how to plan a lesson that met their needs and captured their interest. Curriculum would have made classtime easier for teacher and class. When teaching adults, creative Bible teachers must go beyond the limits of their curriculum. Some adult curriculum is not well designed and should not dictate the approach or content that an effective teacher can bring to the class. Remember, curriculum is a tool, not a task master, especially in teaching adults. But it's never easy for a layman, or even a Bible college or seminary graduate for that matter, to teach without curriculum—and for a variety of reasons it's usually not wise either.

In this chapter we'll see why. We'll look at the values of using published curriculum and some of the things to look for when you try to find good teaching materials. (Not everything published that is conservative and evangelical is good, by any means!) Finally we'll suggest how a teacher can best use the resources a good curriculum provides.

DEFINING CURRICULUM

The word *curriculum* comes from a Latin word meaning a racecourse. It shares the same root as the English word *current*, which speaks of the flow of water in a stream or an ocean moving in a certain direction. From these images we can grasp the meaning of the word *curriculum* as used in education. Curriculum is the course or direction set by a teacher through which the student is to progress educationally. Curriculum is the sum of all of the experiences of the teaching-learning process. In its simplest terms, *curriculum* is the content that you plan to teach. But the term can be used in a wider sense than just class content. In education, the term curriculum is used to speak of all the studies, activities, resources, or experiences a student encounters in an educational endeavor.

Curriculum can be considered in three categories. First there is the *formal curriculum*. The formal curriculum is the planned content and experiences that the teacher seeks to convey to the students. Second is the *informal curriculum*. This involves the unplanned, yet still instructive, experiences and content that occur in a teaching setting. For example, as youth workers we teach not only by what we say, but by how we behave as well. How we react to unexpected situations, how we treat people, the way we live our lives around students, and our attitudes and actions all communicate to those we seek to teach. How we react when the bus breaks down on the way to camp may teach more than anything we actually say once we get to camp. That is what is meant by *informal* curriculum.

The third category of curriculum is what educators term the *null* curriculum. The word *null* means "not" or "none." The null curriculum is what we choose not to teach. For example, a high school science class that excludes any reference to creationism when studying human origins is teaching something by the exclusion of the subject. The message the student receives is that creationism isn't a viable alternative. Evolution is extensively studied because the teacher believes it has merit. Creationism is not even mentioned because, to the teacher, it is invalid. The point is that what we choose not to teach or exclude from our teaching of a subject also teaches. For our purposes in this chapter, we will concentrate on choosing and using formal curriculum in educational ministry.

CHOOSING CURRICULUM

In the view of most conservatives, the Bible speaks for itself. We resent (rightly) the idea that some church authority must speak before we can know the true meaning of a passage, or before we can respond to God, who communicates Himself to us in His Word. In some churches, and to some individuals, this resentment carries over to Sunday school and other curricula. Writers and editors are viewed suspiciously as claimants of an authority not really theirs.

Certainly no writer or editor can stand as an authority. Even Paul, who actually had apostolic authority, commended the Berean believers for *not* taking his word for truth without checking. Each of us is personally responsible to search the Scriptures to see if the things taught are true. But users of curriculum materials normally aren't seeking an extrabiblical authority. They're users because they need help. They need the help of men trained in theology, just as a pastor needs the help of his commentaries and study resources. And laymen definitely need the help of those with educational expertise. It's a tool—not an authority—that is the nature of curriculum.

Values of Curriculum

We see the values of curricular materials when we look at a few of the educational challenges facing most lay Christian education staff.

Developmental issues. First there is the matter of developmental change. As children mature, they pass through stages marked by changing needs, interests, and patterns of thinking and response. This is important, as the Hebrew text of Proverbs 22:6 points out. Children, when they become old, will not depart from the "way" they have been taught—*when taught the truths needed in the manner suitable at each stage of development.* To do less is not really teaching—it's filling time.

Most of us know that children pass through characteristic periods of change and development. But how many of us have mastered an understanding of the developmental characteristics of students in the age group we most often teach? Do we know the implications of these developmental patterns well enough to be sure that a particular approach we have selected is geared to the way they think, feel, and behave? Few know the Word and the learner well enough to choose concepts and passages and stories that fit their students' changing pattern of needs. This is one advantage of using a curriculum. Curriculum writers can be (and usually are) experts on the characteristics of the age groups for which they write curricular materials. Most laymen, and even some public school teachers, need the expert help and guidance such people can give.

Educational methodology. Another factor that published curriculum helps to address for the Bible teacher is the ability to remain current and effective in methodology selection. In the rapidly changing environment of educational theory and programming it is a challenge for teachers to keep current. Each year new teaching technologies and techniques are developed. Although it is difficult for a lay Sunday school teacher to keep up, a curriculum editor or writer can. Take, for instance, the primary education department editor of one evangelical publisher. Go into her office, and you'll find master lists of vocabulary levels expected in various stages of first, second, and third grades. You'll find current school texts, local school curriculum, and numerous reference books on the age group that is her specialization. From these resources teaching approaches are constantly checked and revised, and new ways of assisting learning are introduced into the design of Sunday school lessons. Challenging and interesting lessons are developed.

Another closely related benefit of published curriculum is found in the variety of resources now used in education. A Christian publisher can develop a variety of learning materials, including visuals, workbooks, and take-home papers that would simply be too time consuming or expensive for the average Sunday school teacher to produce independently. When these aids are used, interest is increased, truths better grasped, and practical applications encouraged. Although computer programs like PowerPoint™ produced by the Microsoft Corporation™ and WordPerfect™ Presentations by the Corel™ Corporation offer excellent graphics programs for developing classroom teaching aids, most laymen cannot produce the quantity and quality of supplementary teaching aids that publishing houses make available today.

Lesson planning. Finally, there's the need for overall planning. Not only does the short view need to be considered (what we will teach this week, this month, this quarter, or even this year in a class), we must track the long view as well. How do we want students to change over several years? What content do we want to expose them to as they develop or mature? How do we know what others have taught before us? What will they learn after they leave our class and move on into another teacher's classroom? How do we avoid teaching the same few Bible stories over and over again? These kinds of questions point to the need for a comprehensive curricular plan.

Most churches fail to develop curricular plans. People are busy just trying to be ready to teach this week. Lack of planning can mean that everyone does what seems right in his own eyes. Although any one class may be an exceptionally effective learning experience, the overall experience of the learner can be repetitive and, at points, wanting. Without a master plan, students can move through a church's educational ministry and miss entire areas of study. Published curriculums (or curricula) help to prevent this by offering a total curricular plan or varied aspects of their curricular plan for inclusion in a plan developed by a local church. (This advantage is undercut by churches that don't stick to one publisher but allow teachers of each class to choose their own curriculum. Such churches need to be particularly careful to avoid excessive repetition.)

For these and other reasons, good curriculum materials are an aid to creative Bible teaching. The creative teacher can draw on and adapt resources that few, if any, laymen can bring to their teaching without curriculum. The problem, then, isn't whether or not to use a curriculum; it's how to choose a good curriculum to use.

Words of Caution in Using Curriculum

John H. Walton, Laurie D. Bailey, and Craig Williford tell a story in their article "Bible-Based Curricula and the Crisis of Scriptural Authority" that is worth repeating at this juncture, for it provides an important warning.

> "What was your story about today?" I asked my 3-year-old.
> "Cain and Abel," he answered. I began to feel concern, wondering how such a sensitive story would be presented to 3-year-olds.
> "Well, what did you find out about Cain and Abel?"
> "God made their bodies" came the nonchalant reply. I quickly affirmed the truth of that but pressed for more.
> "What did Cain and Abel do?" I was probing to find out how the issue of sacrifice had been handled. "They didn't do anything," was the reply.
> As it turned out my son had been neither forgetful nor inattentive. The story card sent home confirmed that (thankfully) neither sacrifice nor treachery were discussed at this tender age. The point of the lesson was "God gave us bodies." I was left to muse about what this curriculum was teaching my son indirectly about interpreting the Bible when stories were manipulated in this way. He was being raised in an evangelical church that used evangelical curriculum. But would he learn how to interpret the Bible properly if the curriculum that shaped his education often ignored the actual teaching of the text and molded the stories to its own purposes?[1]

It is essential that curriculum enhance the teaching of the Bible, not obscure it. Teachers must take care to ask if the curriculum is actually teaching the Word of God or simply seeking to meet the objectives of a curriculum writer. All curriculum, even if it was produced by an evangelical publisher, must be carefully reviewed and its message scrutinized.

Marks of a Good Curriculum

It takes a rare teacher to do the kind of planning necessary to develop a comprehensive curricular plan and then write appropriate curriculum for the entire range of developmental stages. Some churches have done so, but most often the task is undertaken with the help of a trained educational and curricular expert. For most churches and most educational ministry leaders, a quality curriculum produced by a recognized publisher is still welcomed. But how does one select curriculum from among the many possible offerings? It's a complicated task, evaluating curriculum. First the overall grading plan is studied. The theology of the materials is determined. The pedagogy and relevance of the lessons at each age level are tested. A program leader, teacher, or pastor can see crucial areas that must be considered if a curriculum is to be used by laymen to teach the Bible. What are the important areas that must be considered in selecting curricular materials?

A correct view of Scripture and its function. Conservatives hold to a propositional concept of revelation: that God reveals true information in His Word. Materials that teach and reflect other views of biblical authority and revelation simply are not acceptable, although some churches use them because of denominational pressures. Many evangelical publishers, independent and denominational alike, provide materials that are based securely on orthodox belief. But too few of these are as clear in their focus on the function of propositional revelation. They lose sight of the fact that revelation takes us beyond information to contact with God, and that such contact calls for appropriate response. Take the senior high lesson on the apostle Paul we looked at in chapter 10. It was designed to communicate information. It did communicate information, but the lesson was not structured to lead the student beyond the information to confront God and His demands for a personal response. Because of this failure, the lesson is not acceptably designed. To teach content without reference to the student's need for personal response is not teaching the Bible in a way consistent with its nature and purpose.

Another error, often found in materials for children and youth, is to call for a conduct response, but not the response demanded by the passage studied. At times even the lessons of most conservative publishers fall into this error. The writer wants children to be kind and to share. So a passage, such as the feeding of the five thousand, is selected. The focus is on the little boy who shared his lunch. And from this passage, "You ought to share" is taught. But is this the meaning of the passage? Is "you ought to share" the passage's teaching principle? Is sharing the appropriate response? Actually, little is said of the boy. He's not focal; Christ is. The child's act of sharing isn't held up for others to imitate. Jesus Christ's power to meet every need is demonstrated for us to trust. This is the concern expressed earlier by Walton, Bailey, and Williford. A good curriculum will teach what the passage teaches and will call for responses that are rooted in the text of Scripture.

It's easy to set up our rules of conduct and then to find passages that seem to indicate some biblical support. But this isn't teaching the Bible. It's teaching a legalism that can become crushing. Such teaching obscures, for teacher and learner alike, the God who reveals Himself, and who demands not conformity to a code, but response to a Person; a life lived not in cold conformity, but in willing and flexible response to God the Spirit. When a publisher's lessons characteristically fall into either pattern—information without response, or distorted response—the lessons should be rejected.

A creative concept of Bible teaching. Good curriculum seeks to raise students' levels of Bible learning. To achieve this, good curriculum follows (either in individual lessons or units of lessons) the pattern suggested in chapter 9. This is not to say that the Hook, Book, Look, Took structure itself is required. But the general flow is important. Does the material gain attention and draw the learner to the subject being addressed? Does the material present solid biblical content and explore the central principle of the passage accurately? Does the curriculum reflect an awareness of the gaps that block response to God? Are the lesson aims clearly stated and life-response oriented? Do the aims exhibit a structure that leads into the Word, explores the Word, and guides students to explore relevance and plan response? In a good curriculum, application is planned for flexibility, maximum student participation, and student self-discovery of the life implications of Bible truths. And good lessons reflect the writer's awareness of structural factors that help create the desire to learn.

What it really boils down to is this: Good curriculum has a distinctive philosophy of Bible teaching, and this philosophy is carefully applied in developing each lesson series. In point of fact, few publishers spell out their position on the theological and educational issues raised in this book. Even if they did, users would still have to check their practice against their claimed philosophy! And so the responsibility returns to the users, who expect and pay publishers for Bible teaching help. Ultimately, it's up to the men and women in our local churches to select lessons that are theologically and educationally sound. Table 17 provides a very helpful list of questions that can guide curriculum evaluation.

USING CURRICULUM EFFECTIVELY

It is important to remember that published curricula are an aid, but not the answer. All lesson materials are limited in value. When used as a crutch even the best can stifle the freedom and flexibility, so essential to creative Bible teaching, which the writer hopes to encourage. Teachers need a healthy attitude toward their lesson materials. They must look to them with appreciation for guidance in the choice of truths relevant to the age group they teach. They should expect ideas on the meaning of the passages taught and a teaching plan that will lead to student response. They will be glad for new methods and approaches lessons may suggest and for visuals and other teaching materials. But they must not view the curriculum materials as setting a pattern the teacher must follow at all points in class. Creative Bible teachers use curriculum as a teaching tool, not a taskmaster.

A slavish reliance on printed plans, while helpful perhaps for an inexperienced teacher, cuts deeply into the potential for creativity. It's

Table 17a

CURRICULUM EVALUATION GUIDE		
Publisher of Curriculum:_____		
Use of Content		
Regards the Bible as the objective, propositional Word of God	Yes	No
Regards the Bible as authoritative and inerrant	Yes	No
Emphasizes biblical essentials: salvation, discipleship, service	Yes	No
Presents biblical facts in accurate manner	Yes	No
Uses sound hermeneutics when interpreting and applying passages	Yes	No
Develops the central idea of study passage and appropriately applies that idea to the learner's life	Yes	No
Supports use of best translations and current scholarship	Yes	No
Communicates biblical values and a Christian worldview	Yes	No
Promotes internalization and application of truth by the student	Yes	No
Contemporary life problems and issues are addressed from a truly biblical perspective	Yes	No
Use of Experience		
Aids the individual in growth toward maturity in Christ	Yes	No
Makes provision for student interaction and expression of life experiences	Yes	No
Encourages active student participation in discovering life response	Yes	No
Provides practical suggestions for life application in the contexts of home, work, school, and neighborhood	Yes	No
Provides relevant connections to typical life experiences	Yes	No
Promotes open-ended discussion around common matters of concern appropriate to the truths being taught	Yes	No
Provides up-to-date and appropriate examples that are culturally relevant to the students	Yes	No
Teaches one major transferable principle or truth that is clearly rooted in the passage under study	Yes	No

Table 17b

CURRICULUM EVALUATION GUIDE (Continued)

Educational Approach and Preparation Support

Is the Bible used as a tool to produce change in the life of the students?	Yes	No
Does the material meet the developmental needs and capabilities of the students?	Yes	No
Are lesson aims written in terms of the students?	Yes	No
Does the material demonstrate an understanding of the teaching-learning process as it relates to the age group?	Yes	No
Does the material encourage use of contemporary teaching strategies?	Yes	No
Does the material provide sufficient aids for the teacher?	Yes	No
Is instruction provided on the use of aids included?	Yes	No
Are study aids supplied for the teacher, including background on the passage being taught?	Yes	No
Does supplementary material (including visual aids) deal adequately with the Scripture passages studied?	Yes	No
Does the material follow the creative Bible teaching process in a way similar to the Hook, Book, Look, Took format?	Yes	No
Are supplementary materials provided for students? (Take-home papers, etc.)	Yes	No
Is the quality of supplementary materials equal to the curricular materials?	Yes	No

Mechanical Features

Is the material pleasing in its look and design?	Yes	No
Is the layout conducive to effective study and preparation?	Yes	No
Is the material colorful?	Yes	No
Does the material have quality illustrative content?	Yes	No
Is the printing and binding quality of the material acceptable?	Yes	No
Are the materials affordable for the group?	Yes	No
Can the material be adapted to the local church setting and size?	Yes	No

not hard to see why. Creative teaching is a process in which students are vitally involved. Often in this process, ideas are developed and needs revealed that no writer can plan for, nor teacher predict. The teacher has to feel free in such cases to respond to the lead of his class and, when appropriate, modify his plan in order to follow the guidance of the Holy Spirit. This may mean shortening some learning activities, adding unplanned ones, and eliminating some that were planned. This kind of freedom just isn't possible for the teacher who relies completely on printed materials.

We have written this book to help equip you to develop your own lesson plans. We have provided a structure and some help on how to prepare. But the curriculum your church uses or the materials you might pick up yourself in a Christian bookstore are wonderfully useful tools to construct creative teaching plans.

What then does the teacher need as he enters class? Not a detailed series of steps he plans to take. He needs, instead, an overview of the process he hopes to stimulate. He needs a flexible view of the end toward which that process must move. And he needs a view so clear that he can feel free to adapt or change his plans in response to classroom developments, so clear that even with changes he still can lead his students to the climax of learning—response to the God who has spoken to them in His Word. So, even if curriculum is used, it is still the teacher who must design the learning endeavor.

This need for structure with flexibility helps us see more clearly what it takes to become a creative Bible teacher. It takes, first of all, an understanding of the nature of the Bible we teach. Second, it requires a knowledge as to how to study the Bible in order to determine the bridge principle. Next, a teacher needs a clear understanding of how to focus the lesson on student needs so that life application and change result. Finally, teachers need to develop skill in planning and using learning activities (methods) that will enable them to achieve their ministry purposes. This has been the focus of this book thus far.

It is time now to turn our attention to the matter of actually teaching the class. The fourth step in the creative Bible teaching model is teaching the lesson. The next section is designed to provide needed instruction in the major factors relevant to teaching various age groups and to illustrate learning activities suitable to those age groups. So let's get to it. Let's see how we can more effectively teach our students.

NOTES

1. John H. Walton, Laurie D. Bailey, Craig Williford, "Bible-Based Curricula and the Crisis of Scriptural Authority," *Christian Education Journal*. Vol. XIII. Number 3, 83.
2. Table contents compiled and revised from R. E. Clark, L. Johnson, A. K. Sloat, *Christian Education: Foundations for the Future*. (Chicago: Moody, 1991), 499–501; D. Eldridge, *The Teaching Ministry of the Church* (Nashville: Broadman and Holman, 1995), 291–92; and L. E. LeBar, J. E. Plueddemann, *Education That Is Christian* (Wheaton, Ill.: Victor, 1989), 271–72.

Figure 16

THE CREATIVE BIBLE
TEACHING MODEL

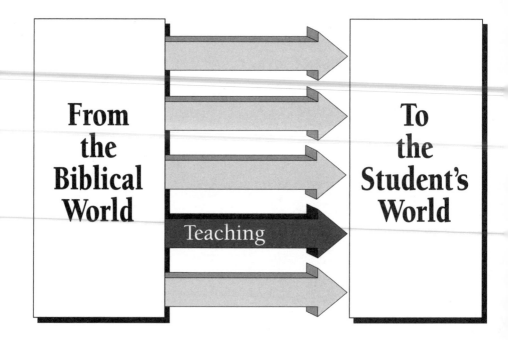

From
the
Biblical
World

Teaching

To
the
Student's
World

TEACHING THE CLASS

Diane and Sean had planned their wedding for months. They wanted their wedding ceremony to honor Christ in every possible way. They wanted it to present a message to those in attendance. Through the music, the words spoken, the symbolism, and the vows they would recite, they hoped to communicate the truth about Christ and His relationship with His bride, the church.

Diane and Sean selected music that would say just what they wanted to say. They met with the pastor to discuss what they wished his message to convey. They met with each participant: the musicians, the soloist, even the people who would stand with them at the front of the church. The order of the service was established, and everyone was brought in on the plan. This was to be a wedding with a theme—a message. It was to be more than a legal service or a religious ceremony uniting a man and a woman. It was to be a living lesson.

The days went by. And eventually it was time for the big day. The plans were in place. The church was decorated. The dresses and tuxedos were donned. The guests were seated. The music began. The bride readied herself at the back of the sanctuary and prepared to walk the aisle. And off in a room to the right side at the front of the church stood the groom, the groomsmen, and the pastor. They had prayer together. And then the pastor commented, "Sean, this is what all the planning was for. It's time to say 'I do'!" With that comment, the men left the room and took their places at the front of the congregation, and the service began.

Planning—it is an essential part of almost every human activity. But at some point the planning leads to action. Game plans lead to games, flight plans lead to flights, building plans lead to buildings, and lesson plans lead to lessons. Eventually it is time to say "I do." We have reached that point in this book. Consider what you have accomplished. You have studied your passage, focused your message, and structured your lesson. Now you're ready to actually teach the class. In this section of the book, we will provide some help in doing that well.

Six chapters are in this section. Chapter 13 will begin by introducing you to some essential principles of effective teaching by looking at the things truly great teachers do by habit. Then, in chapter 14 we will discuss the important matter of motivating student learning. The next four chapters will deal with the specific matters related to teaching various age groups. Starting with adult learners, then adolescents, and finally grade-school children and pre-schoolers, we will discuss some transferable principles, as well as some models for creative Bible teaching with students in each of these age ranges. So let's continue our look at creative Bible teaching. It's time to say "I do."

Chapter Thirteen

TEACHING PRINCIPLES:
COMMON PRACTICES OF
TRULY GREAT TEACHERS

Warren Benson is a truly great teacher. He has credibility with his students, communicates with clarity, stimulates interest in learning, teaches with style, seeks to be creative, and values and respects his students. There are very few like him. He is worth emulating. Once, while he lay on his back nursing a severe muscle strain, he met with a student struggling in a difficult work situation. Even while in pain, he took the time to provide needed support and guidance to a young seminarian he was mentoring. His action went beyond the call of duty. Why? Because Warren Benson is a truly great teacher!

Some teachers are simply better than others. Research studies seem to indicate that effective classroom communicators have certain characteristics and behaviors in common. The practices of truly great teachers can serve as guidelines for those who desire to teach the Bible with skill and influence.

GREAT TEACHERS HAVE CREDIBILITY

One element essential to teaching effectiveness is the credibility of the teacher. "How is the teacher perceived? Are the teacher's statements trustworthy?" These are the first questions that a student considers when evaluating the quality of a teacher, especially a Bible teacher. Credibility as a communicator is influenced by six factors, according to research done by David W. Johnson and Frank P. Johnson.[1] These include: relia-

bility of information, purity of motives, warmth and friendliness, reputation, expertise, and passion.

Application of this research to Bible teaching should be obvious.
Credibility is fundamental to communication, and a Bible teacher who
lacks it is facing more than an uphill battle to be effective. If the Bible
teacher lacks credibility, listeners will likely doubt the teacher's message.
This seems to be Paul's point when instructing Timothy about his ministry as a pastor. He writes,

> Don't let anyone look down on you because you are young, but set an ex-
> ample for the believers in speech, in life, in love, in faith and in purity.
> Until I come, devote yourself to the public reading of Scripture, to
> preaching and to teaching. Do not neglect your gift, which was given you
> through a prophetic message when the body of elders laid their hands on
> you. Be diligent in these matters; give yourself wholly to them, so that
> everyone may see your progress. Watch your life and doctrine closely. Per-
> severe in them, because if you do, you will save both yourself and your
> hearers. (1 Tim. 4:12–16)

Paul's message to Timothy is that credibility is essential to ministry success. Paul is telling young Timothy to build a reservoir of respect
among those he is called to teach. To do this would require his life,
study, actions, and attitudes to underscore the trustworthy nature of his
teaching. A similar injunction could be made to all who desire to teach
the Bible.

Reliability of information, purity of motives, warmth and friendliness, reputation, expertise, and passion—research indicates that *all six*
characteristics are essential to building and maintaining credibility.
Lacking just one of these measures of credibility renders the teacher less
effective. The student will devalue the teacher's message if credibility is
not attained and maintained. Therefore, the first suggestion for increasing your effectiveness as a Bible teacher is to develop and maintain credibility. How does the creative Bible teacher become a credible
communicator of God's Word? Let's examine each of the six measures of
credibility in more detail.

Reliability of Information

Do you know what you are talking about? Is the information you
provide accurate? Do you adequately prepare so that you can anticipate
and deal with questions and misunderstandings about the text? These
are important questions for the Bible teacher to consider in appraising
his effectiveness. Frankly, it takes time to study a passage. It's hard work!
But consider the alternative—a lack of credibility and effectiveness as a

teacher of the Scriptures. That is not to say that you must know every-thing or can answer all questions. That would be impossible and unpro-ductive, even if you could. What it means is that you have done your homework on the passage, and you anticipate some of the questions that might come.

Purity of Motives

Why are you teaching? Does it fulfill a need you have for being in the public eye? Are you seeking to use your role as teacher to achieve some inappropriate personal ends? We all must probe our motives to see if they are pure and right before the Lord.

Hank is a retired professional athlete from the world of hockey. He is a Christian, and he is a sought-after speaker. On a number of occa-sions he has spoken at fundraising banquets and outreaches for various Christian organizations and churches. But Hank has a problem. He tends to move from church to church so that he can be a focal point of people's attention. Hank misses the roar of the crowd and the attention of the media, so he seeks the attention of fellow Christians. He loves it when people notice him. He likes it when people try to get close so they can say they know a once famous hockey star. He likes it when he is in-troduced from the pulpit and invited to say a few words. At some point, after he has been in a church for a while, most pastors ask him to speak. He gets his public kudos, but in time he becomes just another member of the congregation. When that happens, Hank moves on. On to a new church, a new crowd, more cheers, and more recognition.

We, like Hank, may be teaching to meet a personal need rather than to honor Christ. Many teachers need to be up front, the center of attention, the one with the answers. Many want to be noticed for their knowledge, their humor, or their ability. Whatever the reason, when we seek to meet our needs through teaching, eventually our credibility is damaged. And eventually people catch on. Finally we are seen for our real motives. Jesus warned us of such teachers.

> Beware of the teachers of the law. They like to walk around in flowing robes and love to be greeted in the marketplaces and have the most im-portant seats in the synagogues and the places of honor at banquets. They devour widows' houses and for a show make lengthy prayers. Such men will be punished most severely. (Luke 20:46–47)

What happens when we doubt a teacher's motives? What does that doubt do to the person's credibility? If we think a teacher is simply out for his own ends, trust is eroded. And without trust, teaching becomes simply the presentation of information. It is not enough to do the right things as a teacher. We must do the right things for the right reasons.

Warmth and Friendliness

Credibility is gained from being human. Have you ever noticed how radio announcers communicate? The medium of radio allows them to speak to you like a good friend. When a person sits at a microphone in a radio studio there are only two people in the world, the broadcaster and the listener. Most radio broadcasters think this way. They know that effectiveness in communication depends on projecting a sense of warmth and friendliness. That is best done by envisioning a conversation with a single listener. That mind-set also allows the teacher to become more transparent and conversational.

In a similar way, teachers can gain credibility by projecting genuine personal warmth and friendliness. If students detect that you are human, vulnerable, and real, they will themselves become more open and interactive. Humor is one way in which warmth and friendliness can be conveyed. It is important, at times, for a group to laugh together. Of course, humor must be appropriate and never at the expense of a student. Laughter is an indicator of group health and of a teacher who is open and human. Tension in a group will always inhibit laughter, while openness will generate it. This does not mean you have to become a stand up comic. You need not tell jokes. Rather, humor that fits the moment, that simply spills out of a healthy group interaction is all it takes. The result will be a teacher who is received not as a distant information giver, but as a real co-learner and friend.

Dr. Joseph Stowell, president of the Moody Bible Institute, possesses that kind of humor. Through humor, and sometimes even by laughing at himself, he has a way of breaking down barriers between himself and his listener. He becomes a human being, not perfect, but personal. And in the process he gains credibility because his listeners can relate to him. People relax in his presence. Their guard comes down, and they are opened to the truth of the Word in a fresh and relevant way. They become more responsive. Through humor, he skillfully makes learning a pleasure—his ministry is informative and life changing, but still fun.

Another means by which you as a teacher can communicate warmth and friendliness is through being open enough to show how the truth works in your life. By being personal and transparent about your own struggles and experiences, you can interest your students. People are interested in people—especially their personal lives. Just think, an entire magazine is devoted to the lives of great or well-known people.

And tabloids are filled with truths, half-truths, and outright fiction about people because of our fascination with celebrities. People interest us. If you want to connect with your class and gain greater credibility, let the class in on your own efforts to apply the passage—your successes and failures.

Reputation

In a western town a financial consultant led a Sunday school class for those thirty-five to fifty years of age. He preached the need to have a budget and to faithfully pay one's bills. The class went well and was lauded by those in attendance as "eye-opening" and "extremely helpful." Many came up to the front of the room after class to thank the teacher. His ministry seemed to be greatly appreciated by everyone— everyone, that is, except one man who sat toward the back of the room. He was a local Christian dentist. It was all he could do to sit and listen to the teacher. He knew better. The financial consultant had failed to pay for dental work done several years earlier. No matter how dynamic his teaching, no matter how well prepared, no matter how strong his content, he lacked credibility for the dentist in the back row. And if that student were to tell others in the class of his experience, the teacher's ministry would undoubtedly lose its effectiveness.

Reputation is important to a teacher. What is the word out there about you, your life, and your teaching ministry? Proverbs 22:1 says, "A good name is more desirable than great riches; to be esteemed is better than silver or gold." Reputation can involve one's integrity as it did the case of the financial consultant mentioned above, or it can simply relate to the teacher's style and approach to teaching. It has been said that "adults vote with their feet." In other words, adults know what they want. When they find it, they come, and when they don't, they stay away. Often, a teacher's reputation can influence how adults respond. Ask any college student. Most have an opinion about their teachers. That opinion, be it good or bad, is passed from student to student. Students enter the teacher's course predisposed to like the class or to find it boring and unchallenging. The same can be said of Sunday school teachers. Some draw students; others do not. But when it comes to teaching in the church, students do not have to take the course, so reputation is all the more important.

Expertise

We tend to listen to and value those who are experts. When your car is acting up, you want an expert mechanic to give you his opinion. When your children act up, you want expert advice on child development. When your gallbladder is acting up, you need an expert physician. And rightly so. Expertise is a great advantage in most situations because experts know their stuff. It's true that the experts can be too removed from reality at times and can miss the obvious, but more times than not an expert can bring greater knowledge to a given situation or need. In teaching, expertise in a subject area can strengthen the credibility of the teacher.

You may want to focus your efforts in understanding and teaching the Bible in specific areas in order to gain expertise and increase your credibility as a Bible teacher. Some have become experts in teaching on the Old Testament. Others have focused on the Gospels and life of Christ. Some have a thorough understanding of biblical prophecy. By focusing your study and teaching ministry in a particular field, you can increase your effectiveness as a teacher. This may not be feasible if you teach children or teenagers. But you can become an expert in your age group and its needs. We need experts in teaching adolescents as well as experts in teaching children. Wherever you concentrate your study, you will gain credibility with your students by developing a measure of expertise.

Passion

Great teachers have a passion about teaching. When they teach you feel as though they are communicating the most important truths one could ever hear. They have fire in their eyes, sincerity in their words, and conviction in their hearts. And they express that passion dramatically. They generate excitement, and that excitement is truly contagious.

Persons like Zig Zigler in business, Lou Holtz in athletics, and former president Ronald Reagan in politics all are known as people with passion. They love what they do and they love to communicate it to others. In the world of Bible teaching and Christian education we can point to people like Howard Hendricks. Hendricks has often said, "If you are going to bore people, don't bore them with the Gospel. Bore them with calculus, bore them with earth science, bore them with world history. But it is a sin to bore people with the Gospel." Hendricks could never be accused of that failing.

Through your gestures, your voice, and your classroom manner, teach with animation and life. Become passionate about the truth you are seeking to communicate. Teach your passage with a sense that it is indeed life changing. People respond to that kind of passion.

Enthusiasm gives credibility. We know that listeners are more likely to believe a person who is enthusiastic than one who is not. This fact has an upside and a downside. The downside is that they will more likely believe a lie told with enthusiasm than the truth told in deadpan manner. That explains why the cults can be so attractive. Whether we are speaking of David Koresh or Joseph Smith, passion is convincing. But there is also an upside to the power of enthusiasm. The upside is that we have something to be passionate about. We are teaching the Bible, the Word of the living God. It is more desirable than gold, and its message is able to give wisdom that leads to eternal life (Ps. 19:7–11). So we have no reason to feel it inappropriate to teach with passion. We have cause to get fired up and stay that way!

GREAT TEACHERS COMMUNICATE CLEARLY

Clarity doesn't always mean that great teachers' messages are easy to understand or require no mental processing, but that their content, their purpose, their examples, their choice of words, and the structure of their teaching are precisely developed. Jesus was not easy to understand. People had to struggle with the meaning of His message, but He was precise in what He communicated. His words were not haphazard. He knew exactly how He wanted to turn a phrase, and He did so for the sake of learning. Jesus taught with focus and precision.

Clarity of Content

Clarity requires that teachers have something to say. This involves research, time for organization of thoughts, reading widely, and doing adequate preparation for teaching. Think of it! The average rate of speaking is between 120 and 170 words per minute. At that rate teachers produce somewhere near ten thousand words in a one-hour Sunday school class if they do all the talking. That's equivalent to twenty-two pages in this book. Do that each week for a year and you will speak more than one thousand pages of text. That is five or six books a year! The apostle Paul did not produce that much material under the inspiration of the Spirit! This fact alone underlines the difficulty of effective teaching ministry and the necessity of adequate preparation.

Clarity of Purpose

Assuming you have something to say, it is important to boil it down to a single sentence statement of purpose. Students complain that teachers are sometimes hard to follow because they never tell you where they are going. Effective teachers have one unifying theme to each teaching session. They do not simply present an outline of information. They present an idea and develop it.

Haddon Robinson, author of the book *Biblical Preaching* that we referred to earlier, has said this about the importance of putting our thoughts into clear and concise ideas:

Ideas sometimes lurk in the basement of our minds like ghosts difficult to contain. At times we struggle to give ideas expression. "I know what I mean," we say, "but I just can't put it into words." Despite the difficulty of clothing thought in words, the preacher [or, in our case, the teacher] has to do it. Unless ideas are expressed in words, we cannot understand, evaluate, or communicate them.[2]

Great teachers do not teach more; they tend to teach less with more focus. They teach one "big idea" that they attempt to drive home throughout the lesson. They avoid a shotgun approach to teaching in favor of aiming with rifle accuracy. The greatest obstacle to effective teaching is not that we teach too little, but that we teach too much. Great teachers are focused.

Clarity of Structure

People desire structure. Thinking demands structure. And information does not organize itself. Facts are like bricks: They do not simply assemble themselves into a building. Plans are needed. Drawings must be devised. And when the plans are implemented, the drawings become reality. In a similar way, teaching demands structure and planning. Information requires orderly presentation. By creating a structure for the learning experience, teachers enable students to think clearly about a subject and to process the ideas they are taught. One aid to the student in providing structure to learning is an outline or handout. Studies show that students who take notes remember material better than those who do not. Further, research indicates that concepts that are "chunked" are better assimilated by the student than are diverse and separate points.[3] Students appreciate simple class outlines because they help straighten out the zigzag, squirrel-like pattern so often found in classroom learning.

Clarity of Presentation

Outlines are only skeletons for teaching. The actual classroom presentation demands more of a teacher than simply the development of a teaching outline. Teachers must provide illustrations, stories, and examples to put flesh on the bones. One of the responsibilities of a teacher is to take an abstract idea and explain it in concrete terms. Illustrations and stories do this. They render truth believable. They allow students to mentally catch up with the teacher. They prevent weariness on the part of the learner. And they add warmth and vitality to the classroom experience. Clarity of presentation grows out of concrete examples, illustrations, and stories. Effective teachers understand this, and truly great teachers master it.

GREAT TEACHERS STIMULATE INTEREST

Hook the Learner

Researchers tell us that the first twenty-five words spoken by a teacher are the most important in gaining student attention and interest in a subject.[4] We have extensively discussed the "Hook" aspect of the lesson plan introduced in chapter 9, but it is important to remember again the significance of stimulating student interest at the very beginning of our class. That is what great teachers do well. You've got to learn to "hook" your students. Then, once you get their attention, you've got to reel them in. Learners' attention is constantly in demand by other matters, so you cannot assume that their interest in learning is automatic.

Consider television as an example. Most shows use a brief, one or two minute introduction to hook the audience. Tim Allen's show, *Home Improvement*, is a suitable example. Each show begins with a short spot, usually a scene with Tim and his sidekick, Al. These brief clips are often the most humorous part of the show. The segment is entertaining, stimulating, and attention getting. The goal? To hook audience members and keep them watching.

Great teachers get their students' attention right from the start. They know that if they do not gain attention at the beginning of class, they probably never will.

Involve the Learner

Great teachers know that people tend to learn more when they are involved than when they are uninvolved. When you are talking, students may or may not be involved in learning. But when they are talking, students must get involved. So the first principle of involvement in learning is this—to some degree, the less the Bible teacher talks, the more the students learn. It is important to remember that very few teachers are so dynamic that students will sit absorbed in every statement. In fact, all students have a limited attention span. The younger the student, the shorter that attention span. So let's face it, if you teach and they listen, given enough time, your students will become bored. But if you're not talking, then something else must be happening in your class. If planned well, that can be student participation. It will take a lot of planning! But participation minimizes boredom and maximizes learning.

Equip the Learner

Great teachers equip learners for daily living. They seek to be relevant and practical. This is not to say that only truth that is immediately applicable is worth learning, but that students need to see the practicality of what they learn in order to learn it well. "So what difference does all this make?" Usually, your students will not directly ask that question, but you can be sure it is on their minds. It is the question that everyone entertains. It is important to remember that people, particularly adult learners, are not interested in simply gathering more information. They need to see the relationship of the information taught in class to their life on Monday. Our task as Bible teachers is to make sure that God's Word is applied. One way to do that is to be sure it is presented in a practical and applicable manner. Creative Bible teaching is about application. But the response of the learner needs to be to God. The Bible must be applied, but it is not applied in a vacuum as though Scripture were merely a list of good deeds.

GREAT TEACHERS TEACH WITH STYLE

A study conducted in 1963 found that a teacher's delivery is almost twice as important to teaching effectiveness as is the content of the lesson.[5] This is not to minimize the importance and need for adequate content in teaching, but it simply points out that content alone is not sufficient to produce a powerful classroom experience. No simple formula for teaching with style can be given. All teachers must develop their own styles of teaching based on their own strengths and limitations. But there are some principles of teaching style that will enhance any teacher's ministry. Here are a few.

Vivid Words

Mark Twain once said, "The difference between the almost-right word and the right word is . . . the difference between the lightning bug and the lightning." His point is that our choice of words is important to effective communication. Great teachers select words that paint mental pictures for students.

Purposeful Actions

Movement and gestures contribute to the interest of students in the classroom experience. God made the human body to move. By our very nature we link action and gesture with our thoughts as we talk with one another. But something happens when we step in front of a class. A kind of paralysis sets into our joints. Great teachers overcome this paralysis with purposeful actions and gestures. Gestures and movement give needed life to our teaching. Purposeful actions in teaching are like diagrams and charts in a book. They clarify ideas and add interest. Gestures enable students to better understand the point being made. It has been estimated that there are more than seven thousand distinct gestures that can be made with our hands, arms, and wrists. Surely some of these are worth employing in our classroom communication efforts. The result will be that we will become more at ease and our learners will gain more from our teaching.

Eye Contact

Eyes can communicate much. By looking at our students we can communicate interest, we can monitor feedback, and we can gain greater attentiveness. It is a good start to improved teacher effectiveness, and it can begin immediately in your teaching. Look for a supportive person and connect with that person's eyes. When you get more comfortable, try to make eye contact at least once each class with every student, more often in small classes.

Vocal Variety

The voice is a tool of teaching. Through the choice of inflection, volume, rate, and pitch, the teacher can give specific meaning to words. By varying the rate of speech, the range of voice, and the volume of a word, teachers can encourage students to listen more carefully. All of us have had a teacher or professor who has droned on and on in a monotone voice. We know how difficult it was to listen. Like the science teacher in the show *The Wonder Years*, such teachers are better at encouraging sleep than learning. Think of your voice as the punctuation marks in your teaching. Think how much easier it is to read a page accurately when it is punctuated than a page with little or no punctuation.

Visual Display

According to one study of both youth and adults, student attention in a class increases in the first ten minutes and then decreases from that point until the end of the session. Researchers found that students could recall 70 percent of material presented in the first ten minutes of class and only 20 percent from the last ten minutes. The more active the student was in the class, the more was retained. And the more the teacher used visual displays of teaching concepts, the more was retained as well.[6]

Mobil Oil Company studies support the importance of "display devices" in teaching. They found that from hearing alone, 70 percent of material taught was recalled three hours later and 10 percent was recalled three days later. Seeing alone produced a 72 percent recall rate three hours later and a 20 percent recall three days later. But the combination of both seeing and hearing had a dramatic impact on recall. Participants in the study recalled 85 percent of what they both saw and heard three hours later and obtained a 65 percent rate of recall three days later. These figures indicate the important role of visual aids in teaching.[7] But there is a side benefit to using visual aids—increased freedom and flexibility for the teacher. Visual aids allow the teacher to move away from notes while permitting the teacher to retain structure to the lesson.

Note-Free Delivery

Great teachers are not tied to their notes. Most know their material well enough that they could teach it without their notes in hand. Excessive reliance on one's notes tends to restrict the teacher to the podium or a few feet to either side. Too much dependence prevents the teacher from moving about the classroom and interferes with classroom management. When teachers know their subject, few notes are needed. This gives the teacher great freedom to interact with class members and truly hear their comments. It is also true that too many notes give teachers a false sense of security about their mastery of the topic. But, by limiting the use of notes, teachers are forced to think of alternative ways to get the point across.

It is true you are also limited as to what can be covered if you don't use notes, but look at it this way: If you don't know it well enough to teach it without notes, maybe it doesn't need to be covered. Is it reasonable to expect students to know information from memory that you yourself need notes to teach? Instead, detailed material should be in the form of a handout or a transparency. If you teach your class without notes, you will increase your credibility with students as an information source.

So what do we suggest you use if not a detailed set of notes? We would recommend a simple teaching outline like the one we introduced to you in chapter 9. By using a maximum two page lesson plan, teachers become concise and must know their material well. Combine this with other teaching tools and you will have all you need to teach with confidence.

GREAT TEACHERS TAKE THE RISK OF CREATIVITY

It will happen. Those who attempt to be creative will fall flat on their face at some time. Being a creative teacher is risky because it demands that you attempt teaching approaches that you may not have personally tried before or have not even seen used. For example, the use of case study may be intimidating to you if you have used lecture as your primary method of teaching. What if it doesn't work? What if students do not get involved? What if the case is too easy or too hard for the group? There will be days when nothing goes as planned. Eventually, you will attempt a new creative idea, and it will not be as effective as you hoped. At that time you may start to question whether that method of teaching is workable at all and opt for a safer technique. Many concerns, questions, and experiences can come to mind that could convince you that creativity is too risky. But truly great teachers take that risk.

So how do you take the risk? The key is to have a sound philosophy of teaching. You have to believe that engaging the student in meaningful learning is more important than your personal performance or information transfer. When a class session that you have planned fails, your philosophy of teaching becomes the harbor of safety. If your teaching is founded on a commitment to engage learning, when the inevitable questioning of your method selection comes, you will be able to easily chalk off failure to a lack of experience with the method, an approach that doesn't work for your particular class, or just an off day. You will be willing to adjust and try again. But if you are only cautiously convinced of your philosophy of teaching, when creative efforts fail your confidence may be shaken and you will likely travel the easy road of familiarity.

Creative teachers tend to break away from the crowd. They are inventive and imaginative. It is not that they come up with entirely original ideas. Rather, they are focused on student learning, and they plan ways to engage students in the learning process. They have an experimental spirit. Because of their passion for learning, they will move out of their comfort zone to bring students to the point of learning success.

GREAT TEACHERS VALUE AND RESPECT STUDENTS

People are created in the image of God. That fact gives our students worth, value, and dignity. It is important that our theology of human beings filters into our teaching ministry. We must see each and every student as a distinct individual worthy of respect. Great teachers—especially great Bible teachers—see students in this way. Great teachers come to understand that ministry goes beyond just passing on information or stimulating thought. Great teachers give their students the respect due a fellow human being. And students detect it and are changed by it.

Lauri loves teardrop earrings. In fact, she has worn them every day for more than thirteen years. The reason is the influence of a teacher who also wore teardrop earrings—a teacher Lauri will never forget because of the value and respect the teacher showed her as a sixth grade student. Mrs. Lake had auburn hair, sparkling blue eyes, and teardrop earrings that reflected the afternoon sun.

Lauri's family had its problems. Her father was an alcoholic. In his drunken rages he would fight night after night with her mother. She would hear their yelling, the slamming doors, and her mother's sobbing. For Lauri, life was anything but peaceful. It was a life that an eleven-year-old girl should not have to endure. It was a life of agitation, anger, bitterness, and neglect. That's why Lauri's parents never showed up for parent-teacher conferences at school.

All through the afternoon Mrs. Lake greeted parents at the classroom door. Parents who came to see how their children were progressing in school. Parents who shared smiles, pats, and hugs with their children as they expressed their support and pride. But the day passed and Lauri's parents never came. She never actually expected them to, but that didn't lessen the hurt Lauri felt. She imagined what it would be like to have parents who actually cared.

After all of the children had met with their parents and teacher, Mrs. Lake called Lauri into the hallway. Lauri sat in the folding chair near the teacher's desk, which had been moved outside for the conferences. Mrs. Lake sorted through files and then, with a smile, found Lauri's. Lauri focused on the floor, embarrassed by her parents' absence. Mrs. Lake lifted Lauri's chin. She looked Lauri straight in the eye and began. "First of all, I want you to know how much I love you. Second, you need to know it is not your fault that your parents are not here today." Lauri had never heard these kinds of words before. She had never felt such compassion. "Third," Mrs. Lake continued, "you deserve a conference whether your parents are here or not. You deserve to hear how well you are doing and how wonderful I think you are." So Lauri had her conference with Mrs. Lake. She saw her grades, she was told of her strengths, and she was recognized for her worth and value. That day Lauri's life was changed. She became a person with new confidence and a sense of dignity.[8]

Great teachers do more than teach. They value their students and treat them as people should be treated. And it is right that great Bible teachers make special efforts to do so. That perspective should cause us to go the extra mile as teachers. Paul put it this way: "We were gentle among you, like a mother caring for her little children. We loved you so much that we were delighted to share with you not only the gospel of God but our lives as well, because you had become so dear to us" (1 Thess. 2:7–8). Great teachers share their lives, as well as their knowledge, with their students.

NOTES

1. David W. Johnson and Frank P. Johnson, *Joining Together: Group Theory and Group Skills* (Englewood Cliffs, N.J.: Prentice Hall, 1982), 186.
2. Haddon Robinson, *Biblical Preaching* (Grand Rapids: Baker, 1980), 39.
3. R. J. Peper and R. E. Mayer, "Note-taking as a Generative Activity," *Journal of Educational Psychology* (1978): 70(4), 514–22.
4. K. E. Anderson, *Persuasion Theory and Practice* (Boston: Allyn and Bacon, 1971), 98 ff.
5. Paul Heinberg, "Relationships of Content and Delivery to General Effectiveness," *Speech Monographs* (1963): 30, pp. 105–7.
6. J. Hartley and I. K. Davies, "Note-taking: A Critical Review." *Programmed Learning and Educational Technology* (1978): 15, pp. 207–24.
7. O. E. Lancaster, *Effective Teaching and Learning* (New York: Gordon and Breach, 1974), 81.
8. This story was recapped from a story entitled "Tear Drops of Hope," written by Nancy Sullivan Geng. It appeared in the September 1997 *Reader's Digest*. It was originally published by Focus on the Family (8605 Explorer Dr., Colorado Springs, CO 80920) in their November 1996 magazine.

Chapter Fourteen

TEACHING EFFECTIVENESS:

MOTIVATING THE LEARNER

B ob Michaels leads a class that people can't wait to attend. Each week in his church in suburban Toronto he teaches an excited group of high school students. He is known for his wit and his ability to make a passage come alive. But what is most remarkable about his class is the participation and interaction it generates. Bob insists on small group Bible exploration sessions with those who attend. In these small groups, students are guided in the process of application of truth to their lives.

Perhaps it looks too ideal, this picture of students eagerly and excitedly exploring the Bible together. If you teach teens or adults, you may wonder how in the world to get them to speak, much less do the kind of thing described in the earlier chapters of this book. If you teach children, you may wonder how to make them keep still or at least to keep on the subject. How could they be guided to explore Bible truths? They don't think as adults do, and when they get started talking, there's no controlling them.

No one ever suggested that creative Bible teaching is easy. All these problems exist. But all can be solved. Even older adults, soberly stacked side by side on pews in the left front of the sanctuary in many churches, can be actively involved. And they can love it! The solution lies partly in the area of teacher skills and in training the class to take part in the creative process. But only partly. More basic is student motivation: that indispensable *desire* to take part, that *want* to learn.

THE IMPORTANCE OF MOTIVATION IN TEACHING

General and Specific Motivation

General motivation refers to the student's overall attitude toward learning. General motivation tends to remain stable over time and in a variety of situations. It is the most difficult to alter by a teacher. Some students seem to have an innate desire to learn. They are constantly drawn to new learning experiences, to books, to teachers. Although not all motivated learners seek to learn in a classroom situation, all seem to be motivated by the sheer love of fresh discovery. Other learners are less enthralled with learning for learning's sake. This is not to say that they cannot learn or do not learn. They simply do not seek out learning experiences. They require great motivation from teachers and parents to pursue learning goals.

Specific motivation is less stable and refers to a person's motivation at a given time toward a specific topic or class. One day a student may be highly motivated because the topic being studied is of great interest, while another day the student may find the topic to be without much motivational appeal. It is this aspect of motivation that teachers can most readily affect. To do so the teacher must have an understanding of the students' interests and must identify ministry contact points. A needs assessment, such as the one discussed in chapter 6, can be of great benefit in discovering ways to motivate students.

Extrinsic and Intrinsic Motivation

Extrinsic motivation refers to motivation that comes from outside the student. Sometimes students need help getting started in learning, and extrinsic methods of motivation can play a role. If a student is disinterested in a subject, has a minimal general motivation level toward learning, or is simply discouraged, forms of extrinsic motivation can cause him to respond to the learning situation. Generally, but not always, extrinsic motivators are found in the form of positive and negative reinforcements.

Intrinsic motivation refers to motivation that comes from within the student. Students who are intrinsically motivated find some personal satisfaction in learning. They may enjoy the subject, have a high level of general motivation, be seeking knowledge for a specific reason (such as seeking employment in a particular field or preparing a sermon), or desire to grow personally. For whatever the reason, intrinsically motivated persons tend to seek out learning and are not satisfied until they master a particular subject.

We said in chapter 8 that learning occurs in three domains—cognitive, affective, and behavioral. But for learning to occur in any of these domains, the individual must exercise his will to learn. Human will and attitude play enormously powerful roles in learning. If we can understand what motivates a learner, we can possibly prompt or guide student attitudes. By doing so we can encourage students to exercise their will to learn. Although we cannot make a student learn, we can provide a climate where the student is more likely to choose to become engaged in learning. Researchers have discovered both personal and structural factors in education that motivate student participation in the learning process.

FACTORS THAT MOTIVATE LEARNING

It's an old evangelical cliché: "Visit your students, and spend time with them outside class, and everything will go well in class." Like most clichés it's worn, and true—at least, true to some extent. But what it leaves out is more important than what it says. What's left out deals with the *quality* of the outside contacts, and with the fact that the *in-class* teacher-student relationship is certainly as important as anything that takes place outside, if not more important! It also leaves out that class group-life is involved in motivation too. That's a lot left out that ought to be in!

Personal Factors That Motivate Learning

Student-teacher relationship. Did you ever have a teacher who could say this? "I desire to depart and be with Christ, which is better by far; but it is more necessary for you that I remain in the body. Convinced of this, I know that I will remain, and I will continue with all of you, for your progress and joy in the faith." Or this? "I was gentle among you, like a mother caring for her little children. I loved you so much that I was delighted to share with you not only the gospel of God but my life as well, because you had become so dear to me."

Paul said it, of course. He had that kind of loving relationship with those he taught. It's written down in Philippians 1 and 1 Thessalonians 2. Did you ever have a teacher who *could* say this and be believed? Teachers who care about students to this degree are rare.

Paul claimed to live for those he taught. And he did. When he rebuked them or counseled them or encouraged them, his students knew he spoke from love. His life with them breathed his love for them. In living this kind of love, Paul was more like a lay Bible teacher than a pastor who, after all, is paid to love his flock. Paul worked "night and day in order not to be a burden to anyone" while he preached the gospel of God

(1 Thess. 2:9). Toiling over canvas in a tent shop, he earned his own living and gave his free time to his students.

Most lay Bible teachers have families, friends, neighbors. We're not suggesting these be neglected. We are simply pointing out that the depth of Paul's love for his students *could not be questioned.* In the context of unquestioned love, students can be motivated to learn. Involvement in student lives—this is what love leads to. It can be expressed in different ways. We all have seen it. We have seen it in a preschool teacher who comes in Saturdays to prepare her room, who is always there Sunday to lovingly greet her earliest arrival. We have seen it in the teacher of eight-year-old boys who has his Sunday school class over for a pancake breakfast at his house followed by a miniature golf expedition. But it's not just these activities that make him popular. The boys know he cares, and they respond. We've seen it, too, in the teacher of teens, busy already with his teaching and serving on the church board, who cares enough to take on additional duty as a youth sponsor. And in the adult teacher whose concern leads him to meet with small groups for special study, and even to go weekly to meet with one man until a need is met.

There are many ways love can be expressed. But *real* love must be expressed. The prescription of a home visit or class activity is meaningless in itself. It may be done as a duty commanded by a restless conscience. As far as motivating learners is concerned, such empty activities are worthless. But involvement that flows from a selfless love is recognized. Such a teacher has won a hearing.

The teacher-student relationship can be cultivated or destroyed by the teacher's attitude in class. Even a teacher who loves can hinder student motivation in class faster than he can create it outside class. What do we mean? *Motivating students to learn is largely a function of teacher-student relationship in the class situation.* No matter how a teacher relates to his students out of class as a person, how he relates *as a teacher* is crucial.

Often people feel threatened when asked to teach. This shows up in little ways in the classroom situation: the extra demand that children pay attention, the irritation when a teen tries to express a different point of view, the sense of threat when someone asks a question that's hard to answer, the unwillingness to admit, "I don't know."

Each of these is an indicator that a person has taken on the job of teaching with a distorted view of what a teacher is supposed to be. What is this distorted view? That a teacher is primarily an "authority." It's dangerous to equate the words *teacher* and *authority.* An authority is, by definition, a person with power to settle issues, the right (even duty) to control, command, and determine. And each of these activities is destructive of student motivation, a denial of the teacher's true role!

If the teacher is an authority, she must have the answers. She must give the answers. Her students must look to her for answers, and, to be good students, accept her answers. This view subtly affects the relationship between the teacher and student. Even when the class is made up of children and the teacher must exercise classroom management and control, classroom management is not the teacher's primary role. If the teacher sees herself principally as an authority or a classroom manager, she begins to treat students as objects, not as people. They become minds to be filled and subjects to be ruled. As she tries to fill, to control, to rule, she ceases to teach.

People are not objects. They don't like to be treated as objects, and they will not want to learn if they are. God is the true authority, God speaking through the Word. The teacher is no mediator between God and man, no high priest. The teacher is a learner with his students, one who comes to the Word of God as they do—eagerly, expectantly, humbly—looking to the Spirit of God to minister. Only when the teacher teaches the Word of God does he have authority.

Teachers who see themselves this way have a different attitude toward their students. They don't have power to settle every educational or social issue. God does. While the teacher is the manager of the classroom experience, it is Christ who is ultimately in control or command of the class; the teacher is to lead the class in learning together. Teachers with this vantage point share with their students in a great adventure—an adventure in which God directs the outcomes. In this situation teachers treat students as people—people to whom and through whom God can speak. Teachers who value students and treat them with dignity listen and encourage questions. They are not afraid to admit, "I don't know," for they have no false status to maintain. Teachers who see themselves as facilitators of learning come to expect God to speak to them through students; they expect to learn from the class.

A teacher who sees his role this way, and who sees his students as fully human, full partners in the day's adventure in God's Word, treats them differently. There's a different attitude that shows up in the things the teacher says and in the way they are said. When teachers by their attitude set the tone of shared adventure in learning, the majority of students will want to learn.

Group dynamics. The words "group dynamics" describe the relationships and atmosphere within a group as the group interacts and grows together. A teacher can set the tone for expectant learning by encouraging a sense of community within a group and by encouraging effective group interaction. When the whole class shares his attitude, even deeper motivation develops. Students begin to see each other as persons, sharing a common life in Christ. Motivation that grows from such shared life spills over from Sundays into the weekday relationships and activities of each.

It's important to a class of older youth or adults to develop such a group life. In the New Testament, this life is called fellowship. Fellowship is shared Christian life, far more than the casual acquaintances that characterize relationships in so many churches and classes. What in the learning situation leads to growth in fellowship? Basic is the attitude of the teacher, just described. He treats his students as fully human, fully partners. Also basic is the focus on life. When the study centers only on content, life is not shared; only information is. Only when a class moves into the creative process of looking together at implications and responses is life introduced. Even then, growth into fellowship takes time. It may be six months, or it may be a year. People hold back at first. They don't really talk about themselves, about their problems and their needs. There's a reason for this. It's dangerous to open your life to the scrutiny of others. There are too many in our churches ready to gossip; too many ready to nod, clucking piously, "I knew there was something wrong with her."

It takes time to develop a climate for opening ourselves. Carl knew that, so he was patient and persistent. Each week he encouraged discussion and prayer and open interaction. He planned several out-of-class times together, enjoying everything from meals to baseball games. It took a long time to build group cohesion and genuine Christian caring. Then one day in a class exploring the biblical concept of judging, a woman saw a fault of her own and almost involuntarily began, "Then I was wrong when I . . ." As she talked, one could see it in the faces of the others. No one was sitting back, detached. All were fully involved, fully sympathetic, fully sharing the experience as participants in her failure and admitted need of grace. From this point the class became more and more open, more and more willing to open themselves up honestly, to "carry each other's burdens, and in this way . . . fulfill the law of Christ" (Gal. 6:2). The class became a fellowship. It took eight months to begin. But the group life makes the teaching times dynamic as application is discussed freely.

Group life isn't only important for motivation. It's required for maximum spiritual growth. Paul points out in Ephesians that the body grows "as each part does its work" (4:16). For growth, all must contribute. This isn't to say, of course, that contribution necessarily means speaking up in class. It doesn't. It means participating in the real lives of others, meeting in a variety of ways a wide range of needs. But the context for contribution is developed through talking together over a study of God's Word. It's here, focusing together on the God of the Word, that the Holy Spirit melts hearts and creates a unity that is genuine. The result is a harmony of minds and hearts united in responsiveness to God's revealed will.

The personal factors, then, cannot be overlooked by the creative Bible teacher. Students must want to learn if they are to learn. Such desire is most certainly kindled or killed by interpersonal relations. Do your students know without question that you love them? All of us respond to a real (not selfish or forced) love. In class, do you treat your students as people or as objects? Are you an "authority"? Or are you a learner too, a learner who can lead others, but one who learns with them in a mutual quest for truth? Finally, if you teach teens or adults, is your class becoming a fellowship? If you teach as a co-learner, and if you lead your students in a process that causes them to explore together their lives in light of the Word, this will come. God will bring it. Then, in the community of unified life and purpose, your students will truly want to learn.

Structural Factors That Motivate Learning

When Christian educators look at motivation, they usually see the personal factors. The Bible forces them to. In a book that tells of a unique community, a unique oneness in Christ, of a life that develops through the contributions of all, you just can't overlook the personal dimensions. But often the structural factors are overlooked.

What are structural factors? They include elements built into the structure of the lesson. These elements range from the kind of methods selected to the way the material is presented.

Educators have taken many different approaches to the study of learning. Some have tried to define learning, to discover how people learn. They haven't had much success. Others have looked at situations in which people seem to learn best and tried to isolate conditions that facilitate learning. They've made more progress, but even they have not found buttons a teacher can push to turn on every student. But in situations where most people seem to learn, certain conditions do seem to exist. The Sunday school teacher and curriculum writer ought to be aware of these conditions, in order to build lessons that encourage the desire to learn. We're going to look briefly at five of these factors.

People learn best when learning is patterned. What do we mean by patterned? Patterned learning involves having a structured learning experience—one that is organized around a goal students can see and progress toward. We used the Hook, Book, Look, Took pattern to give structure to the classroom learning experience. People need to sense that there is an orderly plan to the class. They need to know too that the content that is presented has been organized in a logical manner. Otherwise, without careful patterning of the class, students are left to feel that the class was aimless and wandering. It's a feeling most people find demotivating if it occurs on a regular basis.

John Franks thought he could just read his passage each week, write a few stimulating questions, and "let things just happen" in class. He reasoned that his was a class of young adults and that they would come up with all sorts of ideas. Well, he was right about one thing. His class did get involved, and many people gave their opinions, but each class seemed aimless. One day one of the members suggested that the class needed more planning. John was surprised. He thought everyone liked his free-flowing style. But when the others confirmed that they too felt the class needed more structure, John got the message. At first he was a bit hurt by the comments because he heard them as criticism and as unfair expectations of him. After all, who has the time to do thorough preparation?

But then John stopped to think about it. He really was concerned that people learn something and that God's Word be taught in a way that would affect people. So John decided to make some changes. Soon he used stimulating news stories from the paper to introduce the class. He would then lead a study of a relevant passage and let people discuss implications of the passage to life. John was pleased. The class members became much more excited about the class and even brought friends because they were learning so much. John had discovered the hard way that people need structure if they are going to learn effectively.

Remember the Hook? Its function is to gain student interest and to introduce the lesson goal in a way that has meaning to the student. Based upon the class aims, the lesson is designed around a structure that moves students from their world, back to the world of the Bible, and then again into their own world to discover application. Finally, the structure we presented moves the student to contemplate and commit to applications that extend into the future beyond the classroom.

Hook, Book, Look, Took—its purpose is to provide the organizational pattern necessary for effective learning. It is only one approach, but it does give students a sense of order and direction to their learning. By starting with a defined aim, each activity is clearly related to reaching that aim. When learning activities have no apparent relationship to the goal, students lose interest. This is why we have introduced you to this method of lesson patterning. It is not the only possible way to structure a lesson. But it is a remarkably effective one, one people have returned to over and over again since it was first presented more than twenty-five years ago. We recommend it because of its proven ability to aid student learning.

People learn best when learning is sequenced. Not only do we like some structure to our learning experiences, but human beings like to have an overall plan to learning that provides a logical sequence. We prefer ideas to build on one another. When students can see progress in the learning endeavor, they remain motivated and feel that they are gaining in their understanding of a subject. Whether it is a sequence of thought followed in a single class or a sequence that builds over time through a series of lessons, concepts must build on one another.

Imagine learning algebra or geometry on a haphazard basis. One week we study right triangles and the next week we learn about discrete lines. The information may be fine in itself, but there seems to be no building of ideas. Soon a student becomes confused and finds it difficult to recall prior learning. A good mathematics textbook will carefully sequence ideas so that the student can gain from prior learning. Each chapter takes the student further into the field of mathematics. A haphazard, what-do-you-want-to-study-this-week approach would be a disaster. Most students would have at best a patchwork concept of math. As learners, we depend upon teachers to sequence our learning, and when they don't we get discouraged and want to quit.

In many ways this is how the Bible is often taught. It is a series of disconnected sermons and lessons that may be stimulating in themselves but that do not lead us to a growing knowledge of the Bible. As a result, most people do not have an understanding of the flow, history, or even theology of the Bible. Most have a disjointed awareness of the Bible's message and its content. Unfortunately, published curriculum often adds to this problem. The creative teacher must be intentional in finding creative ways to help his class understand how lessons fit into the bigger picture of the Bible.

People learn best when learning is encouraged. Believe it or not, some teachers really do not want their students to learn. They want to teach. But real learning means that students are engaged mentally and are participants in the learning experience. Learning environments that allow discovery and exploration, questions and debate are superior to those that allow only one opinion, the teacher's. Participation is key. Students must be active in the learning experience if they are to gain from what is taught. They learn best when they feel successful as learners, when they have evidence that they are mastering in a real and personal way the material taught. In a teacher-centered class, information passes one way—from teacher to learner. This doesn't give students a chance to test their learning, to find out if they really understand the truths. But when students have a chance to participate, they can express their ideas and in this way test their learning. They prove to themselves that they understand. In a Sunday school class this takes place in a climate of acceptance, where misunderstanding isn't held up to ridicule. Students are encouraged to ask questions and to think critically.

Thinking causes learning to occur at more advanced levels. But some teachers find that threatening. They are afraid that they will not be able to answer the questions that arise. Others feel that their content is too important to "waste time" on discussions and people's opinions. *After all*, they reason, *I am the teacher. I am the one who did the Bible study all week.* What could students possibly add? Creative Bible teachers are different. They know that if they are to be effective as teachers, they must seek ways to encourage students to wrestle with ideas and to learn in active and meaningful ways.

People learn best when learning is stimulated. Teachers can create stimulating learning environments. Such environments enhance and promote learning. We know, for example, that children are attracted to bright and colorful rooms, finding those settings preferable to more drab environments. We also know that adults are more likely to participate in a class discussion in a setting where the seating arrangement is casual and the dress less formal than when everyone is in dress attire and seated in rows.

But more significant than the learning environment is the selection of learning methodology. Learning can be stimulated by methods that promote curiosity and interaction between learners rather than simply providing information from a single source. This is not to say that lecture methods have no place, or that there are not some outstandingly gifted speakers who can motivate learning. But, generally speaking, people learn more in participatory and mentally engaging classrooms.

Often learning is motivated by a need to resolve a problem. Sue Phillips had no interest in learning how to fix a broken toilet. She certainly would not watch a home improvement show on that subject by choice. But when the toilet in the bathroom just off her family room began to leak all over the new carpet, she was willing to learn. Not wanting to pay a plumber, she shut off the water supply to the toilet and went to the local home improvement center where she bought a repair kit and a video on plumbing repairs. Two hours later she had it fixed as good as new. The need to solve a problem prompted learning.

This principle of learning also applies in learning biblical truths. Sometimes events in life prompt us to study the Bible in a way we might not otherwise. Teachers can also use problem-posing approaches to stimulate learning. Remember John, the teacher whose class wanted more structure? He found that the use of articles from the Sunday morning paper that related to his lesson could prompt discussion and gain interest. He feels that when he selects articles from that very day's paper, students are naturally interested in what the Scripture has to say in response. Most students, he finds, have opinions on current events and are stimulated by controversial matters. John has discovered that students do indeed learn best when learning is stimulated.

People learn best when learning is relevant. Creative Bible teachers know that they must build on students' prior knowledge and teach in a way that relates to the students' experience. An effective approach to teaching is to start with what a student knows and move to what he does not know. That is true not only in Bible study, but in all kinds of learning situations. Take, for example, the introduction of the computer. Computers share the same keyboard as typewriters. Typewriter keyboards were designed back when typewriters had manual keys that had to strike a page without jamming. The key placement was a matter of practicality. When the computer was introduced, key jamming was not the issue. The real issue was learning. Computer manufacturers used the typewriter keyboard as their standard data entry device because new computer users could relate to it easily. Manufacturers knew that if people were to learn to use this new technology, they needed an old familiar point of initial contact. So the keyboard remained largely unchanged. People learn best when learning moves from known to unknown.

This is what relevance is all about. By seeking points of relevance in teaching, teachers are able to build on something students already know. New information has an old point of contact. Students remain motivated because they have a platform from which to start their learning. By finding ways to relate learning to students' prior experience, teachers are able to teach new concepts.

Jesus used this principle when He taught. He often told stories that began with experiences and knowledge people already understood, and then He introduced a new twist or concept that took student learning a step further. For example, He declared Himself to be the vine and His disciples the branches. He knew that His students were very familiar with vines and branches. They already had seen vinedressers pruning the dead branches and throwing them into the fire. So when Jesus selected this analogy to explain the need to have an abiding relationship with Him, His disciples were able to grasp His message. By using prior knowledge, Jesus was able to teach something new.

An idea is relevant when students can relate it to their existing knowledge base or experience. If they sense a place that they can use the information taught and can find mental "hooks" to place ideas on, they are more easily able to process those ideas. Students need to see a relationship of what is being learned to their own lives and motives. When a lesson presents truth that's important to the students, and when the class process involves a meaningful exploration of Bible truth in terms of life, students are motivated.

People learn best when learning is applied. When a person responds to God, he discovers that truths he has learned in class help him live successfully as a Christian. Such a person comes to class motivated, ready to learn. This, too, is encouraged by the lesson structure suggested in chapter 9. An effectively motivating class should encourage the student to respond. There is something about actually applying a truth in life, seeing our lives change, that keeps us coming back for more. As students apply biblical truth to life, they are motivated to go further in their understanding of the Word of God.

The old adage that we "learn by doing" is true. Somehow, when we begin to live out what we have learned, we are interested in learning more. The heart is like a sponge. Fill it with knowledge of the Word that remains unapplied, and it becomes stagnant. But use the knowledge and the heart becomes ready to soak in more. Application has a way of motivating learning.

Take a look at your class. Do students want to learn? Do your classes have a goal, one your students can see and one they feel is meaningful? Is there time for them to discuss the relationship of truth to life, to interact, and in talking to test their mastery of the truth studied? Do they see in culmination of the lesson just how they are to respond? Lessons structured to provide such opportunities motivate. Your lessons can too.

Chapter Fifteen

TEACHING THE BIBLE
TO ADULTS:
CAN WE GET PRACTICAL HERE?

S ALT—Serving And Learning Together—was the name the group chose for their new adult Sunday school class. Started by a handful of adults, the class grew over a four-year period to fifty, and sometimes even sixty, in attendance. It was a class designed around a very defined concept of how adult learning occurs. It was structured around the observation that adults seek continuing education for a variety of reasons. This class began with the belief that diversity of learning styles and gifts is an asset. Students were helped to see that they needed each other to avoid the pitfalls of classes catering to a single learning style. Rather than segregating the class, the leadership helped the students understand that diversity in the body of Christ is God's plan. So everyone had to learn to adjust to each other and not simply focus on their own needs. Five members illustrate some of the motivations adults have in coming to SALT.

Marty is a regular attendee of the SALT class. He is a thirty-year-old bachelor who works as the head librarian at the local community college. Marty is truly a student. He loves to learn. Widely read, Marty is known for his informed insights—when he does offer comments in class, which is infrequent. Marty is interested in Bible study. He is motivated to gain Bible knowledge, so he often reads books that parallel the material taught in class. Because of his desire is to understand the Bible, Marty prefers classes that use a lecture format. Marty is a *content-oriented adult learner*.

241

Karen is an achiever. She loves the exhilarating feeling she gets when she completes a task or accomplishes a goal. She enjoys order, structure, and planning. Her home is managed like a Fortune 500 company. She finds great satisfaction in her orderly lifestyle. When she comes to church, she wants to get something out of the experience. She wants to learn in an orderly way. She has a low tolerance for adult Sunday school classes that, in her words, "sit around and pool their ignorance." She prefers a teacher who has a great deal of expertise in the subject being taught and divulges that knowledge in a well-planned, systematic way. She also prefers a class that has a definite sense of closure. She is most satisfied when the class completes a study. She likes to feel that something has been accomplished. She is a *goal-oriented adult learner.*

Barb never finds Sunday morning to be anything like a day of rest. With four children, it is all she can do, even with her husband's help, to get the children and herself dressed, everyone fed, the van loaded, and then to make the fifteen minute drive to church and get everyone off to Sunday school classes on time. But she feels it's worth the effort. After all, not only do the children benefit from the teaching they receive, but she also gets out of the house, socializes with friends, and enjoys the fellowship of other believers who have some similar life experiences. Barb loves to serve people. She often teaches children herself. But when she goes to adult Sunday school, it is not as much the content that draws her as it is the context. She is an *activity-oriented adult learner.*

Liz wants some answers. She wants to see how the Bible applies in her life situation, and she wants to investigate ways others have connected biblical truth to their lives. She prefers methods that cause the class to explore the implications of a text, rather than simply studying its meaning. For her, small groups are essential. They allow her to hear how others have dealt with their struggles. She wants a group that is open to talk about real difficulties, failures, and fears. She wants to hear about victories as well. She enjoys thinking through ideas with others. In her estimation, lecture is totally boring and demotivating. Liz needs to see how a passage is relevant. She wants practical teaching related to her own situation. Liz is an *application-oriented adult learner.*

Carl has a difficult time sitting in an adult Sunday school class. It's not that he doesn't enjoy learning. Actually, it is quite the opposite of that. Carl enjoys studying and reading intellectually stimulating material. But Carl is most excited about learning when he is teaching others. He learns best by preparing to teach, rather than by sitting in class. He has leadership qualities and enjoys communicating the Scriptures. So, when his business schedule makes it impossible for him to teach for a period, he struggles. Right now he wants to be teaching, but he must become a participant. He knows that others are gifted to teach and lead as well, but he tends to contemplate how he would have handled the class, the passage, or a discussion differently. Carl is a *leadership-oriented adult learner.*

One of the most difficult things about teaching adults is defining the form adult teaching should take. Some argue for a formal and more content-centered approach to adult teaching termed *pedagogy.* Others argue for an informal, interactive approach called *androgogy.* Still others speak of the benefits of a middle ground approach called *synergogy.* How shall we go about teaching adults? Why do they seek out adult education in the first place? How do we structure teaching for the diverse range of adult learners? To answer these questions, we must come to a better understanding of the nature of adult learners and then look at some strategies for teaching adults using the HBLT structure. Finally, we will summarize some principles that teachers will want to keep in mind as they prepare to teach adults.

UNDERSTANDING THE ADULT LEARNER

Teaching adults demands an understanding of adults as learners. Adult learners differ in many regards. That is one reason teaching adults can be a challenging task. But research conducted by Stephen Brookfield points to some common characteristics in adult learners as well. Brookfield calls these commonalties "adult learning rhythms or patterns." Adults seem to follow these patterns in a fairly consistent way; therefore, it is wise for the adult Bible teacher to be aware of these patterns of learning.

Patterns of Adult Learning

Desire for a safe environment. We tend to think of adults as confident, self-directed, and comfortable in the learning environment and of children as uncomfortable and fearful. Actually, the opposite appears to be the case. Stephen Brookfield has observed that most adult learners feel like "impostors" when in adult learning situations.[1] They often feel that others in the group are brighter, are more experienced, and have greater promise. These views generate enormous negative baggage in adult teaching. Every adult teacher must understand that adults generally feel inhibited by and fearful of the educational setting. This means that there is a need to aid all students by creating a comfortable, safe environment where relationships are mutually supportive. We must create "safe zones" in our adult classes where fear of failure is minimized and freedom to explore and discover is maximized.

Desire to be emotionally engaged. When adults report positive learning outcomes from an educational experience, they are spoken of most often in emotional terms, not cognitive terms. "That class is great. We have some really intense sharing and openness. I have learned so much from our discussions. Bob is such a great teacher," is a more likely comment than, "Bob has so many great concepts in his class. I learn important information from his lectures." This is not to say that the second statement might not be heard at one time or another in our adult Sunday schools when an exceptional lecturer teaches. But the first is the far more likely of the two. Adults prefer teaching that causes them to become emotionally engaged, and they seem to speak more highly of their experience in education when their affective side is stirred.

Desire to meet a challenge. Brookfield found that the most significant adult learning occurred when adults sense the successful completion of a significant intellectual challenge. Most adults feel uncomfortable when faced with a difficult intellectual dilemma, but they feel enormous exhilaration when the dilemma is effectively resolved. The result is a satisfaction with the learning experience and high levels of retention of new information.

Desire for a reflective opportunity. Most adults feel they do not have enough time in class to reflect adequately on the information given in adult education situations. They often feel they receive too much information to process in a satisfactory way. Adult learners often feel that they have experienced information overload because teachers do not give time to assimilate new information into past experiences and understandings.

Desire to feel like they are being stretched. Adult learners actually desire to be stretched. But they seem to prefer that stretching to happen in what Brookfield termed "incremental fluctuation." By this he means that adult learners begin with feelings of enthusiasm for new information but then become somewhat frustrated by their inability to assimilate the new information into their existing patterns and experiences. So, the result is that adults give mental assent to the idea but return to the comfort of their previously held perspectives and patterns of life. But they can no longer be comfortable there. New thinking has made the old patterns binding. Again the adult learner musters the courage to consider the new idea. Finally, the person may take one aspect of the new thought and implement it. This forward-backward-forward pattern of adult learning is normal. It does not indicate a lack of commitment, but rather the nature of adults as learners.

Desire for the unexpected. We think of adults as people of routine. This is true to some degree, but it is also true that adults enjoy and respond most actively to the unexpected. Learners will often say that learning happened unexpectedly. It is as if there is a breakthrough moment that occurs for adults when their thinking is brought from the anticipated to the unforeseen.

Desire for a learning community. Adult learners often report how important a group dynamic is to their own learning experience. Adult learners seem to prefer a learning setting that fosters a sense of mutual support as opposed to competition. Adults seem to need a smaller group within the large group to support their learning and provide a sense of belonging.

Strengths of Adult Learners

Adults have many wonderful strengths as learners. These strengths need to the understood by the creative Bible teacher. Effective teachers know that they must build on the strengths of a group rather than try to counter all of the potential weaknesses. So, what are the strengths of adult learners?

Self-Motivated. Unlike children and youth, no one is making the adult attend the Sunday school class. When adults show up in your class it is because they chose to be there. Adult learners tend to come with at least some measure of self-motivation.

Self-Disciplined. Classroom management and discipline is probably the single greatest concern for those who teach children and adolescents. But with adults, that simply is not an issue. Occasionally situations arise in which people say something inappropriate or when someone monopolizes the discussion, but for the most part adults are self-disciplined enough to manage their own classroom behavior. Often because of self-motivation and self-discipline, adults will go the extra mile in learning and will even seek to support the classroom and out-of-classroom efforts of the teacher.

Variety of Experiences. Adults come to class with a wealth of experience. That experience is the key to effectively teaching adults and engaging them in learning. By tapping into the experiences of a group, teachers can make abstract concepts concrete and can involve adults actively in the learning process.

Relevance Focused. Adults tend to be practical and pragmatic. Often they enter into adult learning to gain something. Adults seek immediate application of concepts learned. On occasion they may enjoy a cerebral discussion of dispensational versus covenantal theology, but when it gets right down to it, they want to know what difference it makes in their lives. Adults want teaching that is applicable. Teachers of adults must factor this into their approach to instruction.

Independent Learning. Adults do not need the teacher. They are capable of independent learning. That is not to say that they will all be independent learners or that they know what resources to employ in the learning task, but that they do have the ability. Almost all adults can learn more independently, and often do, than teachers of adults are aware.

Insightful Contributions. Those who teach adults should recognize the fact that their students might have better and more valuable contributions to make to group learning than they, the teacher, might bring. That can be threatening to some adult teachers. Instead of being threatened, the adult teacher should see class insights and feedback as one of the greatest assets of adult education. Adults can take an average class and make it outstanding, if only adult teachers would tap into this quality of the adult learner.

Learning Beyond the Classroom. Adults are able to fill gaps between what is covered in the class and what they desire or need to know. The teacher of adults need not feel that he must cover every point or bring total closure to a subject. In most cases, it is better not to bring closure. Open-ended learning can motivate further learning on the part of adults. Not all adults will do it, but the vast majority can do some personal study apart from the class to enhance their own learning.

Learning in a Group Setting. Another asset in teaching adults is the fact that most adults can function well in groups. Teachers of adults need not worry about turning a group loose with a set of questions. The group will usually establish a leader and find direction, even when direction from the teacher is lacking. This ability to attack a task in an adequate manner helps the adult teacher in facilitating adult learning.

Adults bring much to the learning experience. They are far from "blank slates" to be written on by the teacher. Adults can become active in the learning process. We turn our attention now to providing concrete examples as to how adults can be encouraged to fully become learning partners in the study of the Bible.

USING THE HBLT STRUCTURE WITH ADULTS

The Bible is a book written by adults, for adults. So we begin with the matter of how to teach the Bible to adults. Teaching other age groups always requires some modification to any teaching strategy. In this section we will consider how adults can become engaged in the creative Bible teaching approach using the HBLT structure.

The Hook: Focusing the Attention of Adult Learners

Adults are able to understand and to respond to God's Word in ways children simply cannot. In teaching adults the teacher's goal is one of stimulating a deeply personal, shared interaction with the Word. Because of their mature perspective, adults can be taken into the learning experience by the teacher as full partners. In fact, it's the teacher's task to build toward such a responsive, responsible fellowship of co-learning adults. We believe that the best structure for an adult class is one in which the curriculum is developed inductively, relating the issues, concerns, tensions, and needs of students to the life-changing truth of the Word of God. When teaching adults, the Hook helps to bring these matters into focus, and then to direct attention to the Word, seeking God's solutions, direction, and perspectives for life.

Awakening a sense of need takes place in the Hook step. This is especially important when teaching adults who are oriented toward practical, relevant learning. Each adult learner must see that he or she has a stake in the learning. Adults must become engaged in the first moments of the class, and this is most likely to occur when attention is gained and a need is surfaced. A number of learning activities can be used to focus attention and raise a sense of need.

We have chosen to use John 14:22–24 as an example passage to show how to hook adults into the learning process. This short segment records Jesus' answer to a question one of His disciples raised before He was to be crucified. Christ had told of His departure. He had promised that, although He would not be physically present and thus could not be seen by the world, He would again show Himself to His followers. We pick up the account with the question.

> Then Judas (not Judas Iscariot) said, "But, Lord, why do you intend to show yourself to us and not to the world?" Jesus replied, "If anyone loves me, he will obey my teaching. My Father will love him, and we will come to him and make our home with him. He who does not love me will not obey my teaching. These words you hear are not my own; they belong to the Father who sent me." (John 14:22–24)

The bridge principle of the passage is this: Christ is experienced as a real, present person when the believer is responsive and obedient to His word. The teaching aim, framed in terms of the response desired, is stated as follows: Learners will come to experience Jesus Christ as a Person who is real and present with them.

The Hook activities for this lesson should be geared to awaken the learner's sense of need for personal experience with Christ—for a faith that exists as a vital relationship, not merely as a mental assent to biblical doctrines. But they must be activities that take the nature of adult learners into consideration. They should be open-ended enough to motivate student thinking and interaction by relating to real matters of concern to the student. Here are three possible Hook strategies that could be used in teaching adults.

Teaching Strategy 1

Display the following statement and ask for your students' reactions: "If I couldn't experience Christ's presence every day, I'd doubt the truth of Christianity." You might attempt a circular conversation (asking each to give his reaction in a sentence or two, and moving from left to right around the circle) or neighbor nudging (pairs of students discussing their thinking with each other before throwing their ideas out to the whole group).

As reactions come, there will probably be both agreement and disagreement with the statement. Help bring the issue into focus with questions: How important is it that the Christian actually experience Christ? What is the role of a daily personal relationship with Christ in the believer's life? Are we satisfied that our Christian experience is real and vital and meaningful? Why or why not? What makes Christian experience "vital and meaningful"? What does it mean to "experience Christ"? Is it just limited to feelings, or does it mean something beyond that?

Teaching Strategy 2

Read the following letter to the religion editor of suburban Chicago area newspaper, the *Kane County Chronicle,* that appeared in the September 25, 1997, edition.

> **Dear Lee:** Your column is so inspirational to all readers! Our Lord prophesied in the last days He would perform miracles in the heavens and marvels on earth (Acts 2:1–21). Also, in John 3:11, He states that we are to "speak of what we know and bear witness to what we have seen." I want to share the most astounding miracle of my life:
>
> One sunny August afternoon, my husband and I were driving in our town. I heard a rustling sound outside my car window. I looked up at the heavens—and there was a magnificent vision of Jesus, in a black cloud forming against a sunny sky! I could not speak as I ran the gamut of emotions, crying silently.
>
> This is one of many miracles I have personally witnessed, but is, by far, the most magnificent! C.T.—Rural Houston, MN

Ask the class to express their reactions to the "vision." Ask the class: "If you were Lee, how would you respond to the letter? What does it mean to experience Christ?" Use the letter as a means of introducing the passage and the concept of knowing Christ personally.

Teaching Strategy 3

Give each student a blank sheet of paper and ask him to write a brief description of one time recently when he was aware of the presence of Christ, when he might say that Christ "showed" Himself to him. Anyone who is uncertain can either leave the sheet blank or briefly tell uncertainties he has about the task. Collect the papers and read one or two. Then invite discussion of the task assigned. Should we be able to describe such a time? Can we expect Christ to be real in our daily experience? How? Or why not? What is the role of personal relationship with Christ in Christian experience? In each case a simple statement of the goal of the day's learning—that we might each actually experience Jesus Christ as a Person who is real and really with us—can serve as a transition into the study of the biblical content, the Book section.

The Book: Communicating Bible Content to Adult Learners

Teaching, for evangelicals, is *Bible* teaching. And so the communication of content takes a central and often dominating role in the class session. It is, of course, right that the communication of content be considered basic. Content is basic. We meet God in His Word. He communicates truth and Himself to us there. And thus it is essential that the Word be taught and that the words of Scripture be rightly interpreted and understood.

But it is not necessary that communication of content—particularly a teacher-given monologue or sermon—dominate class time. It's possible to communicate content creatively. It's possible to encourage each class member to take responsibility for personal study. It's possible to make the study of the Book an interactive process.

In this segment of the lesson, then, we are concerned with discovering what God is actually saying in the passage studied and with helping the learners to a clear understanding of His message. You will recall that we were using John 14:22–24 as an example passage in considering how to apply the HBLT structure to teaching adults. The passage dealt with what is involved in truly experiencing Christ. We had written an aim that read: *Learners will come to experience Jesus Christ as a Person who is real and present with them.* Here are some example strategies for teaching the Book section of our lesson to adult learners.

Teaching Strategy 1

The key points in these verses hinge on the meaning of *to show* and the role given here to the Word. These can be covered by explaining that the word in the original is "to make visible," "to make known, or clear." Thus Jesus' disciple was asking how Christ can be an experienced reality to the believer, while He is not so known by the world. The Word, which, Christ stresses, is the Father's, is to be obeyed by the believer. Only when the believer lives in obedience to the words of Christ will the Father and Son be present in his life in such a way that this presence is experienced.

Rather than cover the material yourself, ask two students to research the two key words (*to show* and *obey*) and prepare reports for the class. Anyone with a concordance that distinguishes the words used in the original (such as *Young's Analytical Concordance to the Bible*) can discover which Greek word was used and what it means. Further research might be done in a commentary or in one of the excellent Greek-English helps available. After the reports are given, summarize and integrate the information they provide.

Teaching Strategy 2

Divide your class into twos, giving each pair a list of key questions they are to attempt to answer from a study of the passage. Encourage your class members to use different translations when undertaking such a study.

Questions that might be used with this passage are

1. What led up to the disciple's question (cf. 14:18–21)?
2. What does "to show" seem to mean in this context?
3. What condition(s) does Christ set down that must be met if He is to show Himself to the believer?
4. What promises are associated with the conditions?
5. What reason is suggested or implied for the importance of obeying Christ's Word? Why does the Word play such a vital role?

When the questions have been discussed by the twosomes, their answers can be discussed with the entire group; then a summary can follow.

Teaching Strategy 3

Divide the class into buzz groups of four to six individuals for a study of related passages that may clarify the meaning and impact of this passage. Sketch the background of the question and point out the nature of the question Christ's disciple was asking. Have prepared slips of paper on which assignments for the buzz groups are written. Give each group two or more of the questions suggested above. Or choose other parallel passages of Scripture (such as James 1:19–25; 1 John 3:19–24) that may give your students insights into the passage being studied.

Teaching Strategy 4

The week before you cover this passage in class, ask each class member to read the larger context at home and to look up John 14:22–24 in at least one commentary. If you wish, you may also give out a guide question list (such as is included in strategy 2). Class time can then be used by the students to tell their discoveries and broaden the understanding of Christ's answer to His disciple's question.

There are many methods available for encouraging preparation by the students for the class hour. This example illustrates just one. Here is a partial listing of other approaches that might be taken, depending on their suitability to the particular passage to be covered.

Readings
1. Read different interpretations of the passage to be studied.
2. Read from a preselected bibliography.
3. Read parallel accounts in Scripture.
4. Read various versions.
5. Read as specific preparation for discussion.
6. Read to prepare an oral or written report.
7. Read looking for relationships (why, where, when, which, how).
8. Read to survey, evaluate, defend, compare, solve.
9. Read to outline or summarize.
10. Read repeatedly.
11. Read to memorize.
12. Read to answer prepared questions.

Projects
1. Construct charts and graphs.
2. Diagram a passage of Scripture.
3. Prepare a quiz or test on the subject being studied.
4. Develop an outline of the subject.
5. Prepare an oral report.
6. Prepare a research paper on the topic.
7. Prepare for a drama in class.
8. Prepare for a panel, forum, or discussion.
9. Prepare with others for a debate.
10. Prepare audiovisuals to present topic.
11. Write subject up as a story or newspaper article.
12. Define terms without any outside aid.
13. Conduct a personal-opinion poll on the topic.
14. Develop a time line for history.

15. Create a poster, display, or exhibit for the hour.
16. Read to the class a poem or story in your own words.

Interviews and Surveys
1. Interview resource individuals on the subject.
2. Interview a "man on the street" for his opinion.
3. Prepare and distribute a questionnaire.
4. Collate and analyze responses to a survey.
5. Make a list of problems people have with this subject.

Questions
1. Give questions to be answered in class.
2. Give questions to be answered by selected readings.
3. Give questions to be answered in writing.
4. Give questions to be answered by experience.
5. Give questions based on previous classes as foundation for next session.
6. Have students prepare a list of personal questions they have regarding the subject.
7. Give thought-provoking questions.
8. Have students prepare a set of questions they would ask on an examination of the subject.

Problem Solving
1. Give a real-life problem to be solved.
2. Give opposing views of the problem and evaluate possible solutions.
3. Use case studies as problems for solving.
4. Make up a hypothetical problem related to subject.
5. Set up a problem in class, then dismiss and allow class to work on it.
6. State a problem and various solutions, asking class to pick the best.
7. Allow students to create or relate their own problems and then solve them.
8. Have students list all possible solutions to a problem.
9. Have students develop a method for solving problems.
10. Give erroneous information or materials on some problem.

Written Assignments
1. List implications of truth on this subject.
2. Write a commentary, report, paper, etc.

3. Write out answers to questions and a solution to a problem.
4. Write a defense for your position.
5. Write out a list of personal definitions on topic.
6. Write letters, tracts, poems, drama, testimony, etc.
7. Outline a reading or Scripture passage.
8. Paraphrase a Scripture portion.
9. Write a paper on "What _____ Means to Me."

Group Work
1. Discuss with others in small informal groups before class session.
2. Discuss with "opponents" who hold a different view on topic.
3. Meet in a group to plan and prepare to teach the class.
4. Do group work on projects to present in class.
5. Meet to prepare a debate, panel, drama, etc., for class.
6. Assign different groups to work on separate aspects of the subject and report to class.
7. Meet after individual readings and preparation to discuss topic.

The Look: Guiding Insight with Adult Learners

In chapter 10, we discussed the importance of encouraging and guiding our learners to openly and personally discuss the application of Scripture. The Look step in the process we've described in this book demands just this kind of open discussion—discussion that is clearly centered on the Word of God and that encourages expression of each person's experience with Christ. It is this context that gives maximum opportunity for spiritual growth through the application of truth to life. And it is this context of openness that Look learning activities must encourage and develop.

Openness and meaningful discussion do not come quickly or easily. But they do come. They come when the teacher understands the Look's purpose. They come when the teacher resists taking an authoritarian role and instead stimulates his students to take full responsibility for discovering and discussing the implications of the Word studied. They come when the teacher encourages inductive discussion.

Let's see some learning activities that can be used to help reach this goal. Again we will consider activities for teaching adults the John 14:22–24 passage. You will recall that our lesson aim was: Learners will come to experience Jesus Christ as a Person who is real and present with them. The emphasis in this passage, as developed in the last section, is on the relationship of obeying Christ's words to experiencing Christ as a reality in our lives. We sought to teach that Christ is experienced as a real, present Person when the believer is responsive and obedient to His Word. The Look activities should help adults explore the implications of this truth and help them define areas of life where they need to become more responsive and obedient.

Teaching Strategy 1

Ask your class to analyze one or more of the following case histories and apply the teaching of John 14:22–24 as it seems relevant. The cases are designed to bring into focus different points at which an individual's ability or willingness to respond to God might break down. Encourage the class to identify these points as they discuss the cases, then to develop constructive suggestions on how to help each person.

Case One

Jack is a new believer who expected that becoming a Christian would solve all his problems. After his conversion, life at first seemed very exciting—sort of a daily adventure. But then things began to go wrong. Jack discovered he still had many of his old habits and desires and that their pull was as strong as ever. He had a setback at work, and he discovered that being a Christian didn't guarantee a comfortable life either. About now Jack is wondering if what he felt in those first weeks as a Christian wasn't just self-delusion.

Case Two

Frank is one of the leaders of the church, a person who knows his Bible well. But no one in the church really likes or trusts Frank. He has the reputation of being a politician and a manipulator. He's been known to cut down other Christians behind their backs. And in the business community he's regarded as too sharp to be trusted.

Teaching Strategy 2

Write on the chalkboard several statements for the class to evaluate in view of John 14:22–24. Here are some examples.

Most Christians today are only interested in God's second best for their lives.
Members of this class experience daily all that a relationship with Christ makes possible.
We can help each other, as families and as friends, to experience Christ in the way He promised in this passage.

There is only one possible cause for our failure to go on as Christians and to develop a vital daily relationship with Christ.

Experiencing Christ sounds great, but there are a lot of good reasons why it's not for me.

I'd be willing to "do Christ's words" if I wasn't afraid of all the changes I'd have to make.

I don't really know anyone who honestly makes it his goal to do daily just what Christ wants him to do—in everything.

Is there a "first class" and "second class" for Christians, or do we all have to be in such terrible subjection?

If obedience to Christ is the measurement of our love for God, I guess we (I) rate . . .

One or more of these statements, or statements like them, should help to stimulate discussion and to guide your class toward exploring the implications of the truth studied in this passage. Note that not all the statements are "true." Some even express a warped view. But each demands evaluation, not a yes or no reaction. And each is related to the truth revealed in the Bible passage studied.

The Took: Encouraging Response in Adult Learners

"How should I respond to God?" This is ultimately and intensely a personal question. Each of us must respond as God the Holy Spirit leads—and He may lead each of us differently. The single command to witness, given to us all, may be used by God to point me to a neighbor, to direct another to establish a home Bible class, and to send you to the mission field. Each life is different from each other—with its own opportunities, its own contacts, its own experiences. And only Jesus Christ, as Lord of our lives and head of the church, has a right to direct us, by His words, into His perfect will for each individual. Certainly God has given only one Word, but our opportunities for response are infinite.

How, then, do we in teaching help each learner face the necessity of a personal response to God? How do we encourage each student to seek God's leading for his own "doing" of the Word? We must be careful that we do not treat our students like mass-produced products. People aren't duplicates of each other. We're each hand-crafted originals. We're all shaped by God's own hand, and each of us is unique, each fitted to just the tasks He has planned especially for us. And only God Himself can show a believer what his task is and how he is to perform it. Thus the creative Bible teacher resists the temptation to make mass applications. Instead, creative Bible teachers seek ways to encourage learners to face the necessity of personal response and to seek God's leading for the specific response that he is to make.

But what kind of learning activities can a teacher structure that will help each realize his own need for response? What kind of learning activities will move the learner toward a personal decision to respond? Let's return to John 14:22–24 as our example. Our lesson aim was: Learners will come to experience Jesus Christ as a Person who is real and present with them. In the class we have sought to communicate the idea that Christ is experienced as a real, present Person when the believer is responsive and obedient to His Word.

The Look activities for this lesson were designed to help the group explore some reasons for unresponsiveness and some ways a believer might become more responsive. Through these Look activities, the class was led to explore specific areas of life in which responsiveness to God was particularly needed. Now we move to the Took. Here we teach for carryover outside of the class. The focus moves to application in the future. Here, the teacher seeks to guide adult learners in identifying a personal application for the future and making a commitment to take the action of the lesson. Generally, the Took activities correlate with the activities undertaken in the Look section. Let's consider a few possible Took activities appropriate to adult learners who have just studied John 14:22–24.

Teaching Strategy 1

Give each person a 3x5 card. Ask each individual to identify and write a needed action or response he must take to become more responsive to God. Conclude class by asking several class members to pray. Ask the Lord to help each member experience Christ's presence as he seeks to know and do God's will in the area he identified.

Teaching Strategy 2

At the conclusion of the case history analyses suggested in the last section, ask each student to decide which of the individuals discussed he is more like. What steps does he need to take to become more responsive to God? Give time for a short written self-analysis, then close in conversational prayer.

Teaching Strategy 3

Ask the group to pray together about each one's responsiveness to God this coming week. Tell the group that you'll give time next week for telling what God has done in their lives. If the class has become a fellowship, in which each can trust the others, take time at the end of the discussion to list prayer requests. Encourage individuals to ask for support of the group as they sense personal problems and needs.

Teaching Strategy 4

Give or send each person a follow-up question to discuss during the week. For instance, a question for a couple who have children might be "How can we guide our children to be more responsive to God?" or "How does our conversation at home show our children that Christ is real to us?"

PRINCIPLES FOR TEACHING ADULTS

We have looked at adults as learners and have provided some examples of how we might engage them in the study of the Word of God. Let's conclude with a summary of six principles for adult education in the church. By keeping these in mind as you prepare and as you teach, we believe you can become a more capable and creative teacher of adults.

Adults Want to Learn

Through many years of working with adults, and through the support of research into adult education, it is our view that the vast majority of adults do indeed want to learn. A case in point is the growing number of adult education programs. Adult education is one of the fastest growing segments in the educational market in America.

Adults Are Motivated to Learn

Adults seek continued education for three basic reasons: pleasure, need, or knowledge. Although adults may not be interested in learning some highly theoretical information, they are often interested in understanding theory as it relates to life. An adult may not be interested in "the theory of the combustion engine," but may be highly motivated to read about "how to do minor repairs and save money." Given the right subject, approach, and context, adults are highly motivated learners.

Adults Are Practical and Problem Oriented

One of the most satisfying and powerful ways that adults learn is through the solving of problems. Whether it is a leaking toilet that needs to be fixed or a friend who is facing marital problems, adults learn best when they are dealing with a problem and seeking to solve it. Teachers of adults know this, so they use problem-posing, practical approaches to teaching. Adults have opinions and information that can lead to solutions to problems. Effective teachers of adults learn to facilitate adult interactions so that adult learning can be maximized.

Adults Are Self-Directed

Adults decide how they prefer to learn. They decide if it will be a class setting, a book, a video, or "The Learning Channel." They manage their own learning experience. Adults need not be dependent learners. They can become independent and self-directed as they mutually support each other's quest for understanding and application.

Adults Fear Failure

As mentioned earlier, almost all adults have some measure of discomfort in classroom learning situations. Because adults fear failure, we must create environments that are "learner friendly." Teachers of adults know that part of their role is to reduce the sense of personal risk felt by adult students.

Adult Education Must Offer Diversity

When we began this chapter we told you of five members of the SALT Sunday school class. Each of these adults had his or her own blend of characteristics and backgrounds. Each had his or her own expectations and needs. It is imperative that adult education in the church be designed to meet the diverse characteristics and needs of adults. We must help all adult learners in a class understand the diversity of the group and the benefits of that diversity. In doing so, we can function as the body of Christ. No adult class will ever meet everyone's needs every time. But everyone can become a part of meeting the range of needs in the class as we seek to equip one another. This is the essence of adult ministry and education in the church.

For those who seek alternatives to classes that incorporate diversity within their structure, elective classes that focus on individual interests and learning styles can be offered. The risk here is in the creation of separate homogenous groups in the church, but for some this can prove beneficial, at least initially. Offering a variety of electives for adults can provide an initial draw for adult learners. We believe, however, that in the long run it is best to help adults understand their need for those who are different from themselves. While classes of like persons are often more comfortable, they can inhibit Christian growth.

NOTE

1. Stephen Brookfield, *Understanding and Facilitating Adult Learning* (San Francisco: Jossey-Bass, 1990), 43–56.

Chapter Sixteen

TEACHING THE BIBLE TO YOUTH: WHAT DIFFERENCE DOES THIS MAKE?

I n teaching youth, there is no more powerful instructor than experience. Kurt found that out when he took several of the teens in his youth group on a mission trip to Mexico.

Kurt works with youth in a large evangelical church located on the east coast. Many of the students' parents are upper level corporate executives. The church is very wealthy and the students he works with have experienced a life of abundance. Kurt wanted to teach his students about biblical servanthood, so he planned a trip to the Mexican border town of Juarez, where students provided necessary construction and painting work for a Christian orphanage. He arranged housing across the border in the dormitories of the University of Texas at El Paso (UTEP).

It was a stark contrast—on one side of the border was a well manicured, nicely appointed dorm with an indoor pool and health center. On the other side was a section of town steeped in poverty. No paved streets. Open sewers and outhouses. And homes made from one-by-two strips of wood and cardboard.

Each day they traveled by bus across the border to work at the orphanage. The heat was almost unbearable. By noon each day the temperature reached 106 degrees.

The university food service workers prepared lunches for the students to take to the work sites. The lunch usually included a piece of fruit, some chips, a snack cake, and a bologna sandwich, which was made with wet lettuce and mustard. More often than not, the sandwich would become almost glued together in the heat and was anything but appetizing.

Students were assigned to different sites and tasks. Five of the teens went with Kurt. They were the guys with the reputation of being tough to work with and too "cool" for their own good. Since none of the other sponsors wanted them in their group, they became Kurt's work team. Their task was to dig an outhouse hole. In an area where the ground was almost rock hard, picks and shovels were the tools of choice.

For two days they worked, and the teens complained. After two days, the hole was only a few feet deep. On the third day, the hottest of the week, Kurt and his team took their lunch break. They ate the fruit, the snack cakes, and the chips, but no one ate the sandwiches. When they were finished they threw their garbage away and went back to their digging. Then they heard laughter. The boys and Kurt turned to see several little children standing around the garbage can. The children were joyful as they shared the sandwiches Kurt and the guys had discarded. What was inedible trash to Kurt's crew was a feast to these hungry little children. The impact on Kurt's guys was obvious. Kurt turned and looked at the boys as they watched the children. Tears streamed down each of these tough, image-conscious young men's faces. Each was moved by what he saw.

One of the guys shared his reaction that evening in a group debriefing session. He said, "I just can't understand it. Why has God given me so much when these children have so little? I don't think I will ever look at my world the same. I am leaving here a different person than I was when I came."

That night Kurt was able to lead his group in a devotional time. They studied Luke 10:25–37 where Jesus tells the story of the Samaritan traveler who cares for the man attacked by bandits. Kurt had the opportunity to draw on the experience the guys in the youth group had earlier that day to explain the need for Christians to have compassion and take action to care for those in need. He then turned the group's attention to James 1:26–27 and led in a discussion of "true religion." Finally, Kurt led the group in considering ways they could express their faith in Christ to those in need back home. The group decided that once each month they would serve at a homeless shelter in the inner city. As a result, regular service-related projects became part of this youth group's planning and activities.

UNDERSTANDING HOW YOUTH LEARN

It is important for those who work with youth to understand how adolescents learn best. Here are five principles as to how youth learn. Although several more could be identified, we believe these five to be non-negotiables of youth ministry effectiveness.

Youth Learn Best Through Direct Experience

It may not seem like it, but Kurt made use of the Hook, Book, Look, Took structure in teaching his students. His Hook was the trip itself. Kurt was seeking to raise his group's awareness of human needs and the necessity of Christians to become involved in meeting those needs. But the wealth and plenty of the group stood as an enormous obstacle to actually initiating any kind of ministry with the group. So Kurt, in consultation with the pastor and church board, decided that a trip to Mexico would stretch the teens out of their comfort zones and open them to the needs of people. Kurt knew that *youth learn experientially.*

But experiential learning need not require an expensive trip to another country. Missions trips are powerful teachers, but opportunities to experience Christianity working are all around us. One youth leader involved his students in a "hike for life," a march that raised money for a local crisis pregnancy center. Another youth leader involved his students in a Passover Meal led by a Messianic Jewish organization. In teaching youth, firsthand experience is essential.

Youth Learn Best from Caring Role Models

A few years ago, basketball star Charles Barkley told the press that he was not interested in being a role model. But role models do not get a chance to choose whether they will or will not serve. Anyone who is watched by youth is likely to be emulated by youth. That includes youth workers.

It is possible that you will teach more to your students by your treatment of other staff members at the youth retreat than in the formal teaching sessions themselves. They watch those who teach them. It matters little how effective your methods of teaching are or how great your ability to tell a story is if youth do not sense that you are genuine in your faith and caring as a teacher. As much as we have focused in this book on lesson preparation and methodology, we must stress that apart from the student the single most important variable in the teaching-learning process is the teacher.

In an introductory education course the professor asked a roomful of college freshmen to describe the attributes of effective teachers by recalling those teachers who most powerfully affected their lives. The responses included such qualities as open, approachable, able to listen, patient, kind, willing to give the extra effort to help the student learn, and genuine. Overwhelmingly, students' comments focused on character issues and modeling matters. Few comments addressed the matters of content or style. One student said it this way: "I probably won't ever remember the lessons he taught, but I will never forget how much my junior high Sunday school teacher cared about me as a person." Modeling will not replace developmentally appropriate teaching or lack of content, but a superior teaching style will never substitute for being the person you are teaching your students to be.

It is best to develop a team of adults to work with adolescents in order to provide a variety of role models. We suggest that you use college students, married couples, singles, middle-aged adults, and even older adults in your program where appropriate. Young people respond to these models in different ways. Really, there is no "stereotypical" youth worker who should be sought. In fact, youth need a wide range of personalities. The primary requirements must be dedication to Christ, desire to understand and minister to teens, and willingness to be available.

Youth Learn Best When They Are Active in Discovering Truth

Leslie is a master when it comes to teaching high school students. She knows how to engage them. Her secret—never tell them something they can discover for themselves. Her methods often employ case studies and small group discussions. She establishes study teams in class and trains student leaders to give direction to the study groups. Her view is that if she provides the structure and her students provide the small group leadership, the class will work. So she meets each week to prepare the lesson with the small group teachers. These are juniors and seniors in the high school group, as well as a few recent graduates. Together they decide what will work to get students interested in Bible study. She has taught them the Hook, Book, Look, Took structure, which they use as their framework for teaching. Within this structure, they build discovery learning approaches and activities.

In the context of discovery, freedom to ask questions is essential. Youth must come to the point where they own faith themselves. This only happens when questions can be comfortably asked without any fear of negative reactions. Teachers should create an environment where doubts and questions are seen as normal and important means to growth and understanding. If a mature faith is to be achieved, students must be able to form their own personal convictions.

In a discussion on the authority of the Bible, one student made this comment: "It seems like the Bible is a lot of myths and things. Really, Adam and Eve and a talking serpent?! Isn't that just ancient, non-scientific people's ways of explaining something? How is that different from the Greek gods?" Here was an honest and well-considered question. Here was a student trying to think through what the teacher was saying. Imagine if the teacher's reaction was something like this: "We all know that the Bible is the Word of God. If God said it that is enough for me! Of course Adam and Eve and the serpent were real. It wouldn't be recorded in the Bible if it weren't true. We all just need to learn to trust the Bible and eventually we will not have these doubts." Do you think that student will ask questions again? Unlikely!

Students need freedom to question. It would be far better for the teacher to say, "That is a really good question. I've had similar questions myself. Let me tell you how I have worked that one through." Then the teacher is free to address his perspective on the question. Or the teacher might have said, "You have raised one of the most important questions anyone can ask. Can we really trust the Bible and its historical accuracy? It shows that you're not willing to just take 'pat answers.' I respect that. I wish all Christians would seek out answers to their questions so honestly. Let's set aside our next class to deal with that. Does that sound like a good approach?" Now the teacher has affirmed the student and has allowed time for adequate preparation in addressing a hard question.

Youth Learn Best When a Variety of Methods Are Used

Youth tire of the same predictable class experiences. No matter how creative an activity might be, if you use it week after week you'll soon hear, "This class is boring." And boredom is the unforgivable sin in youth ministry. Youth do not learn as adults learn. They tend to demand much more variety in their learning experience. Since youth are often very social, methods must be employed that allow interaction. Those who work with youth must employ many different learning activities in their lesson plans. The HBLT structure will still work, but methods selection is the key to its effectiveness. Later in this chapter we will review some of the more effective methods for use with adolescents.

Youth Learn Best When Lessons Are Relevant and Needs Focused

Erin really likes the Bible study group she attends once each week. When asked why, she responded, "Because the leader understands what it's like to be a teenager and makes the Bible so relevant." Knowing the issues that matter to your students and the events that are shaping their lives is crucial to effectiveness in working with teens. It is also important to know what they *need* to know that they will not immediately find relevant—teaching such material will be particularly hard with high school students.

Remember Alex, the teacher who works with urban teens? By doing a needs assessment, Alex was able to better connect his teaching to his students. Understanding needs and then matching teaching to those needs is important with all age groups but is especially necessary in teaching youth. You'll want to review chapter 6, which deals with needs assessment, to guide you in this process.

Teaching in a relevant, need-focused manner is not as easy as it might sound, especially in the evangelical church. Pamela and Stanton Campbell explain why.

> Teaching of any kind is an intense and demanding obligation, but teachers in traditional evangelical churches have an even greater challenge. To be effective, they must learn to teach on two different levels. One large segment of their students are those who have been brought up in the church. They have accumulated hundreds of hours of Sunday school, vacation Bible school, youth group and other church functions. They have been subjected to all kinds of teachers and curricula. And frankly, by now they are beginning to think that they have heard it all. You are going to have to go beyond the basic stories and applications to hold the attention of these kids.
>
> But then there is the other segment of students—those occasional attenders, the "fringe" kids. This segment may not even know who was in the lions' den, who taught the Sermon on the Mount, or in which testament those stories are located.
>
> Standing before these two segments is the teacher. If the leader tries to challenge the knowledgeable kids, the others feel stupid, complain the meetings are boring or quietly drift away. But if the leader shifts the focus to the unchurched kids, regulars are quick to exclaim: "We already know this story!"[1]

The answer is far more difficult than stating the problem. In all likelihood the answer will require more than one action. In the classroom, the churched students can be used to teach the unchurched. Outside the classroom, small discipleship groups can be formed. These can more readily be focused on the needs of students who are involved. Teaching in a fresh way can unearth Bible treasure that is new to both groups and neither boring nor incomprehensible to either. Getting students into Scripture for themselves allows them to see things they've never seen before, and it gives them a chance to begin to study the Bible for themselves in a setting with people who can answer questions they have. "Graduating" the more knowledgeable kids into service for the church is another way to cope with the boredom factor—and simultaneously encouraging application of truth they have learned.

USING THE HBLT STRUCTURE WITH YOUTH

Some modification of the Hook, Book, Look, Took format is needed when teaching youth. Our focus here is on using the HBLT model in the adolescent Sunday school, but many of the ideas can be used in small groups, and other ministry settings.

As with adults, the Hook must gain attention, but relevance is paramount. Use of humorous or emotionally moving skits can be effective. Showing excerpts from a popular movie, playing a song, or showing a music video can all get students interested in listening to a biblical viewpoint. Shortly after Princess Diana died, one teacher used a clip from her funeral. He understood that students were anxious to talk about why so many people were moved by her death. The lesson was on "Christ, the King of Hearts," and he used the idea of Princess Di being termed the Queen of Hearts. If teachers know their teens well—their music, the movies they are watching, the events they are responding to—finding a hook to draw students into a study of the Bible is much easier. Start with your teens. Hook them by connecting your teaching to their world.

The Book section can be conducted in a large group or in smaller groups. We prefer the large group with a gifted youth communicator presenting a biblical concept or passage. It is best to keep this to a maximum of twenty minutes. The average attention span of a fifteen year old is between fifteen and twenty minutes. Any longer is counter-productive. In smaller groups, various discovery methods can be employed in looking at the passage. In the large group approach, the teacher will probably deliver a "youth talk." The focus must be on the Word of God. This section should present the Bible truth and explain it in a way that is both comprehensible and motivating. Use of illustrations, stories, and analogies are a must. Appropriate humor can be an enormous asset in the presentation. The goal of this part of the lesson plan is to bring students face-to-face with the Bible truth. The large group teacher must be sure that one idea is clearly communicated.

The Look section can occur in small groups of five to ten students led by adult team members or mature students in the youth group. The goal of the small group time is to identify implications of the topic presented in the large group session. This segment can run about thirty minutes, because discussion often takes time. Questions for discussion should be prepared in advance by the team. A variety of methods can be employed to encourage student involvement and participation.

The Took section should involve a commitment from students to act in the week ahead on the message and ideas they have heard. It is best to develop a group application, because students seem to find strength in numbers. By having a group or a couple of individuals to be accountable to, youth are more likely to follow through on their intended application. This can be clearly seen in the application jewelry for

Christian teens that has become popular in recent years, including "WWJD" (What Would Jesus Do?) and "Key to My Heart" (rings and necklaces with a heart and key displayed to indicate a girl's commitment to remain a virgin until marriage). These "tooks" are commitments to apply godly principles to daily living. Teens find it much easier to stand for Christ when they stand with others. Group applications can be a means of helping teens make needed individual commitments.

METHODS THAT WORK WITH YOUTH

Some methods are more effective with youth than others. In his excellent chapter on teaching youth, Daryl Eldridge suggests a few of these.

Art. Youth appreciate the aesthetic. Many youth are visual learners. Some youth have difficulty expressing themselves verbally but can express their faith through drawings, cartoons, collages, bumper stickers, T-shirt logos, murals, photography, posters, and sculptures.

Drama. Drama doesn't have to be professional or scripted. It may be done live or shown on video. Drama can make the biblical story come alive. Some forms of drama include acting out a Bible event, contemporary skits, choral speaking, and dialogues. Teachers can use drama as a discussion starter to create interest in the lesson. Youth enjoy playing a role and acting out a solution to a contemporary problem. Drama also can be used to interview a biblical personality. Other forms of drama might include monologues, pantomimes, puppet shows, and radio or television formats.

Music. Teenagers fill their world with music. When they get into the car, youth turn on the radio and listen to their favorite music. Find out what music your youth like. Use their music to illustrate biblical principles. . . . Use contemporary Christian music to illustrate biblical truth. Analyze secular music and help them see the values and messages contained in some music.

Pencil and Paper. Paper and pencils provide an economical way to get youth involved in studying God's Word. Use a variety of approaches to prevent youth from perceiving it as school work. Teachers can design activities that require youth to research the Bible. Letter writing is another excellent method. Teachers can ask youth to write a letter to God, friends, or significant persons in their lives. Youth can write simulated newspaper articles, poetry, lyrics, stories, and skits.

Verbal Techniques. Verbal methods are probably the most commonly used activities in Youth Bible study. Teachers must be taught
how to use them effectively. Remember that [not all youth are] verbal learners. . . . Youth enjoy brainstorming, discussing, case studies, debating, and problem-solving. . . . Youth will respond to
lecturing if you use visuals, listening teams, and jot sheets, and tell
stories or personal experiences.

Visual Techniques. Our challenge is to teach a timeless Book to a
generation living in a multimedia world. Youth are accustomed to
a collage of images interrupted every ten minutes by a commer-
cial. They are not linear and sequential thinkers. They watch several scenarios at once. Life is not black and white, it's digital
cinematography. So how can we compete? We don't. We can't. . . .
But we can use the visual techniques available to us.

Personal Experience. Youth learn best by doing. Find ways for them
to apply what they have learned. Youth need avenues to share their
faith and to serve others. Teachers can involve youth in mission action projects, outreach visitation, ministering to the homebound,
and personal witnessing. The idealism of youth can be channeled
to do great things for God.[2]

PEOPLE IN TRANSITION

A transition has been defined as "a period of instability preceded
by and followed by a period of stability." Youth are in that period of instability. They are no longer children but not yet adults. They need spe-
cialized ministry care. If God has called you to work with teens you have
been called to a unique and essential mission field. As if you were a missionary going overseas, there is a culture to understand, a language to
learn, music to appreciate, and clothing and customs to comprehend.
As a youth culture missionary, you will not only have to bridge the
world between the Bible and the present, but between adults and youth
as well. It is a great challenge, but a rewarding one as you see lives affected
for Christ. Your task is to teach the Bible in a culturally sensitive and relevant way. Given the willingness to try, fail, learn, and grow, it can be done!

NOTES

1. Pamela T. and Stanton D. Campbell, "Junior and Senior Highers" in Clark, Johnson, and Sloat, *Christian Education: Foundations for the Future* (Chicago: Moody, 1991), 257–58.

2. Daryl Eldridge, *The Teaching Ministry of the Church* (Nashville: Broadman and Holman, 1995), 250–53.

Chapter Seventeen

TEACHING THE BIBLE
TO CHILDREN:
PLEASE UNDERSTAND ME

L arry's son Paul was in third grade. Like many third-grade children he developed a fear of the dark. Of course, he didn't come out and say, "I'm afraid of the dark." In fact, he denied the idea vigorously. But when bedtime came, it was amazing how many different excuses he could find for not going down the long dark hall to his room alone.

"Dad, will you get my pj's? I want to finish this picture." "Dad, I don't think my pj's are on my bed. Will you go look?" "Dad, come on down to my room with me. I want to show you something." The fear was there—denied, but there.

Then, one evening, Larry suggested they write a book together. The book was to be one he could later read to his younger brother and sister to help them not to fear. Paul's father pointed out that as children grow, they often experience different kinds of fear. About the age of three, children often develop a fear of loud noises. Sometimes they have a fear of other children—and fears in the Sunday school as mom or dad leave. The book Paul and his father were writing was going to help the little ones learn how to overcome their fears.

The first night they went through a concordance, looking for Bible portions where the words *fear* or *afraid* and *trust* occur. Together they narrowed down the list to forty verses that spoke of fear and trust, and they were ready to start the book. They bought a composition book and some construction paper and went to work. Paul first chose the verse for the title page: "Fear not, Abram," God had said, "for I am thy shield."

Paul cut out a construction paper shield, and then a number of paper spears, which he showed striking the shield and breaking. The idea was his own, as was the insight: "This shows God protects us." That night he named the book and printed the title on the cover: *Paul's Not Being Afraid Book*.

Paul and Dad wrote several chapters. "What time I am afraid, I will trust" was one. Together they thought of a Bible character who might have had reason to be afraid. Paul thought of Daniel and drew several fearsome lions for illustrations. On the next page he listed times when children his age—the boys and girls he knew in school—might be afraid. His listing included fear of tornadoes, of kidnaping, and—of course—of the dark. Thinking in terms of others and understanding that fears were natural even for adults, Paul found it easier to face his own fears. And in the context of the Word it was easier for him to see that even when a believer is afraid, he is to trust in God.

Paul never quite finished that book. But as he worked on it with his dad, something happened in Paul. His terror of the dark gradually lessened. His calls on dad at bedtime, to go into the dark for him, diminished. And somehow his awareness that God went into the dark *with* him grew, until he was able to trust even in his fear.

It's not only adults who have needs that must be met by the Lord. Children do too. Trust in God, and personal experience with Him, do not suddenly become relevant when a person reaches his teens. Childhood is a time for foundational experiences with God: finding Him able to help us in our fears, to comfort us in disappointment, to strengthen us for challenges we face. God does speak to children with the message of comfort or strength or encouragement that they need in their now, even as He speaks to us. Children, then, need to meet God in the same way that adults need to meet Him. Children, too, need to hear His voice and learn the joy of responding.

Since God's point of communication with all of us is the Word, it's clear that the Bible must be for children too. It's through the Bible that children come to know the person of God, to understand His love and steadfastness, to discern His character and care, and to know His will that they might be guided in their responses to Him in daily life. Through the Bible children too can become aware of the God who reveals Himself there. God does speak to children. Our task is to communicate all that He has to say to them as meaningfully as we can.

THE PROBLEM OF TEACHING CHILDREN THE BIBLE

The Bible really is an adult book, written by adults and for adults. Major sections of the Bible, such as the prophets, most poetical books, and much of the closely reasoned teaching of the New Testament are beyond a child's understanding. Who can imagine teaching seven-year-olds Zephaniah, verse by verse! And so, teaching children the Bible presents a problem. What parts of the Bible should we teach? What aspects of its message can children comprehend? How shall we go about teaching children the Bible?

Children can't delve into deep theological truths, but faith is more natural to them than to adults. Adults have learned self-sufficiency and have to unlearn it; children eat and sleep because someone else provides the means. They can trust Christ readily, and they pray in a way that seems naive but that God—surprise—answers. Their love of song, their creativity, the fact that much of the Bible is brand new to them, and their almost intuitive understanding of God's presence can more than compensate for the difficulties enumerated here. God does have something to say in His Word to elementary age children. And it's our task to communicate what He is actually saying to them. There are two primary requirements for Bible teaching that will best help children understand what God has to say to them. The first is being sure that what we teach is actually what God is saying. The second is creative structuring of the teaching/learning situation.

How Shall We Teach the Bible to Children?

There are several factors a children's Bible teacher must recognize when ministering to his or her class.

First, the teaching must be true to God's Word. Often, children are taught "truths" they must unlearn in later life—like the idea that the Bible is a book of moral rules, of lists of dos and don'ts. The Christian life can't really be summed up as sharing or helping or being kind or obeying parents or being friendly. Yet sometimes this impression is given to children. The feeding of the five thousand is taught to promote sharing and the little boy is exalted; Dorcas is held up as the shining example of a person who was kind to others; David and Jonathan are praised for their unusual friendship.

When this kind of thing becomes the central core of a curriculum, where is God? A merit-centered works righteousness replaces the biblical core of grace, and the biblical concept that human response is an expression of love to a God whose grace enables it is clouded and lost.

This isn't, of course, to suggest that the Bible doesn't reveal a distinctive moral expression of God's will for us all. It does. "Obey your parents" is a distinct command. "Love one another" is too. But these commands are given in the context of a response to God. Most of the stories through which children are taught do not teach morals at all!

Both the feeding of the five thousand and the story of Dorcas focus on Christ and His power. The history of David and Jonathan is a wonderful story of human friendship, but the glory of it is that God should enable Jonathan to love David to the detriment of his own self-interest. The stories in context are not really there to be examples of morality principles.

The Bible is given to us that we might know and respond to God. How dare we tear incidents out of this context and use them to teach ideas they were never meant to communicate? Stories of Christ's life and ministry recorded in the New Testament are a rich source of teaching material. How thrilling is the story of Christ's stilling of the storm, when the focus is placed on Christ and we (as did the disciples) learn the power of our Lord. How deeply meaningful the feeding of the five thousand can be when the focus is on Christ's compassion and His willingness to act for those in need. So stories, taught in harmony with their purpose in the context, have an important place in children's Bible teaching.

Not every biblical theme, truth, or story can be taught to six through eleven year olds. But they do need to understand truth that tells them who God is and what He is like. They need to understand doctrines (though perhaps their understanding will be rudimentary) that relate to their own Christian experience: doctrines such as those of Christ's indwelling and His personal presence providing power to obey Him.

Clear teaching of God's moral will has a place also. We are to love one another. This has meaning to a child, who can express love in his own home and in school and play situations. Surely God's moral will must be known if children are to know how to respond to Him. But God's will should never be taught apart from Him; never as a set of rules, but always as the response of love and as a means of emulating God's character.

Our teaching of children must be true to God's revelation. Surely the Bible contains objective truth, objective dos and don'ts. But the Bible is given primarily that we might meet and come to know God Himself. Only when behavior is presented as a response to God, whom we have met and come to love, is Bible teaching true to His revelation. The weak moralizing of many lessons simply is not *Bible* teaching!

Second, teaching should relate to a child's present needs and experiences. The goal in Bible teaching is not primarily to instill ideas that students will need to know "someday." The goal is to bring pupils into vital relationship with God today! Children, as suggested earlier in this chapter, do have experiences in which they need God. Children have fears that can be quieted by coming to trust God. Children sin and need to know God's forgiveness. Children are faced with choices and need to find strength to do what they know is right. God is eager to become real to each child, now, in his present life experiences.

Third, the teaching must make Scripture relevant on the child's own level. It's one thing to say to a child who fears the dark, "Don't be afraid; God will take care of you." It's quite another to structure a situation in which the child himself comes to recognize this truth and respond to God with trust. Too often in teaching children, pat solutions to problems and easy formulas for meeting needs are offered. "Trust and obey, Jimmy." "Ask God to help you, Paul." "Sue, ask your friends to come to Sunday school." The pat solutions may well be the right ones. Trust and obedience are central in our life with God. But simply passing on truth as advice is not making God's revelation relevant to life—for children or adults.

What is involved in making revelation relevant? Our teaching must help the learner become aware of the crucial issues in his own life. It must lead him into contact with God, not rules. It must let him discover how God relates to his needs. It must help him discover his own opportunities to respond to God appropriately. Although no child will have as deep an understanding of the Lord's relationship to the issues of his life as an adult may potentially have, the insights a child *does* have will be meaningful to him. And so, our teaching must be structured to help children make their own discoveries and respond to God on their own level and in their own ways. When teaching children, the basic concepts outlined in earlier chapters must guide our expression.

How Do Children Learn?

Children do not learn in the same ways that adults and adolescents learn. It is important that we understand the nature of learning as it applies to children before we discuss how best to teach children. Doris Freese has identified ways children process ideas and what those ways mean for the teacher. Understanding these principles is helpful in designing effective childhood education programs.

Children learn by experiencing and doing. Discovering, interacting, playing and manipulating, children experience what is around them in their world. Although developing a growing use of language, children still need to have direct experiences. Talking about things (abstract) does not give enough input for concept development.

Allow for hands-on experiences rather than just talking with children. Use visuals, videos, recordings, role playing, and dramatization that allows them to be involved in the learning process. For example let them look up Bible verses rather than just memorize them.

Children learn by example. They learn by observing peers, siblings, parents and teachers. They try out behaviors and learn from the reactions. A child will often observe a peer talk to her parents in a certain way, then return home and try that out on her parents. The reaction of her parents will teach her the appropriate behavior.

Be aware of the behaviors and attitudes you model as a teacher. Use stories of persons who set the right example. Compliment students for their learning and appropriate behavior so that [other] students can observe their example.

Children learn by repetition with variation. Children enjoy reading the same books and doing the same activities over and over again. But gradually, they will begin to vary their repetitions, adding to or enlarging their activities.

Provide familiar books and use stories and concepts repeatedly. The more exposure to concepts, the deeper the understanding.

Children learn through concrete language and experiences, and they think literally and concretely. Although they can repeat correct answers, that does not mean they understand a concept. Misconceptions often occur when teachers use abstract concepts like describing Jesus as the "rock" or "the lily of the valley." Do not use object lessons with young children. They cannot understand how a lighthouse represents the Bible or rocks represent sin.[1]

METHODS FOR TEACHING CHILDREN

Norma Hedin suggests several methods that are applicable to teaching children the Bible. Here are her six categories of childhood teaching methodology.

Storytelling. Children are imaginative. They love stories. Bible stories, your stories, classic tales, role plays, and pantomime will capture their attention and stimulate their thinking. Stories help to prepare children for the ups and downs of reality. Through Bible stories children learn about the joys and problems of human relationships. Stories of God-motivated heroes provide role models for young lives.

Dramatics. Story playing, drama, skits, role play, mime, fingerplays, and action rhymes all have value in helping children apply what they learn. As they put themselves in the shoes of other people, they begin to think and feel as other people do. Pretending is part of children's growth and provides them with the opportunity to act out their feelings and impressions. Pretending also serves the very important function of revealing the children's thoughts to the teacher.

Questions. Questions are used by teachers as a means to stimulate interest, test knowledge, help students express their thoughts, and review past learning. Factual questions and thought questions stimulate thought and deepen understanding. Bible games make use of questions to review material.

Discussion. Discussion, or guided conversation with children, encourages students to participate in learning, share their ideas, test their knowledge, and get feedback from the teacher. Children love to talk and they love to express their ideas. Discussion gives them the chance to talk about concepts which reinforces their knowledge.

Projects. Projects help learners to do something related to their learning. Whether inside or outside of class, learners spend time actively involved in creating a plan and carrying it to completion. Research activities using Bible handbooks, dictionaries, maps, atlases, and books involve children in understanding and applying Bible truths.

Creative Activities. Creative writing, music activities, constructive arts and crafts, art, and mosaics are all creative activities. Creative activities bring new dimensions into learning experiences. Children become active in creating and expressing themselves. Creative activities make learning more enjoyable, lasting, and meaningful. They provide opportunities for self-expression and they instill pride of accomplishment.[2]

USING THE HBLT STRUCTURE WITH CHILDREN

The process described and illustrated in chapters 9 through 12 can and should be used with children as well as adults. The principles developed there apply to elementary children, but the teacher may find it more difficult to plan learning activities that will help children discover relevant truth and motivate appropriate response. Therefore, modifications to the HBLT structure are necessary when teaching children. In this section we will provide examples of a variety of learning activities that can be used to guide children through each step.

Learning activities are meaningful only when viewed in relation to the role they play in the structure of a lesson. In this section we will develop a lesson for children, step-by-step, using a variety of learning activities. By illustrating this process we hope to enable you to visualize methods that will fit your teaching purposes.

Let us assume that we will be teaching about the event where Jesus stilled the raging Sea of Galilee. It's recorded in Matthew 8:23–27, Mark 4:37–41, and Luke 8:22–25. In each book the section containing the record of this event is concerned with developing awareness of the person and power of Christ. And in each book the record contains a clear rebuke to the unbelief of the disciples, who had failed to trust a sleeping Savior, and expresses the wonder of the disciples as the deity of Christ was vividly demonstrated to them. The event, a private miracle for the disciples, clearly served to nurture a growing faith in this Man to whom they had entrusted themselves. This is a lesson we all need, adults and children. Christ stands to us as a Savior who is involved in our lives, who is with us, although unseen and—sometimes, we fear—unseeing. Yet His power, as His love, is unlimited. And we, too, can trust ourselves fully to Him.

We will look at how this story might be developed if taught to elementary age children, say about seven to nine years of age. The aim, growing out of the response that this recorded event clearly calls for, will be: *The students will identify ways they can trust Jesus when they are afraid.* So let's turn our attention to the beginning of each of these lessons and discover what learning activities are available for use by the creative teacher who desires to (1) gain and focus attention, (2) lead into the Bible study, and (3) help the pupils set a learning goal that will be meaningful to them.

The Hook: Focusing the Attention of Children

"All right, children. Let's review what we learned last week. David, what was our lesson about? Karen, do you remember who we talked about last week?"

Hardly a fascinating beginning to a Sunday school class! Hardly the kind of activity that will grab the pupils' interest and focus it. Hardly the kind of thing that will help them see and set a goal that will be meaningful to them. Somehow, at the very beginning of your time together, interest has to be gained and focused, and a learning goal set. How? Let's see some ways.

Teaching Strategy 1

To encourage your elementary students to think of situations in which they fear, play a "what's happening" game at the beginning of class. Tell your pupils that you'll describe how an eight-year-old friend of yours feels, and ask them to guess what he's doing or what's happening. Begin by saying, "Jack is very excited." Let them tell you what they think might be happening. Then suggest, "Jack is sad," "Jack is happy." When the pupils are enthusiastically involved, tell them, "Jack is afraid."

Write down the possible "afraid" situations they suggest on the chalkboard. Encourage them to think of as many likely situations as possible. Normally they'll mention situations in which they themselves feel fear. Then ask, "Is it fun to feel afraid? How do you think a person can keep from feeling so afraid?" As your transition, after the class discusses this last question, state the learning goal that they are able to sense as important to them: "Today we'll see how Jesus helped His friends not to be afraid, and how Jesus can help us when we're afraid."

Teaching Strategy 2

Tell your pupils this "open-ended" story. Explain that you're going to start a story about eight-year-old Jack, and ask each one to think of how he would finish it.

> It was terribly dark in the big, empty school. Jack pushed his back up against the corridor wall, afraid to move down the shadowy hall. How could he have been dumb enough to fall asleep in the gym behind that rolled-up wrestling pad? When he woke up, it was dark. The school doors were locked, all the lights were out, and the trees outside made weird shadows that looked like giants creeping through the empty rooms.
>
> Suddenly Jack heard a loud thump against the outside doors, and someone or something began to shake them violently. They burst open with a loud crash, and a giant figure stood blackly in the entrance.
>
> "Jack!" a voice cried. It was Dad! "Dad!" Jack yelled and dashed down the corridor to throw himself against the warm strong arms.
>
> Later, at home, after a warm meal, Jack told Mom and Dad all about his experience. "It was awful, Mom!" Jack said. "I felt . . ."

Let each child tell what he thinks Jack told his mother. Write the words and phrases that describe the feelings on the chalkboard. Then ask, "Can you think of other times when boys and girls might feel as Jack did?" Let your class think together for several minutes and list other occasions when they feel fear. Move to the transition, as suggested in strategy number 1.

Teaching Strategy 3

Divide your class into twos, and ask each pair to plan and act out (pantomime) one or two situations in which children their age might be afraid. Other teams will try to guess what is being represented. Write each situation on the chalkboard as it is guessed. When each team has presented one or two pantomimes, discuss the situations they chose. Let the children talk about these questions: "Is it fun to be in situations like these? How do you think we could be helped when we're afraid?" Move into the lesson by stating, "Today we'll see how Jesus helped His friends when they were afraid, and how Jesus can help us when we're afraid too."

The Book: Communicating Bible Content to Children

The Bible—that "adult" book—is central in evangelical teaching. So the Bible must be communicated to children. Such communication encounters two main difficulties. First, what is communicated must be true to the Scriptures. The Word must be presented accurately, interpreted in full harmony with its literal, historical, grammatical meaning, with full attention given to the inspired writer's purpose. Second, what is communicated must be on the level of the children. The Word must be presented so that they can understand it—understand it as fully as possible not only within the framework of their mental level, but also within the framework of their current experience. Teaching the Bible to children isn't easy. But it's necessary. And it can be done. The following examples will demonstrate how. We return to our lesson on Jesus' calming of the storm. In the biblical record this incident is sketched sharply and briefly.

> That day when evening came, he said to his disciples, "Let us go over to the other side." Leaving the crowd behind, they took him along, just as he was, in the boat. There were also other boats with him. A furious squall came up, and the waves broke over the boat, so that it was nearly swamped. Jesus was in the stern, sleeping on a cushion. The disciples woke him and said to him, "Teacher, don't you care if we drown?" He got up, rebuked the wind and said to the waves, "Quiet! Be still!" Then the wind died down and it was completely calm. He said to his disciples,
>
> "Why are you so afraid? Do you still have no faith?" They were terrified and asked each other, "Who is this? Even the wind and the waves obey him!" (Mark 4:35–41)

The situation is clear: the raging storm; the terror of the disciples (many of whom were experienced fishermen) as they became convinced that they were about to die; the calm Christ; His quiet rebuke of the raging elements and their miraculous response; His gentle rebuke of the disciples for their fears; the awed response of those who had traveled with Him as, once again, they came face to face with His power.

Although the fear of the disciples was surely justified by the circumstances, the presence of Christ transformed the situation and should have enabled the disciples to trust even in their fear. The more you and I and our children are aware of the power and the presence of Christ in our experiences, the more we too will be able to trust, even in our fears.

The basic approach taken in teaching younger children is storytelling. The elements of the biblical narrative are woven into a word picture that will interest and impress the children. It's built to appeal not only to the children's minds, but also to their emotions; built with "tugs" to draw the listener and move him to think and feel and to experience and decide. And storytelling, as we'll see, is also a method that provides for an almost infinite variety of learning experiences.

Teaching Strategy 1

When the first dark clouds began to pile up in the night sky, the men in the boat weren't worried. They were fishermen and had seen many storms. They weren't worried when the wind began to blow. They weren't worried when the waves began to pound against the side of their boat. They weren't even worried when the lightning started to flash and the thunder boomed out louder and louder.

But the wind blew harder and harder. And the waves got bigger and bigger. Now drops of cold water began to spray over the side of the boat. And the men began to shiver in the cold and wet. They shivered even more as the thunder crashed louder and louder, and the lightning cracked nearer and nearer.

Even then the men weren't worried. When they began to feel a little frightened, they looked toward the back of their little boat. And they saw someone lying there, fast asleep. It was Jesus. *If Jesus can sleep,* the men must have thought, *the storm can't be too bad. If Jesus can sleep, we'll probably be all right.*

But the storm kept getting worse and worse! With a crash, crash, crash, the pounding waves beat against the boat. The waves began to surge over the side of the boat, pouring gallons and gallons of water onto the men. All Jesus' friends grabbed buckets and basins and tried to throw water out of the boat. They dipped as fast and as hard as they could. But the waves poured more water in, faster and faster. The boat began to fill up! And now the men were really afraid. In the darkness and terrible noise of the great storm, they knew their boat was going to sink. And soon! They were lost.

But wait! What about Jesus? Where was Jesus? In the brightness of another lightning flash they saw Him. He was still asleep! Terrified now, one of Jesus' friends shook Him and cried out, "Lord! Don't You care? We're sinking! We'll all be drowned!"

Then Jesus woke up. He looked around and saw the terrible storm. He saw the fear on the faces of His friends. He stood up in the boat and told the wind, "Stop." And the wind stopped, just like that! Jesus told the waves, "Be still." And they were still. Just like that. And suddenly, instead of being in a great storm, the boat was floating quietly on a flat, still sea. Then Jesus turned to look at His friends. Sadly He said to them, "Why were you afraid? Don't you trust Me?"

Jesus' friends were amazed. Who else could have made the storm stop and the seas be calm? No one, no one but Jesus. *Who can this Jesus really be?* Jesus' friends wondered. And deep down inside they must have thought, *We really could have trusted Jesus all the time. We didn't have to be afraid, because Jesus was with us. We'll never forget to trust Jesus when we're afraid again.*

And you know, boys and girls, we can trust Jesus when we're afraid, too. Jesus loves us, and He has promised, "I will never leave thee" [Heb. 13:5 KJV]. We don't have to be afraid, because Jesus is with us!

Teaching Strategy 2

By cutting the last two paragraphs off the story and substituting a series of questions, the teachers can lead children to discover the central bridge principle of the story themselves. Here are some questions that might be used.

Question	Expected Response Pattern
Why were Jesus' friends afraid?	They were afraid of the storm.
Why wasn't Jesus afraid?	Jesus knew He could stop the storm, had more power, was God, etc.
How did Jesus show His power to help?	Jesus stopped the storm.
Now, stop and think a minute. If Jesus was in the boat, did His friends have to be afraid? Why? Why not?	No, because Jesus was with them. He could and would take care of them.

Question	Expected Response Pattern
Do you think Jesus takes care of us today?	Normally, children who have been brought up in church or in Christian homes will respond with yes. Either yes or no responses call for a verse like Hebrews 13:5, which may serve as a memory verse or key verse.

Teaching Strategy 3

Another variation is to let the children act out the story after they have heard it. This kind of experience uniquely lets the children enter into and participate in the total experience, to thus sense vicariously the comforting presence of Christ.

Teaching Strategy 4

A variation that can be very effective is to encourage the children to pretend they were actually in the boat and "interview" them. A tape recorder or video camera for the "reporter" makes the experience especially exciting. In using this technique with older children, divide the class into two groups, one of which is to be reporters and the others disciples who were in the boat. The reporters can decide what questions they would like to ask, and the disciples can discuss the experience, before the interview takes place.

The Look: Guiding Insight with Children

Children need to participate actively if they are to apply the Scripture to life. The teacher's task, then, is to structure learning activities in a concrete manner with solid enough handles for children to grasp, and to find learning activities that help children work with concrete situations and ideas rather than with concepts and abstractions.

In working with children, it is important also to recall that the response that is appropriate to a given truth about or from God may be an action, but it may be a change in attitude or motivation as well. These later responses are not immediately perceptible to the teacher or even to the learner! The learning activity chosen, then, must help children focus for themselves on what the appropriate response to the truth studied actually is, and it must facilitate that response.

The Look step in this lesson should focus on developing the children's awareness of uncomfortable situations in which they can trust themselves to an ever present Christ. Or it can focus on encouraging the children to think through how they might turn to Him when afraid. The

learning activities suggested here focus on one or the other. In the class
you may want to use two activities, which would permit you to help the
children in both these ways.

Teaching Strategy 1

With young elementary age children (grades one and two), cut
from a catalog pictures of a man, a woman, and two or three children.
Back the pictures with cardboard. Introduce the "family" to your class
and tell a story about one primary-age child who became lost. Move the
figures appropriately as you tell the story. Tell how worried the mother
and father were, and how frightened the child was when he (or she) realized he was lost. Then tell how each remembered that the Lord was
with the lost child, for He has promised never to leave or forsake us. Tell
how each prayed and asked the Lord for help (as the disciples in the
boat had), and how they then were comforted as they trusted Him until
the child was found.

Then let each child who wants to use the family tell his or her own
story about trusting. Remind the class of the various situations they discussed at the beginning of the period. Thus primed, the children will
have plenty of ideas for their own stories.

This same approach may be used with finger puppets, paper bag
puppets, etc.

Teaching Strategy 2

Prepare for each child four picture panels that show a situation in
which a child or adult feels fear. One of the panels ought to show the child
in the situation. A second should be a close-up of his face showing his fear
or unhappiness. A third might show him praying or thinking of the Lord.
And the fourth should show him trusting the Lord with fears lessened.

Ask the children to make up a story about the child in the four pictures, telling in some detail what is happening. You may wish to write
the story down as the children dictate.

Another variation on this approach is to leave one of the four picture squares blank (preferably either frame 3 or frame 4) and ask each
child to draw in the picture that he feels will help complete the story.

Teaching Strategy 3

For older elementary students, have the class develop a skit or story to act out that applies the lesson concept to the everyday life of a
child their age. Talk together about ideas for the skits, and then let the
children write scripts together. Break into groups if the class is larger

than a few children. Have the class do their skit, and then let the class identify the application point being made.

The Took: Encouraging Response in Children

Response to God is always an intimately personal thing. Only God knows the heart; only He can sovereignly move to touch our motives and our wills and to create the love that makes an action a true response to Him. Yet from the point of view of our perception, response is our choice, our decision. And from the point of view of the teacher's responsibility, our students must and can be encouraged to respond, to decide, to choose to do God's will.

The teacher in the class has the task of leading the learner to the brink of decision. That is, the teacher needs to help the young learner face the necessity to respond, giving whatever help is appropriate to the age group without coercing a response. Children often need an external stimulus to help them respond, but not the stimulus of a prize or an award, which stimulates response to the reward rather than to God. Children need the kind of stimulus that will help them respond appropriately in the life situation outside of class. They need the kind of support that will help them be alert for response opportunities. What kind of learning activities might serve this function? Let's look at some.

Teaching Strategy 1

Give each child a postcard, addressed to you (the teacher). On the postcard place a picture seal of Christ and print this incomplete statement: "Today I remembered to trust the Lord when . . ." Encourage the children to complete the card during the week whenever they've found the Lord has helped them, then to mail the card to you. Next Sunday bring the cards you received to class and post them. Also, let the children share with the rest of the class how the Lord comforted and helped them.

Teaching Strategy 2

Make from several four-by-six-inch slips of paper, stapled together, a "Chapter-a-Day" book on trusting. Have each child print his name on the cover of his book, and also the day's key verse ("I will never leave you"), or some such phrase as "I can trust Jesus." Encourage the children to keep the daily diary on trusting by drawing in, each day, a picture of some situation in which they were conscious that Jesus was with them and taking care of them. The books can be discussed in class the next Sunday.

Teaching Strategy 3

Phone the children during the week and talk with them about the lesson. Let them tell any times they have trusted the Lord in a special way since class. Or mail each a personal note.

TEACHING CHILDREN IN THE LARGER CONTEXT OF LIFE

Response to God is normally made in the context of life—life lived outside the church and outside the classroom. The Christian teacher and the Christian parent need to be clear on one basic point: the formal instruction in the classroom cannot, in itself, develop strong Christians or nurture children and youth in the Christian faith. To be in harmony with the nature of our faith, Christian education must be integrated with daily living. Students should study the Bible in class, certainly. But they must also be guided to experience the truths studied in the context of daily life. Who is in a position to fulfill this responsibility? Certainly not the Sunday school teacher. Only the parent. For maximum impact on children, teaching in the agencies of the church must be integrated with a ministry of informal guidance in the home. Although such integration is difficult to accomplish, it can be done. What does it take? Here are a few simple suggestions.

1. *Acquaint parents with their responsibility.*

Children's ministry leaders should make sure neither parents nor teachers trust in church-centered training alone to accomplish spiritual nurture goals.

2. *Keep parents aware of what teachers are teaching.*

Acquaint parents with weekly lesson themes. Visit homes and hold parent meetings to explain the goals, materials, and methods employed in the children's educational program.

3. *Program leaders and teachers should be made more sensitive to the need for working with the home.*

Parents need help to relate daily experience to Bible truths. It is important to communicate this need to parents. Parents need to see the children's ministry of the church as a partner in helping them accomplish their responsibility as spiritual mentors of their children. Information sheets can be mailed at the beginning of each unit of lessons that contain ideas, copies of new songs, memory verses the children will learn, etc. Most important, the sheets can summarize the Bible content taught each Sunday and suggest to parents the general trend of application suggested in class. Because limitations are inherent in even the best classroom teaching, we should seriously consider, when teaching children, how the teaching ministry can be integrated with a guidance ministry of the home.

NOTES

1. Doris A. Freese, "How Children Think and Learn," in Robert E. Clark, Joanne Brubaker, and Roy Zuck, *Childhood Education in the Church* (Chicago: Moody, 1986), 74.

2. Norma Hedin, "Teaching Children" in Daryl Eldridge, *The Teaching Ministry of the Church* (Nashville: Broadman and Holman Publishers, 1995), 237.

Chapter Eighteen

TEACHING THE BIBLE
TO PRESCHOOLERS:
MORE THAN BABY-SITTING

One of the announcements in the Sunday morning bulletin said:

Wanted: Someone to work in the twos and threes class. Help adults get more out of worship by caring for their little ones during the service. Only one week per month required. No teaching involved.

Consider what this recruitment announcement is actually saying about twos and threes and those who serve by teaching that age group. There is a message subtly communicated through announcements like this one. The parenthetical statements provide the real, underlying message.

Wanted (*help, we're desperate*): Someone (*anyone, it doesn't matter what your qualifications are*) to work in the twos and threes class (*this is work, not service or ministry*). Help adults get more out of worship (*the real ministry around here is to adults*) by caring for their little ones during the service (*we need to get those crying kids out of the service so we can listen to the pastor's message*). Only one week per month required (*although we would never do it with adults, we rotate people in and out of the little children's classes*). No teaching involved (*we just see this as baby-sitting; you can't actually teach this age group anything, so hey, no big deal*).

The long-standing belief that preschool ministry isn't authentic teaching is the chief problem in recruiting the right kind of people to teach little children. And church leaders are often the ones who promote this misunderstanding. Such a view, sometimes spoken directly, but more often seen in staffing and resourcing decisions, grows out of a faulty definition of teaching and learning. Teaching is seen as formal, classroom presentation of information by the teacher resulting in the students' careful and thoughtful processing of that information. Because twos and threes cannot easily interact in a formal way with content, many conclude that real ministry must begin later. So the church falls back to a baby-sitting approach. In too many churches, the goal becomes *Keep the children entertained until their parents come to pick them up, and pray the sermon doesn't go over again.* We end up providing child care rather than early childhood Christian education.

Some of our programs do a better job. Teachers see their role as one of nurturing faith by providing a safe, secure environment for developing interpersonal relationships. They focus on the nonformal aspects of education. Growing out of a recognition of the developmental needs of children, these programs focus on implicit, rather than explicit, communication of Christian truth. This is certainly commendable and altogether appropriate, but still we believe that Bible content and Bible truth can be taught to little ones. We believe it is possible to lay a foundation, both emotionally and cognitively, that the teacher can build upon as the child develops greater and greater cognitive powers and as he comes to know the Lord as his own Savior.

Teaching preschoolers the Bible is surely a different ballgame than teaching adults, adolescents, or even elementary aged children. Frankly, it requires some significant revision to our Hook, Book, Look, Took strategy. In this chapter we will explore some revisions to the HBLT structure that enable teachers to provide basic concepts and information that preschool children need to formulate the foundation of a biblical view of the world. Our goal is to provide guidance on how to teach preschoolers age-appropriate truths of the Word of God in a developmentally appropriate manner.

We've emphasized the idea that the Bible teacher teaches for response. Response to God is the big must when it comes to spiritual growth. But how about twos and threes and fours and fives? Spiritual *growth* presupposes spiritual birth. And most of the children in the preschool departments aren't born again.

So our first task is to answer this question: What is the purpose of teaching preschoolers? It's not primarily to convert. It's not to produce spiritual growth in those who have no spiritual life. It's certainly not to help tots who aren't Christians act like Christians.

What then is our Bible teaching goal? When we know our goal, then perhaps we can see *how* to teach.

Many times classes are taught with the conscious or unconscious philosophy that through guided "Christian" experiences, preschool children will develop Christian personalities. But it's in truth about God that we contact God. So, somehow, whatever approach we take to preschool Christian education, it cannot neglect the Word and words of God, made understandable to preschool children on the threshold of understanding.

Another thing this sort of thinking doesn't fit is the biblical picture of a Christian. There is no scriptural justification for the idea that "Christian personalities" can be developed naturally through training in Christian moral principles. A Christian personality is produced *supernaturally*. Christian character comes into being when a person exercises personal faith in Jesus Christ as Savior, and a new, supernatural life is imparted by God. This supernatural life, lived out by the indwelling Spirit, is the only kind of life the Bible allows us to call "Christian."

So we can't take the position that church preschool training is for the production of "Christian personalities," or even for helping tots live "the Christian life." But we still haven't answered the question of what it *is* for.

The growing preschooler is eagerly learning information about his world; if we relate that to the nature of Scripture as revealed truth about the nature of reality, we come up with a distinctive purpose for Christian education of preschoolers. Simply stated, it's this: *The primary task of the nursery and beginner Sunday school teacher is to provide the basic concepts and information needed by their children to formulate a biblical view of the world.*

All this talk of a biblical worldview sounds obscure and difficult. But pull it down to the level of *what* is taught, and you can see what we mean. Children need to know who God is. It's vitally important that they look on the world as the creation of a loving God, that they develop the assurance that Jesus, God's Son, is a powerful Friend who loves them and cares for them. They need to know that God speaks to them in the Bible, His book; that He tells them there of His love, and how they can show their love for Him. Children who grow in this knowledge, who have a place for God in their thoughts and a picture of the way things really are, will be ready to respond to the gospel message of God's love expressed in Christ's sacrifice when they've reached an age of understanding. Children who grow up without a biblical concept of God will find the gospel message completely foreign to their way of thinking about life and the world.

What does this mean in practice? *First, the Bible must be taught.* Twos and threes and fours and fives need and must be taught biblical information. The information that's particularly relevant isn't moral in character—not telling them what God wants believers to do. The relevant truths are those that tell who God is—truths that give preschool children a biblical picture of the world, of themselves, of Christ. These ideas must be the core of the curriculum.

Second, response must be encouraged. Preschoolers can respond to Bible truths. A child who knows that "Jesus always sees me" can remember it and react when he's tempted to do something wrong out of Mommy's sight, or when he's alone and afraid in the dark of his bedroom.

In asking for response, we're not expecting preschoolers without spiritual life to grow spiritually. We may encourage young children to share or to pray in response to a particular truth, but by this we're not suggesting that either response pleases God. Before a child or adult can please God, he must be made acceptable to Him in Christ.

Why then the emphasis on response? We're trying to establish early in life a pattern of response to truth. We're trying to help children develop awareness that response is the normal and necessary companion of learning Bible truths. "I learn God's Word" and "I respond to God" are inseparable, and we dare not separate them, even when our teaching goal is primarily informational.

Third, the Bible must be taught effectively. Biblical information must be taught on the preschool level. And it must be taught in ways that preschoolers can most easily grasp and learn. We won't talk about omnipresence or omniscience to threes, but we can teach "Jesus always sees us." In the rest of this chapter, we'll continue to explore how truth can best be communicated to preschoolers.

TEACHING TWOS AND THREES

Visit a Sunday school class for two or three year olds and what you'll see probably won't look like teaching. Children will be on the move, playing with blocks or dolls, or looking at colorful books. The room will be large and spacious—no cubicles for classes. And who can teach without classes! But stay and listen awhile. Watch the pattern of the activities. Watch the teachers near each activity center. Listen to the simple conversations they have with boys and girls as they play. Stay through the hour and you'll observe a simple Bible story, told clearly and with a variety of visuals. Then more activities—motion songs, finger plays, playing of the story, working at simple paper projects—all of which reinforce the total learning impact. A two year old or three year old class may not look like Sunday school; it may not seem that teaching takes place. Yet in a good department, tots *are* taught. In this section we want to explore the keys to effective teaching of twos and threes.

The Way Twos and Threes Learn

Effective teachers teach students. It's not simply "talking truths." Truth has to be communicated in such a way that children can learn. This is important to remember when we think about teaching twos and threes. Children this age simply do not learn meaningfully when taught in the same manner as older children. Learning, for them, starts with activity, not with words. They are pre-logical learners.

Ideas take on meaning for preschoolers *as they're associated with experiences.* Thus the best way to communicate biblical ideas is to teach them in a context of activity and experience. Remember that little children are naturally wiggly. They have a built-in need to move. Twos and threes also come equipped with a wandering attention. As a rule, children have an attention span in minutes equal to their age. Two year olds can attend to a talking adult for about two minutes. Three year olds can focus on verbal learning for about three minutes. When adults talk at them, things on the other side of the room just naturally draw small bodies off to a personal investigation. If your lesson is to be longer than their attention span, you need to change your style, perhaps allowing them to act out part of the lesson as you teach it. Young preschoolers need activity and freedom to move. And so, we need to build activity into our teaching. If you have a one hour time period with two year olds, you may have as many as thirty different changes in learning activities. Imagine—thirty!

Social characteristics, too, play a big part in guiding development of a teaching program for preschoolers. Young twos and threes normally aren't ready for *group* activities. Turn a dozen threes loose in a well equipped room and something interesting happens. They scatter. They'll move away from each other. Even when several go to the same area of the room, these won't be "together." They'll play beside each other, but they won't be playing with each other. Developmental researchers call this *parallel play.* Two will build with blocks—but each will build his own tower. Three may look at books, but each will look at his own book. Others may work simple wooden puzzles, but again each will work his own. Cooperative play—playing with others—comes later.

All this combines to highlight the fact that little children are special and must be taught in special ways. They're individualists who don't fit in groups and who need to be taught and loved individually. They're wiggly and they need freedom to move. They're short on words and they need to learn ideas in association with activities that will give the ideas meaning. To communicate Bible truths meaningfully to children who are like this demands a uniquely structured teaching program.

A Plan for Teaching Twos and Threes

A Sunday school class for twos and threes is a teaching class. It is structured to communicate Bible truths. But in this department, teaching wears an unusual face. The hour is filled with activities, carried on with many shifts between active and quiet times. Yet the whole is carefully patterned. Overall, the hour breaks down into three basic periods in which three *different approaches* to teaching should be followed.

The first of these begins with pre-session and continues approximately fifteen to twenty minutes into the Sunday school hour itself. During this time, the children are free to take part in a variety of activities provided at centers in different parts of the room. In the second period, the Bible story is told. *Only during this short time* are the children together in a group. In the third teaching period, the boys and girls are again engaged in activities (singing, crafts, handwork, etc.). Although they are all working on the same things at approximately the same time, they do them in different areas of the room (*not in a group*), with teachers guiding and helping the children who gather in small clusters around them.

1. Pre-session and Learning-Center Time

Often larger groups distress twos and threes, and, because of little experience in groups, easily overstimulate them. This characteristic is one of the principle reasons for arranging the room as shown in Figure 18 on page 294. Notice that in each corner area an activity center is provided. These activity centers (also called learning centers) provide play materials that will capture and hold interest. Play is the primary means by which children this age learn. And so the materials that are provided are carefully selected to relate to the day's teaching aim and to provide experiences through which the day's Bible truth can be invested with meaning.

Four principles are important in making this "play time" a time of teaching:

First, have available only play materials that relate to the Bible teaching aim. Aims for this age group are always simple and should relate to communication of a basic biblical concept. "Jesus always sees me" is one example of a theme on which to build an hour's teaching activities. Others about Jesus are appropriate. Develop the idea that He is God's Son, the children's friend, who loves and cares for them.

Figure 17

PLAN FOR CLASS
TIME USAGE—AGES
TWO AND THREE

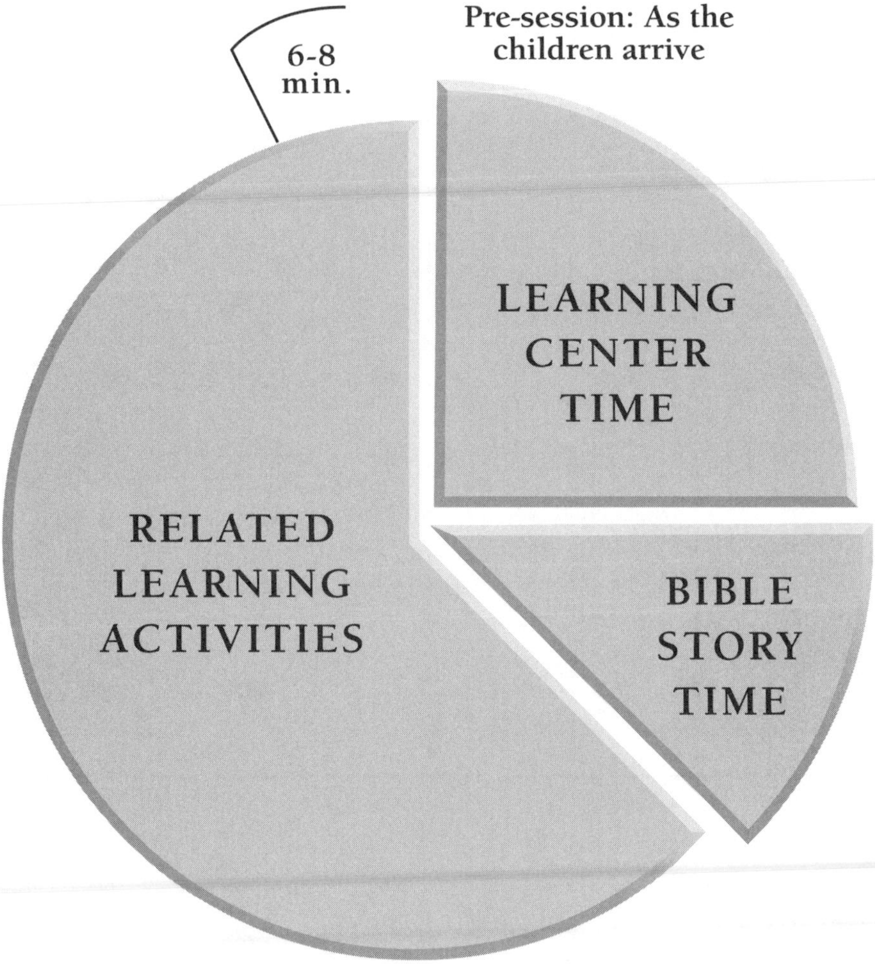

6-8 min.

Pre-session: As the children arrive

LEARNING CENTER TIME

RELATED LEARNING ACTIVITIES

BIBLE STORY TIME

Figure 18

ROOM ARRANGEMENT—
AGES TWO AND THREE

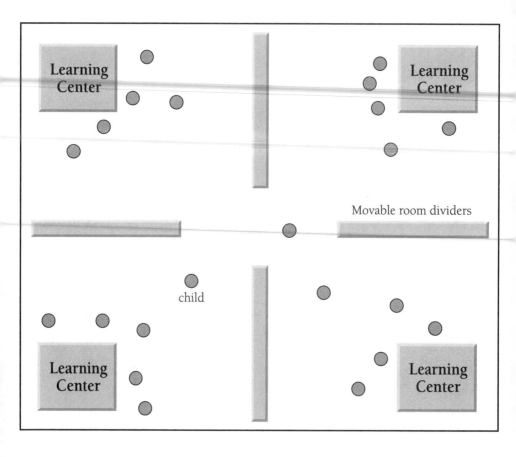

Learning Center

Learning Center

Movable room dividers

child

Learning Center

Learning Center

"Jesus gives us our food" might be another such idea, reflecting the truth that we can trace all blessings back to Him. For such a theme, blocks might become building units for farms, a housekeeping center a place to play at preparing and serving meals, magazine pictures of food a favorite meal to paste on paper plates. Each activity is related to the theme and provides an experience in which the idea can be communicated meaningfully.

Second, station a teacher or worker at each learning center. The play materials and the children's activities must be related to the day's theme. The children won't fall into activity patterns that reinforce the teaching by themselves. Yet twos and threes are highly suggestible. They can easily be guided into play patterns that do fit.

For instance, listen to the teacher at the housekeeping center: "My, Kim, that looks like good food you're cooking. Are you going to put some on my plate? Thank you. It's good to say 'thank you,' isn't it? Whom do we pray to and thank for our food when we sit down at the table? Yes, Jesus. Isn't Jesus good to give us our food? Let's thank Him now, shall we?"

Third, allow the children freedom to move from one center to another. Children have wandering interests and a need to move. So during this period, freedom of movement is important. A child should be allowed to go from center to center as he wishes. The teaching focus of the hour isn't disturbed by this freedom of movement, because no matter what center a child moves to, the same simple truth is repeated.

If Kim tires of cooking and goes to play with the blocks, the teacher there may say, "Hello, Kim. I'm glad you've come. Tommy and Ann are playing farm. They're growing good food for their family. Jesus sends the rain and the sunshine to make the food grow. Isn't Jesus good to give us food this way? Would you like to make a farm too? What will you ask Jesus to help you grow?"

Thus through a variety of activities one simple idea is presented and given meaning in terms of the child's own world and experience. And the child further develops his picture of Jesus, who can do wonderful things, and who loves us.

Fourth, separate the learning centers visually. Although children are given freedom to move, rapid and repeated shifts from center to center aren't encouraged. A movable room divider can cut out distracting sights. Such dividers also give sensitive youngsters a sense of confidence by making them relatively unaware of the number of other children in the room. A divided room reduces contact of child with child and helps the whole program remain quieter and more stable.

Finally, note that this structure for the first period of the hour provides an individualized teaching situation. Teachers and workers are able to talk personally with each child as he joins the small cluster at their centers. And the constant repetition of the lesson's one main Bible truth sinks in.

2. Bible Story Time

In terms of communicating the day's Bible truth, the Bible story time can be the least effective part of the hour. Activities are a better medium for communication than stories. The children will sit in a group for the Bible story—an unnatural situation for twos and threes. It will be hard to hold them together—to say nothing of holding interest and attention. Particularly difficult is the fact that the storyteller will be talking to the group, not to each child as an individual. All of these factors limit the teaching value of the Bible story time. Why then have it? Primarily because each truth taught in the department should be associated with the Bible, God's Book. A Bible should be shown and opened by the teacher as if being read.

Actually, Bible stories can be made interesting and fun for little ones. Visuals are important: sand, tables, figures, murals, surprise aprons (with big pockets out of which can pop unexpected figures) all help arouse interest. If the story isn't too long, if the story is visualized, if the story is well told, a happy excitement about Bible time can grow. And developing an awareness of God's Book as interesting and a source of truth is an important goal of the preschool staff.

3. Related Learning Activities

After the Bible story the group of children will break up. Children can be free to circulate and join one of the small clusters that gather around each teacher. A number of learning activities take place during the rest of the hour. One teacher may lead her cluster in a finger play that reviews the Bible story or restates the lesson taught. In another part of the room a teacher may lead a fun-to-do motion song with words that, again, are related to the day's lesson. Often activity in each cluster will parallel that in the others. All will be working on the handwork project at the same time, for instance. But still, each teacher will work with only four or five children, giving each individual attention and conversation.

Learning activities commonly used with twos and threes include songs and handwork. The teaching aim is central in all activities. It's central in songs too. Most evangelical publishers highlight songs that are especially written to impress Bible truths. Of course, some fun-to-do exercise songs are included for their own sake. But choruses that use symbolic words and phrases beyond the ability of young preschoolers to grasp are definitely ruled out. A piano isn't needed for singing. Children this age find it much easier to match tones with a human voice than a musical instrument. But new songs must be hummed and sung often if little children are to learn their simple words and tunes. Songs are especially good teaching tools, since a preschooler, after learning them, is likely to sing them over and over again at home, further impressing the biblical truth the words convey.

In Sunday school, the handwork project is designed to teach. Handwork projects teach in one of two primary ways: (1) Some permit the child to replay the Bible story. (2) Some projects demonstrate appropriate response to the Bible truth.

Handwork projects like these may often be completed by the teacher before class. In this case, handwork time isn't spent in making the item, but in learning how to use it. The teacher tells the story and shows each child how to move or play with his item. Although often some little thing is reserved for the child to do to "make" his project, the class emphasis still should be on helping him see how to use it. Handwork projects, too, are a teaching tool.

Each curriculum provides other ideas for instructional activities. Some have workbooks. Others suggest ways to play out the story. Still others suggest simple trips outdoors to find items associated with the day's lesson. Whatever methods are used, the basic function remains the same: to repeat, in a variety of situations and through a variety of activities, basic Bible truths that will structure the preschool child's thinking within a biblical framework. And this happens in a relaxed, flexible, truly fun hour at church, highlighted by play activities the children enjoy and through which their adult friends *teach*.

TEACHING FOURS AND FIVES

Fours and fives are different from twos and threes. But there are important similarities too. Older preschoolers are still preschoolers. They haven't yet been to elementary school. They can't read. Although their vocabularies are larger, these children still learn best when words are made meaningful by experience. They still need to move. Like younger children, fours and fives are still building their understanding of the world. And they still need basic truths to help them build a biblical picture of themselves and the world in which they live.

What about differences? These show up particularly in social areas. Older preschoolers are interested in each other. They play together. They listen to each other. They can cooperate. And—very important—

they can feel involved when part of a group. They don't require that talking-just-to-me approach used to hold the attention of a younger child.

All these—the differences and similarities—are important. They, too, need a program tailored just to their developmental characteristics.

The Way Fours and Fives Learn

"Can you growl like a hungry lion?"

"GRRR-rrr. GRRR-RRR!"

"Oh. Look, lions! Someone is opening the door of our den. Let's growl loud, to let him know how hungry we are."

"GRRR-RRR!"

A host of bright-eyed five-year-old "lions" in John's kindergarten department enthusiastically respond. "GRRR-rrr!"

"Look, lions! They're throwing something down to us! It's a 'people'! It's Daniel. Hurry, let's eat him right up. Come on—Oh, dear. Just a minute. What happens now?"

"God shuts the lions' mouths. God wouldn't let the lions eat Daniel. God took care of Daniel."

"Can you all growl like hungry lions—with your mouths shut?"

"GR-MMMmmm."

Tommy plays Daniel. Then Sue wants a turn. Eagerly the children cluster around. "I'm next!" And so the Bible story is played and replayed, as each child *lives* the great event and experiences God's protection. God took care of Daniel. God wouldn't let the lions hurt Daniel.

The students in John's department are learning, in the way they learn best. They're playing. They're experiencing the biblical event, experiencing the joy of deliverance, and finding confidence in God. Later in the hour pictures of preschoolers in familiar situations may lead the kindergartners to think of God's care for *them* while at play or riding in the car or on walks with mom. The children will have a chance to talk, to suggest places where God takes care of them. One may tell about the time he was in a boat, others may think of home, of playing in the yard, of being at church. Perhaps they'll draw pictures representing one of the experiences they talked about. Through it all—the imaginative play, the picture studies, the talking of personal experiences—the great fact of God's care for them will be impressed.

For fours and fives, this is the way to meaningful Bible learning. What's involved in programming for this pattern of learning? "Fitting" learning to the developmental characteristics of the age is especially important.

First, children must become involved. This means physically involved in a variety of activities, as well as verbally involved in talking. Playing the story, motions set to music, acting out applications—all these require movement, activity. Such involvement demands a large and open room—a room with space in which to move and play.

Second, these learning times are group activities. Older preschoolers aren't broken up into little classes and forced to sit at "their" table and learn only through words. These children learn best through activities. They need to move, to be "lions," to be "Daniel" and jump down off a low chair into an imaginary den. Activities like these are noisy. They take space.

But the activities through which beginners learn are the kind of activities the whole group can do. And fours and fives are able to work together in a group. They can listen together to a single storyteller or follow a single song leader. They've come a long way from twos and threes.

Because of this social development, and because an activity-teaching program is needed for maximum learning, keep them together in a group, except during handwork times.

What we need, then, is a teaching program patterned for the whole department group (usually a maximum of twenty-five is desirable). The pattern should provide for activities, yet also allow for quiet times of worship and listening. It's within a program so patterned that Bible truths can be most meaningfully communicated to fours and fives.

A Plan for Teaching Fours and Fives

Sunday school is fun for most four- and five-year-old children. But the fun is purposeful. Through each activity the children learn. As in programs for the other age groups, one main Bible truth is to be communicated during each Sunday's session, and response encouraged. The program, then, isn't "loose" (in the sense that children may choose any of a variety of activities and do as they please); it's "tight" (in that all activities are carefully planned to help children learn the day's Bible truth). Every activity must fit the lesson aim and give added dimension to the truth taught. Yet, even with the "tight" structure, the hour itself is relaxed, flexible, and fun for children and teachers alike. The hour is best broken down into clusters of activity that focus on the Bible story, worship, and expression. And, of course, the teacher has those minutes during which the children arrive before the hour begins. Let's look at each segment in turn.

Figure 19

PLAN FOR CLASS TIME USAGE—AGES FOUR AND FIVE

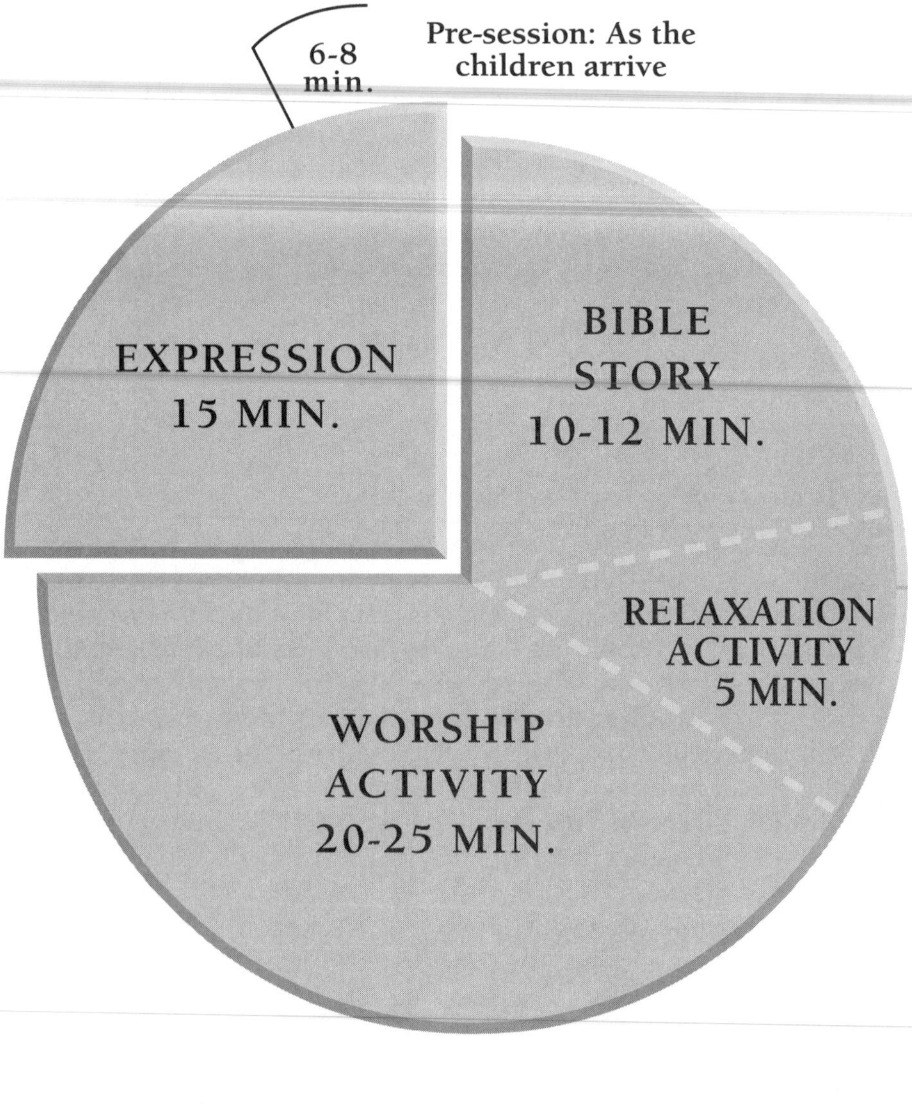

6-8 min.

Pre-session: As the children arrive

EXPRESSION 15 MIN.

BIBLE STORY 10-12 MIN.

RELAXATION ACTIVITY 5 MIN.

WORSHIP ACTIVITY 20-25 MIN.

1. *Pre-session*

Sunday school—and teaching—begins when the first child walks in the door of the room. This is the time when he can talk to one of the teachers, get adjusted to the room and the group, and get involved in activities that help him begin to think along the lines of the day's theme.

In good curricula, pre-session activities that fit the theme are suggested for each lesson. Pre-session activities may include choosing pictures and helping make a bulletin board, learning a new song, coloring or cutting out, making a picture wall, acting out scenes, etc. But, again, these activities are related to the lesson aim. They may introduce new words and ideas the children need in order to understand the Bible story. They may simply help children recall experiences like those of people in the Bible story or situations in which the Bible truth may be applied. In any case, the pre-session activities create a readiness for the lesson and the hour. And this is important.

Normally pre-session play doesn't extend deeply into the hour, as it does with younger children. Activities suggested may be carried on in small groups clustered around different teachers. At times the whole group will be together for pre-session fun. The procedure will depend on the kind of activity suggested for each hour.

2. *The Bible Story*

In most older preschool programs the Bible story comes first. The rest of the hour is structured to lead to response of various sorts. The whole group is together for Bible story time. This minimizes the problem of several noisy small classes trying to teach the lesson at the same time. And with the story told to all by one leader, the children all get to hear one of the department's best storytellers.

Picture studies and conversation are two activities normally clustered in the Bible story time. But relaxation activities are also needed. After ten or twelve minutes of sitting, this age group is ready to move. So movement activities are included. These activities should also be related to the lesson. A trip as thumping elephants going into Noah's ark, or a chance to pretend to be the sick girl Jesus made well and to jump up at His imaginary touch, will meet the need of fours and fives for movement and change, and also contribute to the teaching impact of the hour. For all of these—the listening, the conversation, the relaxation fun —the whole department is together. And one teacher can lead each learning experience.

3. *Worship Activities*

Following Bible story activities and the relaxation fun, beginners reassemble for activities that cluster around the idea of worship. Involved here are songs, prayers, and conversations that help children relate the Bible truth to their lives and their experiences at home and play.

The message of beginner songs is of primary importance. Songs should carry out the teaching aim and be of practical help to fours and fives. Words should contain concepts children can understand, speak of something they can experience, and be worth singing many times. In better curricula, songs that meet these criteria are included. Songs should be used as suggested, and not replaced by choruses that the children sing noisily, yet without understanding.

Songs should be explained as they're taught. This can be done by singing a song as a message before the children realize they're learning a new song, by using its words in conversation, by asking questions that the song answers and letting the children discover the answers, by illustrating the song with pictures as it is sung, etc. As beginner songs are used frequently, each time within a context where meaning is emphasized, they become vital communicators of Bible truths.

This age group can easily learn simple Scripture portions. Here, as with songs, the "learning" must focus on meaning rather than on the words themselves. Simply repeating Bible words isn't really learning God's Word. Meaningful learning has not occurred, only rote level learning. During the worship activities, time will often be given to making words of the day's verse meaningful by relating them to class experiences or to weekday lives.

Opportunities for simple prayers come spontaneously as songs and memory verses are taught and discussed, or as worship stories are told. Prayer should be a natural expression of gratitude or need. Prayer can be a natural and frequent experience with this age group as songs and conversation create a readiness.

4. *Expressional Activities*

The general purpose of this cluster of activities is to guide beginners to actually do in Sunday school that which is stated as the response aim of the lesson. Here fit such activities as playing the Bible story to make events more real or playing out life situations in which a Bible truth is applied. Handwork should be designed to help beginners see how truth fits into their lives. It has a teaching purpose. With adequate adult support, children can do much to make their projects for themselves, and they should be allowed to. Then the rest of the time can be spent showing the children how to use their project for play at church and later at home.

It's only (as a rule) during handwork time that the department group is broken down and seated around tables. During this time it's best to have one adult for every five or six children. As each worker assists her charges, her conversation can key their thinking to the meaning and use of the handwork.

PRINCIPLES FOR TEACHING PRESCHOOL CHILDREN

What can we say, then, in summary as we consider the matter of teaching young children the Bible? We would suggest the following guidelines.

Play Is Key

It has been often said that "play is a child's work." In a very real sense that is true. What is play to adults is for children a learning quest. Simply observe a room full of preschoolers, and you will discover that through play, children are able to collect and process ideas.

Sensing, Experiencing, and Doing Are Essential

From the moment of birth, children act upon, and are acted upon by, their world. Parents shape children, and children shape parents. This is not done in a verbal way, but in an experiential way. Children learn through the senses, through experiences and behavior. That is how God has made them. It is wise for teachers of young children to correlate their efforts with God's design and match methods to development.

Relationships Are Important

The single most important factor in the formal teaching learning process, besides the child, is the teacher. It matters how teachers relate to children. Preschool children learn best when a caring adult builds a meaningful relationship with them.

Concepts Learned Here Are Foundational

The teaching received by children in their preschool years is foundational in nature. It helps to shape their view of the world and life. In these years several foundational concepts are learned, including the nature of trust, love, and human interactions. Equally significant foundational concepts about God, Jesus, the Bible, creation, the world, and sin can be understood, as well. Let's identify more specifically the theological ideas that can be conveyed to preschool children.

> God: He knows and sees and can do all things.
> He takes care of us, hears us when we talk to Him.
> He made all things, and gives us all things to enjoy: eyes to see, strong legs, parents, home, etc.

Jesus: He is God's Son, who loves us.
        Jesus loves all children, and wants them to love Him.
        Jesus can do all things, and will help us when we ask Him.
        Jesus is alive, and watches over us all the time.
        He helps us to obey and to please God.
        He died for our sin, and will forgive us.
        He is our best Friend.

Bible: It is God's Word. God speaks to us through it.
        It tells us about God and Jesus, and it tells us how to please
        God.

World: God created it, and all good things in it.

Sin: Sin is disobeying God and displeasing Him.
        God loves us even when we sin, though this makes Him
        unhappy.
        Jesus can forgive our sin.

A FINAL WORD

Imagine a different recruitment announcement in the church bulletin. Imagine one that was more motivational and accurate—one that reads like this:

Wanted: People dedicated to teaching Bible truth to preschool children. Seeking persons who see preschool children as real people needing genuine ministry. Vision, commitment, and caring all essential. Must have desire to mold a life and model the love of Christ—building a foundation for the future.

Figure 20

THE CREATIVE BIBLE
TEACHING MODEL

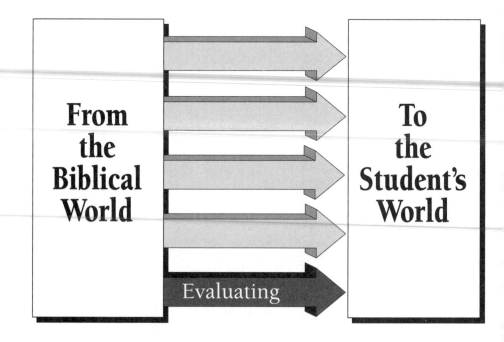

EVALUATING THE RESULTS

Lou Smith is struggling as a teacher. He is not sure how to improve. He prepares the best he knows how and each week comes early to interact with his class of adults from thirty to forty-five years old. But he really doesn't feel he is doing as well as a teacher as he could be, or that his students are growing very much as Christians. Lou needs some help, and he needs some information he simply does not have. Lou needs someone to evaluate what he is doing and what students are learning if he is ever to improve the results and his own abilities.

Evaluation—it is probably the most neglected educational task of the church. Or, should we say formal evaluation is neglected. You see, informal *evaluation happens every time our classes convene. People in our classes judge the quality of teaching each time we stand before them, and those who are old enough to make decisions for themselves choose whether or not to participate. Their actions are a kind of evaluation. Comments about our class are passed along by our students at the dinner table Sundays after church. This is another kind of informal evaluation. But formal evaluation, conducted in a careful and systematic way, is a rare occurrence in most Christian education programs.*

That's probably because evaluation is a threatening idea. Who wants someone to come to their classes to evaluate them? Who really longs for a critique of their teaching? Most people fear such evaluation. But we

*need not. If our goal is to improve and develop as teach-
ers, evaluation is essential. From the information we
gain, we can make necessary adjustments. And we can
identify and build on our teaching strengths. In this last
section of the book we will discuss how you can evaluate
your teaching ministry. In chapter 20 we will provide
some guidelines for self-improvement. Even if no one of-
ficially evaluates you as a teacher, this step is crucial to
your teaching success. In this section you will find a tool
you can use yourself that will reveal much about your
teaching and your students' learning. So you need not
fear. Your self-evaluation effort will simply provide information you can use to enhance your teaching effectiveness. But, then again, that is one reason why you are
reading this book in the first place, isn't it?*

Chapter Nineteen

A MODEL FOR EVALUATION:
SOMETHING TO "STAKE" ON

On October 4, 1957, the Russian satellite Sputnik was launched. With it came technological war, a battle for space. Americans were concerned that Russians had moved ahead technologically. That produced a growing worry that freedom itself was at risk. If the Russians could put a satellite in orbit, how much longer would it be before they placed a nuclear warhead in orbit as well? Such a situation would make every square inch of American soil vulnerable to attack. Americans were justifiably concerned. They demanded a response—a space race. They were determined to dominate space for the sake of safety and freedom on Earth.

But it was not only the space race that was launched that day; so, too, was the modern educational assessment movement. Americans felt that their educational system was adrift in a rising tide of mediocrity. Calls for school reform were rising in the media, at PTA meetings, and in Congress. In response, educators began to devise educational assessment tools, standardized tests, and evaluation instruments with the hope of improving the quality and outcomes of American education. And so, for more than forty years, educators have not only concerned themselves with the planning of teaching, but with the results of teaching as well. From these developments have come the means by which Christian teachers can assess, evaluate, and improve their effectiveness in the classroom.

WHY DO EDUCATIONAL EVALUATION IN THE CHURCH?

We're not teaching math or science or reading skills in Sunday school. We're not preparing the workforce for North American industry. We do not have the task of producing good citizens, although we believe we contribute to that end. We are making disciples of Jesus Christ. If we are teaching the Bible, what more can we expect? Do we really need to do formal evaluation as well? The answer is a clear and resounding *yes.* Of all who are concerned for the outcomes of education, those who conduct Christian education ought to line up first. We desire to do our best and to achieve the greatest possible ends in our programs because we serve Christ and want to honor Him. In addition, we sense a stewardship for which we are accountable. These factors alone should motivate us to ask probing questions about the quality and effectiveness of our ministry. Evaluation offers three very desirable benefits.

First, it helps us determine if we are reaching the objectives we have set for our class. You will recall that we have previously discussed the need to write objectives or lesson aims for our classroom teaching sessions. These aims help us keep all of our lesson planning on course. By establishing a direction and a purpose to our teaching, we can select appropriate content and teaching strategies. But lesson objectives also help us when doing evaluation. Did we achieve what we set out to achieve? In other words, when we complete the teaching session, did our learners change in the ways we were targeting? Did they gain the knowledge and understanding we had hoped they would? Did they adopt the attitudes or values we were seeking to instill? Did they develop the skills or practice the behaviors we were trying to cultivate? It may well be that the answers to these questions are not yes or no. It is possible that the student may have progressed toward the goal but has yet to fully attain the result we had been aiming for. But how would we know this without some form of evaluation? Evaluation enables teachers to make judgments on the results of the teaching-learning endeavor.

Second, evaluation allows teachers to make changes in the future in order to achieve goals more effectively. Assuming that it is rare to be completely satisfied with the outcome of a class session, teachers can make changes to the curriculum, the methodology, or the environment to improve the outcomes of teaching. If, in teaching a session on the priestly ministry of Christ, it becomes obvious that students did not comprehend the concept, the teacher could come at the matter again in a different way. Evaluation may cause the teacher to change his or her assumptions about students' prior knowledge of a subject area. Through evaluation, the teacher might also judge the usefulness of a particular method and consider an alternative means of teaching the idea in the future.

Third, evaluation provides a basis for improving one's teaching skills and abilities. One of the variables at work in education is the teacher. In fact, this is the variable over which we have the greatest control. We may have our curriculum given to us. We have little choice in who attends our class. And we have only limited control over environmental factors affecting our teaching. But we can change our own teaching performance level. We can alter that variable by simply growing as a teacher and making needed changes. And when we change and improve, the results improve as well. Here is the exciting point. Nothing stops us from improving as teachers, except our will to do so. That is not to say that personal change and development is easy. Far from it! It is a process that demands a willingness to see the need for improvement, a desire to be a more capable teacher, and a plan to get there. Evaluation is an essential part of the process of growth and development as a teacher. Teachers who are passionate about teaching are driven to become excellent at their tasks. They are lifelong learners who are unwilling to settle for a static level of teaching competence. No, great teachers are growing teachers. And evaluation is a catalyst for growth.

WHAT SHALL WE EVALUATE?

The teaching-learning process is a function of four fundamental variables—the learner, the teacher, the curriculum, and the environment. We could picture this relationship using the following mathematical equation: $\text{TLP} = f(l, t, c, e)$. What we are saying is that each variable influences the outcomes of teaching. For example, change the age of the learner, and the same lesson can have greater or lesser impact. What works well with junior highs may be entirely ineffective with high school students.

Instead let's say we change the teacher. One teacher might be very ineffective in a group, whereas another has no trouble gaining group respect. The content may be identical, the students the same, and the environment unchanged. Simply changing the teacher can result in a very different classroom experience.

We could alter the curriculum. It may be that our curriculum is undershooting or overshooting our students' developmental level. As a result, it does not have the impact we want. But if we change the curriculum design in a way that fits the class, positive results can occur.

Then there is the environment. Too hot, too cold, too dark, too noisy, too formal, too informal, too crowded, too sparse—in all cases the outcome of teaching can be significantly hindered. We can see, then, that each variable changes the result. Each variable is a dynamic part of the teaching-learning equation.

It stands to reason that each of these variables must be evaluated if educational efforts are to be correctly understood and revised. We may assume that the reason for an ineffective session is due to a poor teacher, when in reality it may be true that no teacher could have done significantly better given the students' attitudes, the curriculum quality, or the environmental limitations. Since all four variables are at work in any educational enterprise, all four must be considered in a careful evaluation of the outcomes of teaching. Here are some questions that you might consider as you evaluate each variable.

The Learner

♦ What was the age, developmental level, and spiritual maturity level of the students?
♦ What needs did students bring to the learning exchange? Were those needs met?
♦ Were students prepared to learn? Did they bring their Bibles? Other needed materials?
♦ Were students motivated to learn? Did they participate? How extensively?
♦ What knowledge, attitudes, and skills did the students bring to the learning exchange?
♦ What knowledge, attitudes, or skills were developed or enriched through the learning exchange?
♦ What level of understanding was achieved by the majority of the students?
♦ How did students change as a result of participating in this class?

The Teacher

♦ Was the teacher clearly heard?
♦ Was the teacher able to clearly articulate the concept under consideration?
♦ Did the teacher provide needed structure to the material?
♦ Did the teacher provide adequate illustrative material?
♦ Did the teacher have credibility as a communicator of God's Word?
♦ Was the teacher enthusiastic? Did the teacher teach heart-to-heart?
♦ Did the teacher pace the lesson well? Did the teacher allow time to drag? Was the teacher rushed?
♦ Did the teacher seek to engage the learners?
♦ Was the teacher sensitive to the individual needs of students where appropriate?

◆ Was the teacher adequately prepared?

◆ Did the teacher have a firm grasp of the material being taught?

◆ Did the teacher manage the classroom and student behavior effectively?

The Curriculum

◆ What was the aim(s) of the lesson? Was it clear? Was it learner-centered?

◆ Was the aim(s) achieved? To what degree?

◆ Was one central concept or pedagogical idea presented?

◆ Was it consistent with the idea of the passage(s) studied?

◆ Did the Hook gain student attention? Did it lead into the study of the Bible?

◆ Were the methods appropriate for the age group? Were they effective?

◆ What worked well? What failed?

◆ Would a different method work better next time this is taught?

◆ Was the passage adequately addressed? Was it understood? Was it taught accurately?

◆ Was application relevant?

◆ Did students enter into the process of determining appropriate application points?

◆ Was the Took appropriate? Did students commit to a response?

The Environment

◆ Was the environment developmentally appropriate for the group? Were chairs the right size? Blackboards and posters the right height? The room contents age appropriate?

◆ Was the environment conducive to learning? Too warm? Too cool? Adequately lit? Limited intrusions and distractions from noise or activity in other classes?

◆ Was the environment appropriately formal or informal for the type of class conducted?

◆ Were chairs arranged for optimal learning?

◆ Were materials available? Were they organized and ready to go?

◆ Were visual aids ready to use? Videos and players available and ready to go?

◆ Did all the equipment work properly?

◆ Was there a sense of community? Did people feel welcome? Were students comfortable together? Was there a sense of the body of Christ at work together?

A MODEL FOR SYSTEMATIC
EVALUATION OF TEACHING AND LEARNING

The teaching and learning process is complex. As we have seen, the teaching-learning process is comprised of several variables that can affect results. In order to simplify the evaluation of the educational process, Robert Stake has devised a helpful model for constructing and evaluating educational efforts.[1] Figure 21 depicts the model. It is comprised of six boxes in two columns labeled "expected" and "actual." Stake believes that evaluators must take both into account. All teachers expect or plan for certain things to happen in their classroom, but those plans never happen exactly as designed. So evaluation is a comparison between the expected and the actual—between the planned and the real.

The left side of the model focuses on what the teacher expects to happen in the teaching-learning encounter. Starting at the top of the page we find the box labeled "Expected Learning Antecedents." An antecedent is something that comes before something else. Learning antecedents are the things that come before our actual teaching session. These include the students' prior experiences, knowledge, skills, and attitudes. An antecedent is something that the student brings to the learning experience. For example, a teacher might expect all students to understand the difference between the Old Testament and the New Testament. Or a teacher might expect students to come prepared for class in some way because of a prior assignment. Any expectations regarding the student, the environment, or resources for learning that the teacher uses to design the learning experience fit in this box.

The second box in the "expected" column is the box labeled "Expected Learning Transactions." Learning transactions are the learning strategies that teachers plan into the classroom experience. This is where the lesson plan fits into the model.

The third box on the left side, the expected side of the model, is labeled "Expected Learning Outcomes." This describes the results the teacher hopes to achieve through the class. This is another term for lesson objectives or learning aims.

Stake suggests a simple and logical structure. When we plan, we plan for students we expect to come to our class. We plan certain activities to take place. These activities are designed to lead to certain outcomes. Wouldn't it be nice if it always worked that way? Imagine if our lesson plans worked in reality as effectively as they worked in our minds when we design them. What we expect is never identical to what we experience. It is the similarity or difference between our expectations and

Figure 21

ROBERT STAKE'S MODEL
FOR EVALUATION OF
EDUCATIONAL PROGRAMS
AND TEACHING SESSIONS

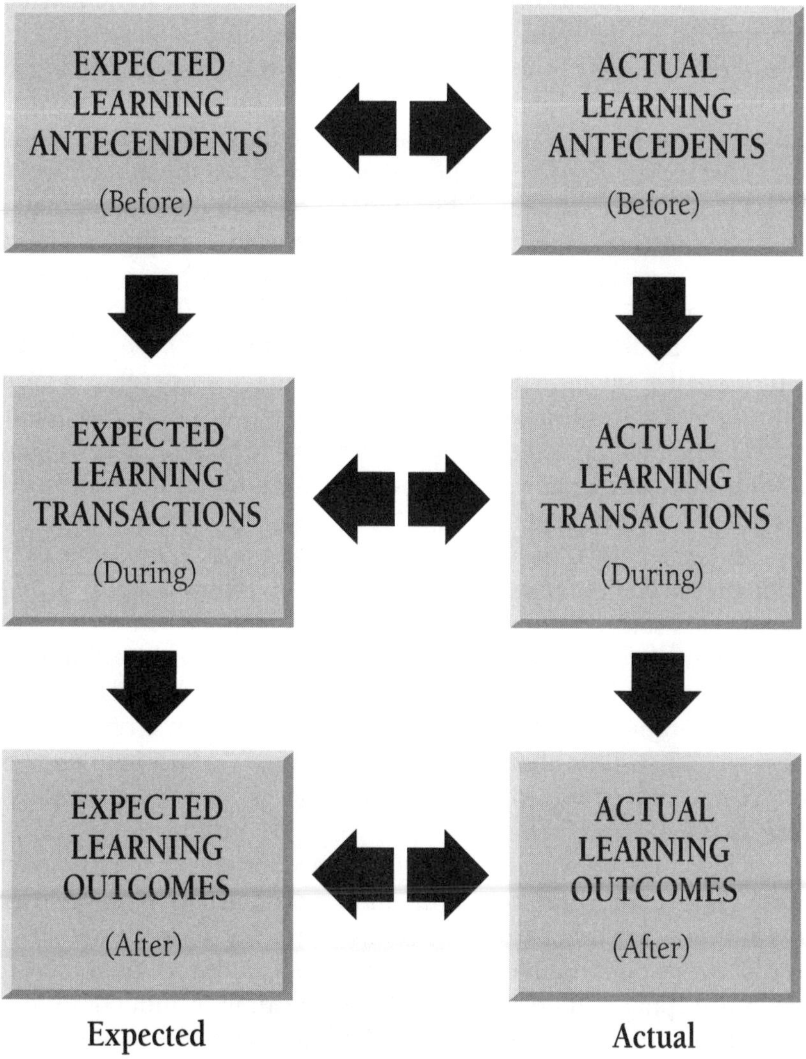

EXPECTED LEARNING ANTECENDENTS (Before)		ACTUAL LEARNING ANTECEDENTS (Before)

EXPECTED LEARNING TRANSACTIONS (During)		ACTUAL LEARNING TRANSACTIONS (During)

EXPECTED LEARNING OUTCOMES (After)		ACTUAL LEARNING OUTCOMES (After)

Expected   Actual

what actually occurs that, Stake suggests, formulates the ground for our evaluation efforts. And so, Stake repeats all of the boxes on the right side of the model. But this side is the "actual" side. Here we record what really happened when we taught so we can make comparisons and judgments about what occurred or did not occur. Ultimately, we do so in order to make adjustments to our expectations, our curriculum, and our teaching in the future. The Stake model provides a simple framework for evaluation—a before, during, and after comparison.

We must look at what comes before we teach, what happens during our teaching, and what happens in the lives of students after we teach. Let's consider an example so we can gain a better understanding of how Stake's model might be applied to the creative Bible teacher's ministry. We return again to Alex Smith, the youth worker we have met on and off throughout the book. Take a look back at Table 13 in chapter 9 to see how Alex designed his study. Table 18 shows how he used the Stake model as he evaluated his small group Bible study on Hebrews 11.

Alex expected eight to ten students for the study. Nine regulars showed up. No surprise there. But only six brought Bibles. Fortunately, Alex had some other Bibles around, so each student was given a Bible to use. Alex was expecting his regular group of students, but this time, two of the teens brought unsaved friends. That affected the group in that these students did not understand much in terms of Bible knowledge. It also made it a bit difficult because Alex planned to develop a group commitment with his group. He went ahead anyway, even though one key teen was missing and the unsaved youth were present. Alex will have to follow up on this to see how these factors affected the outcome of this time of commitment.

As is often the case, the video player didn't work at first. One of the visiting teens had the touch and got it working. That was a plus because the teenager was recognized and appreciated by the entire group. Alex understands that even when things go wrong, some positive things can result. The video led nicely into a discussion just as he had planned. But when the group turned to the Book section, it became obvious that those who knew little about the Bible were bored. So Alex shortened his lecture and moved right into some other learning activities that were more successful.

The outcomes were a bit less dramatic than Alex had envisioned. He had hoped for a deep commitment to a group-devised response. The commitment included involvement in a weekly prayer time before school. Alex would not be able to be there, but students would meet together and pray with a student leading the time. Although students made the commitment, only time will tell what actually happens from

Table 18

USING A STAKE MODEL: EVALUATING A YOUTH BIBLE STUDY	
Expected Learning Antecedents	**Actual Learning Antecedents**
• 8-10 students would attend • All would bring their Bibles • Mostly committed Christians • Video available • Most students are facing some degree of persecution for being a Christian • Students feel a need for mutual support	• 9 regulars attended—only one no show due to school event • Only 6 brought Bibles • Two regular students brought friends with whom they have been sharing Christ. • These students had no Bible knowledge or background. Both are unsaved. • The video equipment wasn't working right at first. One of the students fixed it, and then we were able to show the video.
Expected Learning Transactions	**Actual Learning Transactions**

• Hook:
 	
    Video Clip—SS troops
    Discussion on persecution
 	
• Book:
 	
    Mini-lecture on background material
    Student Report—Research on Priesthood
    Discussion—Need for Prayer, Perseverance, People
 	
• Look:
 	
    Brainstorming: Ways to apply lesson
    Goal Setting: Commitment to support each other
    Commitment: Write group commitment to meet regularly for prayer and encouragement.
 	
• Took:
 	
    Commitment Signing Ceremony
    Group Prayer
	• Students were moved by *The Hiding Place* story. They asked if we could show the entire film.
	• Mini-lecture was hard for students to relate to. Most seemed to become less interested at this point. Student report was a plus. Student did excellent job getting together information for the group and presented it enthusiastically. Discussion was effective. All students entered in with an opinion or a personal experience.
	• Look section seemed to meander a bit. Students need more guidance. Had to actually suggest group commitment details. Once we got commitment written and read it out loud, students became excited about concept.
	• Took section was very effective. Strong sense of commitment present. Prayer time was moving and reflected understanding.

Expected Learning Outcomes	**Actual Learning Outcomes**
• Students would understand implications of Christ's priestly ministry. • Students would desire to encourage one another in times of persecution. • Students would establish a regular meeting time before school for prayer.	• Students seem to grasp the passage. • They were able to intelligently discuss the concept of the priesthood of Christ and the believer. • Students lacked a clear understanding of the priesthood of the believer. They confused it with the priesthood in Roman Catholic theology. • Students committed themselves to a small group prayer time and a group commitment.

the agreement. Alex plans to follow up with students at his next study to see if they actually carried through and met. The students identified a time. But Alex is not sure if they will fulfill their agreement.

From the use of the Stake model, Alex is able to evaluate his own teaching, the needs and level of his students, the effectiveness of planned learning strategies, and points where he must follow up on decisions and commitments made. By evaluating the study, Alex can make adjustments that will continue to improve his ministry with teens. Although his assessment is not foolproof or absolutely objective in nature, it is a more systematic and informed approach than simply speculating as to how things went on a given evening.

A FINAL THOUGHT

When Mike Ditka was the head coach of the Chicago Bears, he was known for making his team watch films of games that they had lost—and watch them over and over again. They would study every false move, every fumble, every interception, and every penalty until the team was absolutely clear on what it had done wrong. Then, and only then, would he talk about the next game. He believed that evaluation is the key to excellence. Even though his players did not want to see their mistakes, they knew that Iron Mike was right.

Evaluation can be uncomfortable. It can be threatening as well. But without evaluation, we teachers are destined to repeat our ineffective practices. Evaluation can be the means by which your teaching moves to a new level of competence.

NOTE

1. Robert Stake, "The Countenance of Educational Evaluation" in *Teachers College Record*, 68 (7), 1967, 523–40. The model has been modified in figure 21 for ease of understanding.

Chapter Twenty

DEVELOPING AND IMPROVING
AS A TEACHER:
YOU CAN GET THERE FROM HERE

E ven in third grade, Mark Eklund had a zest for life. He was neat, joyful, and only occasionally mischievous. With his fun and enthusiastic personality came one drawback—he talked continually. Again and again his third grade teacher had to remind him that talking without permission was not allowed. And, true to form, Mark would sincerely apologize and then thank his teacher for her correction.

Sister Helen Mrosia was a new teacher. And like all new teachers are prone to do, she made a promise to Mark she later regretted. One day when Mark was just a bit too talkative, she said, "If you say one more word, I am going to tape your mouth shut!"

It was just a matter of time before the inevitable occurred. Mark talked when he was supposed to be listening. She had made her threat publicly and so she felt she had to follow through. She walked over to her desk and found a roll of masking tape. She tore off two pieces and made a big X over Mark's mouth. When she looked at Mark a bit later to see how he was responding, he winked at her. With that, Sister Helen started to laugh, the class cheered, and she removed the tape. Mark said, "Thank you for correcting me, Sister."

Years went by, and again Sister Helen had Mark in class. This time she was teaching junior high math. Mark was older, more handsome, and still very polite. But now he had learned to talk less and pay closer attention.

One day when the class material just wasn't getting through and

319

students were edgy with each other, Sister Helen decided to address the tension and crankiness of the class by building a more positive atmosphere. So she had each student list the names of all of the other students in class on a sheet of paper, skipping a line between each name. She then had the students write the nicest thing they could say about each student after each name. When students left class, they handed her the papers. On Monday, she gave each student a list of his or her positive qualities as described by their classmates. It wasn't long before everyone in class was smiling.

Several years later as she returned from vacation, Sister Helen's mother and father picked her up at the airport. On the ride back home her father said, "The Eklunds called last night."

"Oh really," she replied. "I haven't heard from them in years. I wonder how Mark is."

Her dad responded with an obvious tone of sorrow, "Mark was killed in Vietnam. The funeral is tomorrow, and his parents would like it if you could attend."

At the funeral, Mark's body was dressed in his military dress uniform. To Sister Helen he looked so handsome. She couldn't help but recall the masking tape incident so many years earlier. Right now she wished Mark could once again be his talkative self. After one of Mark's elementary school classmates had sung "The Battle Hymn of the Republic" and after all had said their last good-bye, the family and many friends gathered together at Mark's parents' farmhouse for lunch.

Mark's father approached Sister Helen, as did several of Mark's junior high classmates. Mark's father began, "Sister, we want to show you something. They found this on Mark when he was killed. We thought you might recognize it." Mark's father carefully unfolded a piece of paper, torn years before from a notebook. Now it was held together with tape. It was immediately obvious to Sister Helen that the paper was the list of good things Mark's classmates had written about him on that day in ninth grade.

"Thank you so much for doing that," his mother said. "As you can see, Mark treasured it."

Mark's classmates one by one recalled how important their lists were to them. One kept the list in his wedding album, another in her pocketbook, another in her childhood diary. "I think we all saved our lists," said Vicki, one of Mark's friends. At that, Sister Helen cried.[1]

Sister Helen Mrosia enlightens us with an important lesson about teaching: *Teachers can have a profound impact on students!* And often it is through a small thing—positive or negative. A small word of encouragement, a simple act of kindness, a caring incident, little gestures of interest, small changes in one's teaching approach can all have significant, long-term effects on people. It is a bit like a very small course correction to an ocean liner or aircraft. A very small adjustment, just a degree or two, can result in miles saved or miles lost. In this final chapter we want to suggest some small changes you can make that will have profound impact over time. The task may look enormous when you finish reading a book like this, but we suggest you start somewhere, one step at a time, to become the kind of teacher you want to be. And so, we leave you with these suggestions.

1. Teach people, not just lessons.

It is people we are called to serve. It is people Christ died to redeem. Be sure that it is the student who is your focus in teaching, not simply the delivery of Bible content.

2. Teach more by teaching less.

It is preferable to teach one idea well. Too often we try to teach everything we know on a subject. Limit the content of your class so that there is time to illustrate, explain, and discuss truth.

3. Teach using a lesson plan.

Planning is essential to effective teaching. Use the lesson planning sample and worksheet provided in chapter 9.

4. Teach for life change.

Remember, the goal is changed lives, not covering the material. Be willing to stop and take the needed time to interact with people.

5. Teach only after you have gained attention.

Start today developing the Hook portion of your lesson. The first few minutes of your lesson are important to engaging student learning.

6. Teach only what the Bible teaches.

Don't stretch the Bible to say something it doesn't say or to prove your point. Be sure you teach what the passage teaches. Never take passages out of context or use them to teach a concept that they were not intended to teach.

7. Teach in ways appropriate to your age group.

Start reading about the age group you teach. Become more familiar with the issues and needs of your students.

8. Teach using relevant issues.

Read the paper, news magazines, and books. Video tape news broadcasts and special programs. Use clips from recent major movies. Give your class relevance. The Bible speaks to our times. Show students how relevant it is!

9. Teach heart to heart.

Share your passion. Don't simply aim for the intellect or behavioral matters. Aim at people's values and attitudes. Get a little preachy once in a while.

10. Teach from a humble heart.

Be open to grow and develop. Be willing to evaluate your teaching skills and effectiveness. Recognize that you can be taught. Students are teachers too, so be open to learn from them as well.

Teach. Be a creative teacher. Learn all you can about how to handle the Word of God, conscious of whose word it is. Learn all you can of how God works through the Word, and develop skills that will help you lead learners to respond. And when you have done all of that, bow your head and commit all your efforts to God, in complete dependence on His Spirit, who alone can truly teach the Word.

NOTE
1. Helen P. Mrosia, "All the Good Things," *Reader's Digest,* October 1991, 49–52.

BIBLIOGRAPHY

Aleshire, Daniel O. *Faith Care: Ministering to All God's People Through the Ages of Life.* Philadelphia: Westminster, 1988.

Anderson, Ray A., ed. *Theological Foundations for Ministry.* Grand Rapids: Eerdmans, 1979.

Anthony, Michael J. *Foundations of Ministry: An Introduction to Christian Education for a New Generation.* Wheaton, Ill.: Victor, 1992.

Ashley, Jeff. *The Philosophy of Christian Religious Education.* Birmingham: Religious Education Press, 1994.

Barlow, Daniel L. *Educational Psychology: The Teaching-Learning Process.* Chicago: Moody, 1985.

Beechick, Ruth. *A Biblical Psychology of Learning.* Denver: Accent, 1982.

Bennett, David W. *Metaphors of Ministry: Biblical Images for Leaders and Followers.* Grand Rapids: Baker, 1993.

Benson, Clarence H. *A Popular History of Christian Education.* Chicago: Moody, 1943.

Benson, Warren S. "A History of the National Association of Christian Schools During the Period of 1947–1972." Unpublished Ph.D. Dissertation, Loyola University of Chicago, 1974.

Berkhof, Louis and Cornelius Van Til. Edited by Dennis E. Johnson. *Foundations of Christian Education: Addresses to Christian Teachers.* Phillipsburg, N.J.: Pres. & Ref., 1990.

Beverslius, N. H. *Christian Philosophy of Education.* Grand Rapids: National Union of Christian Schools, 1971.

Bloom, Allen. *The Closing of the American Mind.* New York: Simon & Schuster, 1987.

Bloom, Benjamin S., ed. *Taxonomy of Educational Objectives: Cognitive Domain.* New York: David McKay, 1956.

Boehlke, Robert R. *Theories of Learning in Christian Education.* Philadelphia: Westminster, 1962.

Bolton, Barbara, Charles T. Smith, and Wes Haystead. *Everything You Want to Know About Teaching Children.* Ventura, Calif.: Regal, 1987.

Bower, William Clayton. *The Curriculum of Religious Education.* New York: Charles Scribner's Sons, 1925.

Boylan, Anne M. *Sunday School: The Formation of an American Institution, 1790–1880.* New Haven, Conn.: Yale, 1988.

Bruce, A. B. *The Training of the Twelve.* Grand Rapids: Kregel, 1971. (Originally published in 1894.)

Burgess, Harold William. *An Invitation to Religious Education.* Mishawaka, Ind.: Religious Education Press, 1975.

_____. *Models of Religious Education.* Wheaton, Ill.: Victor, 1996.

Bushnell, Horace. *Christian Nurture.* Reprint. Grand Rapids: Baker, 1979.

Carson, D. A., ed. *The Church in the Bible and the World.* Grand Rapids: Baker, 1987.

Carson, D. A. *Hermeneutics, Authority, and a Canon.* Grand Rapids: Zondervan, 1986.

_____. *The Gagging of God: Christianity Confronts Pluralism.* Grand Rapids: Zondervan, 1996.

Carson, D. A. and John D. Woodbridge, eds. *Scripture and Truth.* Grand Rapids: Zondervan, 1983.

Carter, John and Bruce Narramore. *The Integration of Psychology and Theology.* Grand Rapids: Zondervan, 1980.

Chadwick, Ronald P. *Teaching and Learning: An Integrated Approach to Christian Education.* Old Tappan, N.J.: Revell, 1982.

Clark, D. Cecil. *Using Instructional Objectives in Teaching.* Glenview, Ill.: Scott, Foresman, 1972.

Clark, Robert E., Lin Johnson, and Allyn K. Sloat, eds. *Christian Education: Foundations for the Future.* Chicago: Moody, 1991.

Coleman, Robert E. *The Master Plan of Evangelism.* Old Tappan, N.J.: Revell, 1963.

Collins, Gary R. *Psychology and Theology: Prospects for Integration.* Nashville: Abingdon, 1981.

_____. *The Rebuilding of Psychology: An Integration of Psychology and Christianity.* Wheaton, Ill.: Tyndale, 1977.

Colson, Howard P. and Raymond M. Rigdon. *Understanding Your Church's Curriculum.* Revised ed. Nashville: Broadman, 1980.

Cross, K. Patricia. *Adults as Learners.* San Francisco: Jossey-Bass, 1981.

Cullman, Oscar. *Early Christian Worship.* London: SCM Press, 1969.

Daniel, Eleanor, John W. Wade, and Charles Gresham. *Introduction to Christian Education.* Revised ed. Cincinnati: Standard, 1986.

Doll, Ronald. *Curriculum Improvement: Decision Making and Process.* 6th ed. Boston: Allyn and Bacon, 1986.

Drumheller, Sidney J. *Handbook of Curriculum Design for Individualized Instructions: A Systems Approach.* Englewood Cliffs, N.J.: Educational Technology Publications, 1971.

Drushal, Mary Ellen. *On Tablets of Human Hearts: Christian Education with Children.* Grand Rapids: Zondervan, 1991.

Eavey, C. B. *History of Christian Education.* Chicago: Moody, 1964.

Eble, Kenneth E. *The Craft of Teaching.* 2d ed. San Francisco: Jossey-Bass, 1988.

Edge, Findley B. *A Quest for Vitality in Religion.* Nashville: Broadman, 1963.

_____. *Teaching for Results.* Nashville: Broadman, 1956.

_____. *The Greening of the Church.* Waco, Tex.: Word, 1971.

Eldridge, Daryl. *The Teaching Ministry of the Church.* Nashville: Broadman and Holman, 1995.

Elwell, Walter A., ed. *Evangelical Dictionary of Theology.* Grand Rapids: Baker, 1984.

Fee, Gordon D. and Douglas Stuart. *How to Read the Bible for All Its Worth.* Grand Rapids: Zondervan, 1982.

Ferre, Nels F. S. *A Theology for Christian Education.* Philadelphia: Westminster, 1967.

Ford, LeRoy. *Design for Teaching and Training.* Nashville: Broadman, 1979.

Fortunato, Connie. *Children's Music Ministry. A Guide to Philosophy and Practice.* Elgin, Ill.: David C. Cook, 1981.

Foster, Charles R. *Teaching in the Community of Faith.* Nashville: Abingdon, 1982.

Gaebelein, Frank E. *Christian Education and Democracy.* New York: Oxford, 1951.

_____. *The Pattern of God's Truth.* Chicago: Moody, 1968.

Gangel, Kenneth O. and Howard G. Hendricks, eds. *The Christian Educator's Handbook on Teaching.* Wheaton, Ill.: Victor, 1988.

Gangel, Kenneth O. and Warren S. Benson. *Christian Education: Its History and Philosophy.* Chicago: Moody, 1983.

Gangel, Kenneth O., ed. *Toward a Harmony of Faith and Learning.* Farmington Hills, Mich.: Wm. Tyndale College Press, 1983.

Getz, Gene A. *Sharpening the Focus of the Church.* Revised ed. Wheaton, Ill.: Victor, 1984.

Gibbs, Eugene S., ed. *A Reader in Christian Education.* Grand Rapids: Baker, 1992.

Graendorf, Werner C., ed. *Introduction to Biblical Christian Education.* Chicago: Moody, 1981.

Grudem, Wayne. *Systematic Theology.* Grand Rapids: Zondervan, 1994.

Grunlen, Stephen A. and Milton Reimer, eds. *Christian Perspectives on Sociology.* Grand Rapids: Zondervan, 1982.

Habermas, Ronald and Klaus Issler. *Teaching for Reconciliation: Foundations and Practices of Christian Education Ministry.* Grand Rapids: Baker, 1992.

Hakes, J. Edward, ed. *An Introduction to Evangelical Christian Education.* Chicago: Moody, 1964.

Hamachek, Don E. *Behavior Dynamics in Teaching, Learning and Growth.* Boston: Allyn and Bacon, 1975.

Hart, D. G. and R. Albert Mohler, Jr. *Theological Education in the Evangelical Tradition.* Grand Rapids: Baker, 1997.

Haystead, Wesley. *You Can't Begin Too Soon.* 2d ed. Ventura, Calif.: Regal, 1982.

Heck, Glenn and Marshall Shelly. *How Children Learn.* Elgin: David C. Cook, 1979.

Hendricks, Howard G. *Teaching to Change Lives.* Portland: Multnomah, 1987.

Hendricks, William L. *A Theology for Children.* Nashville: Broadman, 1980.

Holmes, Arthur F. *All Truth Is God's Truth.* Downers Grove, Ill.: InterVarsity, 1983.

Horne, Charles M. *Salvation.* Chicago: Moody, 1971.

Ingle, Clifford, ed. *Children and Conversion.* Nashville: Broadman, 1970.

Issler, Klaus and Ronald Habermas. *How We Learn.* Grand Rapids: Baker, 1994.

Jones, Stephen D. *Faith Shaping: Nurturing the Faith Journey of Youth.* Valley Forge: Judson, 1980.

Kaiser, Walter C., Jr., *Toward an Exegetical Theology: Biblical Exegesis for Preaching and Teaching.* Grand Rapids: Baker, 1981.

Knight, George R. *Philosophy and Education.* 2d ed. Berrien Springs, Mich.: Andrews Univ. Press, 1989.

Knoff, Gerald E. *The World Sunday School Movement.* New York: Seabury, 1979.

Knowles, Malcolm. *The Adult Learner: A Neglected Species.* Revised ed. Houston: Gulf, 1984.

_____. *The Making of an Adult Educator: An Autobiographical Journey.* San Francisco: Jossey-Bass, 1989.

_____. *The Modern Practice of Adult Education.* 2d ed. Follett, 1980.

_____. *Self-Directed Learning: A Guide for Learners and Teachers.* New York: Cambridge Book Co., 1975.

Knox, A. B. *Helping Adults Learn.* San Francisco: Jossey-Bass, 1986.

Kotesky, Ronald. *Psychology from a Christian Perspective.* Nashville: Abingdon, 1980.

Krathwohl, David R., Benjamin S. Bloom and Bertram B. Masia. *Taxonomy of Educational Objectives: Affective Domain.* New York: David McKay, 1964.

Kuethe, James L. *The Teaching-Learning Process.* Atlanta: Scott, Foresman and Co., 1968.

Kuhatschek, Jack. *Taking the Guesswork Out of Applying the Bible.* Downers Grove, Ill.: InterVarsity, 1990.

Kuhlman, Edward. *Master Teacher.* Old Tappan, N.J.: Revell, 1987.

Lankard, Frank Glenn. *A History of the American Sunday School Curriculum*. Nashville: Abingdon, 1972.

Larkin, William J., Jr. *Cultural and Biblical Hermeneutics*. Grand Rapids: Baker, 1988.

LeFever, Marlene. *Creative Teaching Methods*. Elgin, Ill.: David C. Cook, 1985.

Lockerbie, D. Bruce. *Asking Questions: A Classroom Model for Teaching the Bible*. Milford, Mich.: Mott Media, 1980.

Loder, James E. *The Transforming Moment*. 2d ed. New York: Harper & Row, 1989.

Lopez, Diane. *Teaching Children: A Curriculum Guide*. Westchester, Ill.: Crossway, 1981, 1988.

Lynn, Robert W. and Elliott Wright. *The Big Little School: Sunday Child of American Protestantism*. 2d ed. Birmingham: Religious Education Press, 1980, and Nashville: Abingdon, 1980.

McCartney, Dan and Charles Clayton. *Let the Reader Understand*. Wheaton, Ill.: Victor, 1994.

McQuilkin, Robertson. *Understanding and Applying the Bible*. Chicago: Moody, 1992.

Mager, Robert F. *Preparing Instructional Objectives*. Revised ed. Belmont, Calif.: Fearon, 1975.

Merriam, Sharon B. and Ralph G. Brockett. *The Profession and Practice of Adult Education*. San Francisco: Jossey-Bass, 1997.

Meyers, Chet and Thomas B. Jones. *Promoting Active Learning*. San Francisco: Jossey-Bass, 1993.

Miller, Donald E. *Story and Context: An Introduction to Christian Education*. Nashville: Abingdon, 1987.

Moran, Gabriel. *Showing How: The Act of Teaching*. Valley Forge: Trinity, 1997.

Morgan, Norah and Juliana Saxton. *Teaching Questioning and Learning*. New York: Routledge, 1991.

Murray, Dick. *Strengthening the Adult Sunday School Class*. Nashville: Abingdon, 1981.

Osmer, Richard Robert. *A Teachable Spirit: Recovering the Teaching Office in the Church*. Louisville: Westminster/John Knox, 1990.

Pardy, Marion. *Teaching Children the Bible: New Models in Christian Education*. San Francisco: Harper & Row, 1988.

Pazmino, Robert W. *By What Authority Do We Teach?* Grand Rapids: Baker, 1994.

_____. *Foundational Issues in Christian Education.* Grand Rapids: Baker, 1988.

_____. *Principles and Practices of Christian Education.* Grand Rapids: Baker, 1992.

_____. *The Seminary in the City: A Study of New York Theological Seminary.* Lanham, Md.: University Press, 1988.

Peterson, Gilbert A., ed. *The Christian Education of Adults.* Chicago: Moody, 1984.

Peterson, Michael L. *Philosophy of Education.* Downers Grove, Ill.: InterVarsity, 1986.

Pitts, Peter. *The God Concept in the Child.* Schnectady: Character Research Press, 1977.

Powers, Bruce P., ed. *Christian Education Handbook.* Rev. ed. Nashville: Broadman and Holman, 1996.

Richards, Lawrence O. *Christian Education.* Grand Rapids: Zondervan, 1975.

_____. *A Theology of Children's Ministry.* Grand Rapids: Zondervan, 1983.

_____. *A Theology of Church Leadership.* Grand Rapids: Zondervan, 1980.

_____. *A Theology of Personal Ministry.* Grand Rapids: Zondervan, 1980.

_____. *A Practical Theology of Spirituality.* Grand Rapids: Zondervan, 1987.

_____. *A New Face for the Church.* Grand Rapids: Zondervan, 1970.

Robinson, Haddon W. *Biblical Preaching.* Grand Rapids: Baker, 1980.

Roehlkepartain, Eugene C. *The Teaching Church: Moving Christian Education to Center Stage.* Nashville: Abingdon, 1993.

Rood, Wayne R. *On Nurturing Christians.* Nashville: Abingdon, 1972.

_____. *Understanding Christian Education.* Nashville: Abingdon, 1970.

Rusboldt, Richard E. *Basic Teacher Skills: Handbook for Church School Teachers.* Valley Forge: Judson, 1981.

Sell, Charles M. *Transition.* Chicago: Moody, 1983.

Seymour, Jack L. and Donald E. Miller. *Contemporary Approaches to Christian Education.* Nashville: Abingdon, 1982.

Shelp, Earl E. and Ronald Sunderlund, eds. *A Biblical Basis for Ministry.* Philadelphia: Westminster, 1981.

Smart, James D. *The Teaching Ministry of the Church.* Philadelphia: Westminster, 1954.

_____. *The Rebirth of Ministry.* Philadelphia: Westminster, 1960.

_____. *The Strange Silence of the Bible in the Church.* Philadelphia: Westminster, 1970.

Stephens, Larry D. *Building a Foundation for Your Child's Faith.* Grand Rapids: Zondervan, 1996.

Stott, John R. W. *Understanding the Bible.* Grand Rapids: Zondervan, 1976.

Stewart, Donald Gordon. *Christian Education and Evangelism.* Philadelphia: Westminster, 1963.

Thiessen, Henry C. *Introductory Lectures in Systematic Theology.* Grand Rapids: Eerdmans, 1949.

Tidwell, Charles A. *Educational Ministry of the Church.* Rev. ed. Nashville: Broadman and Holman, 1996.

Towns, Elmer L., ed. *A History of Religious Educators.* Grand Rapids: Baker, 1975.

Trueblood, Elton. *The Company of the Committed.* New York: Harper & Row, 1961.

_____. *The Teacher.* Nashville: Broadman, 1980.

Tyler, Ralph W. *Basic Principles of Curriculum and Instruction.* Chicago: Univ. of Chicago, 1950.

Vieth, Paul H. *Objectives in Religious Education.* New York: Harper and Brothers, 1930.

_____, ed. *The Church and Christian Education.* St. Louis: Bethany Press, 1963.

Walton, John H., Laurie D. Bailey, and Craig Williford. "Bible-Based Curricula and the Crisis of Scriptural Authority," *Christian Education Journal.* Volume XIII, Number 3.

Walvoord, John F. *Jesus Christ Our Lord.* Chicago: Moody, 1969.

Wilbert, Warren N. *Teaching Christian Adults.* Grand Rapids: Baker, 1980.

Wilhoit, James C. Edited by Kenneth O. Gangel. *The Christian Educator's Handbook on Adult Education.* Wheaton, Ill.: Victor, 1993.

Wilhoit, James C. and Leland Ryken. *Effective Bible Teaching.* Grand Rapids: Baker, 1988.

Wilhoit, James C. and John M. Dettoni, eds. *Nurture That Is Christian: Developmental Perspectives on Christian Education.* Wheaton, Ill.: Victor, 1995.

Willis, Wesley R. *200 Years and Still Counting: Past, Present and Future of the Sunday School.* Wheaton, Ill.: Victor, 1979.

Worley, Robert C. *Preaching and Teaching in the Earliest Church.* Philadelphia: Westminster, 1967.

Wyckoff, D. Campbell. *The Task of Christian Education.* Philadelphia: Westminster, 1965.

_____. *The Gospel and Christian Education.* Philadelphia: Westminster, 1959.

_____, ed. *Renewing the Sunday School and the C.C.D.* Birmingham: Religious Education Press, 1986.

_____. *Theory and Design of Christian Education Curriculum.* Philadelphia: Westminster, 1961.

Yount, William R. *Created to Learn: A Christian Teacher's Introduction to Educational Psychology.* Nashville: Broadman and Holman, 1996.

Zuck, Roy B. "The Theological Basis of Neo-Orthodox Christian Education." *Bibliotheca Sacra.* Vol. 119, No. 474 (April–June 1962), 161–69.

_____. "The Educational Pattern of Neo-Orthodox Christian Education." *Bibliotheca Sacra.* Vol. 119, No. 476 (October–December 1962), 342–51.

_____. *The Holy Spirit in Your Teaching.* Wheaton, Ill.: Victor: 1963.

_____. *Learning from the Sages: Selected Studies on the Book of Proverbs.* Grand Rapids: Baker, 1995.

_____. *Precious in His Sight.* Grand Rapids: Baker, 1997.

QUESTIONS
FOR DISCUSSION
AND FURTHER STUDY

CHAPTER 1

1. In this chapter, the authors distinguish between the immanence view of God and the transcendence view. Create a chart that identifies the key differences between these views of God. On your chart compare the two views of God's nature, how He makes Himself known, how we come to know Him, and the role of the Bible in knowing God.

2. Write out your personal view of the nature of Scripture and explain in detail the implications of your view for the Bible teacher.

3. For discussion: Think of several people you know who have learned much about the Bible but aren't changed by it. How do you explain this?

4. Compare and contrast the liberal, neo-orthodox, and conservative views of the nature of the Bible. How would one approach Bible teaching if he embraced each of these views?

5. First Corinthians 2:9–13 is examined in this chapter. According to this passage, one of the characteristics of the Bible is that it reveals information that could not be otherwise known. Choose a New Testament book and make a list of concepts in it for which there could be no source of sure information except that God has made it known in the Bible.

CHAPTER 2

1. What is meant by "inspiration"? What evidence is there that the Bible indeed is inspired?

2. What does "literal interpretation" mean? Why is this the preferred approach to interpreting the Bible?

3. Find examples of Scripture passages written in various genres. How does the task of interpretation differ when reading different genres of Scripture?

4. Review Gordon D. Fee and Douglas Stuart, *How to Read the Bible for All Its Worth* (Grand Rapids: Zondervan, 1982). Make a list of guiding principles for the study of different scriptural genres.

5. Why do you think God used so many varied styles of writing in Scripture? Why did He use so many different authors?

CHAPTER 3

1. The authors point to the theme of reconciliation as the "unifying motif" of Scripture. Do you agree or disagree? Why, or why not?

2. In this chapter, we examined 2 Corinthians 5:17–21. Why is this passage significant to those who study the Bible? What aspect of this passage is most intriguing and encouraging to you?

3. The authors discussed three specific roles that the Bible plays in the life of the believer—it enlightens, exposes, and equips. Give two examples of how you have personally experienced the Bible's impact in your own life in each of these ways.

4. Why is it important that the Bible teacher understand the message and role of the Bible?

5. The authors contend that, "The purpose of educational ministry from a Christian perspective is to bring the learner into a reconciled relationship with God through Jesus Christ and to enable the learner to order all of life and learning around that relationship." What does this statement mean? Do you agree? Why or why not?

CHAPTER 4

1. According to the authors, what is required to give a Bible teacher authority in a teaching ministry?

2. Why is inductive Bible study the starting point in creative Bible teaching?

3. Select a passage in one of the New Testament epistles, and use the inductive study questions provided by the authors to guide your investigation of the passage.

4. Why is it important to state the central idea or "generalization" of the passage in a single sentence?

5. Many people tend to rush right to application when they read the Bible. Why is this dangerous? What cautions should the student of the Bible keep in mind when making applications of the Bible?

CHAPTER 5

1. Using the model of study given in the chapter, select another segment of the book of Hebrews and conduct your own inductive study of that passage.

2. Looking at Table 2, how might you construct an outline of Hebrews 10:19–25?

3. The authors have identified some key words and repeated words in the Hebrews passage examined in this chapter. Select one of these words, or another word that you believe is important or unclear, and conduct a word study using a concordance and a Bible dictionary.

4. What point of personal application can you draw from studying the Hebrews 10:19–25 passage for your own life? If you were to adjust your life to implement this truth, how would you have to change?

5. Imagine teaching this passage in your own class. What concepts do you believe would be most relevant to your students?

CHAPTER 6

1. What factors make teaching the Bible challenging? Why is it important to understand your student as well as the passage being taught?

2. Review the developmental characteristics charts (Tables 3-6). What characteristics would you add to the charts? How might you use these charts to improve your teaching?

3. Use Table 9 to conduct a "needs assessment" with the students in your class.

4. Why is it important to understand human needs? Should teachers seek to meet all categories of needs or simply those deemed to be "spiritual" in nature? Defend your view biblically.

5. At the end of this chapter the authors encourage Bible teachers to "teach students, not lessons." What do they mean by that injunction? Does this mean that content is unimportant?

CHAPTER 7

1. The authors state that "Children are born with an innate, God-given ability to learn." Do you agree? How have you seen this concept first-hand? Give an example of learning as part of the created nature of people.

2. A principle is presented in this chapter that says that "Learning most powerfully transfers and transforms when the material taught has meaning to the student's life and experience." Give a personal example of this principle from your own life or teaching ministry.

3. What is the value of rote learning? Why do the authors describe rote learning as "meaningless"? By this, do they mean that it is without value?

4. Figure 10 presents five levels of learning transfer. Explain the diagram in your own words. Identify one passage of Scripture that you have taken through all five levels of learning in your own life.

5. The authors define creative teaching as "consciously and effectively focusing on activities that raise the students' learning level." What do you think they mean by that statement? How does that statement differ from typical definitions of creative teaching? Why is creative teaching more than simply the use of a variety of methods?

CHAPTER 8

1. Why is it important to define both what you want a student to learn and how you want him to change because of that learning?

2. How would you distinguish between "the exegetical idea," "the pedagogical idea," and "a lesson aim"? Why are all important?

3. Explain what is meant by the cognitive, affective, and behavioral domains. Why is it important to seek to teach to all three domains of learning?

4. As you evaluate your own teaching, which domain of learning do you typically teach to? Which gets the least attention in your teaching? How do you need to change as a teacher to more effectively teach for life change?

5. Read John 15:1–11. Write out the exegetical idea, pedagogical idea, and three lesson aims—one cognitive, one affective, and one behavioral—for a lesson on this passage.

CHAPTER 9

1. Look over three samples of curriculum. Do they follow the HBLT format even though they do not use the same terms? How do they differ? What do they add? What do they delete?

2. Why is it essential to start with the student when teaching the Bible? How effective are you as a teacher in designing and implementing hooks that draw in your students?

3. Using Table 14, design a lesson using the HBLT structure.

4. What do you believe are the strengths of the HBLT structure? How would you modify it to better fit your teaching style or needs?

5. Notice again Figure 13. Be sure you are clear as to the flow of the HBLT structure. Use the chart to explain to a fellow student or teacher how to prepare a lesson.

CHAPTER 10

1. Why is it so difficult to get students to be more than hearers of the Word?

2. Many people believe that if you can get students to think rightly, they will act rightly. What is wrong with this viewpoint? Does correct thinking produce correct action?

3. Why are generalized applications insufficient? What is the difference between a generalized application and specific, personal, guided self-application?

4. Look again at your study notes on Hebrews 10:19–25. List three personal implications from the passage for your own life. If you were to actually apply this passage to your life, in what ways would you have to change?

5. Evaluate the following statement: "The task of the creative Bible teacher is not to make the Bible relevant to students, for that is its very nature, but to make it meaningful and applicable to students." What is meant by the statement? Do you agree or disagree with the statement?

CHAPTER 11

1. Make a list of methods that you would categorize as most appropriate for teaching to the cognitive domain, the affective domain, and the behavioral domain.

2. Figure 14 identifies seven ways that the ideas taught in your lesson can be supported and clarified for the learner. Can you identify any other ways to support your lesson and clarify classroom communication? Which of the seven do you regularly use in your teaching? Select one new means of supporting your communication and try it the next time you teach.

3. Figure 15 introduces the reader to four questions used in selecting appropriate teaching methods. Are there any other questions that should be considered in methods selection? How do you select methods you use in your Bible teaching lessons?

4. Several methods of teaching are discussed in this chapter. Select one method that is new to you or that you want to learn more about. Review books on methodology to learn more about the use of the method you have selected. If you have access to the Internet, do a search for articles and information about the method you selected. Try to incorporate the method in an upcoming teaching situation.

5. The chapter lists some twenty methods that Jesus used in His teaching ministry. Read the accompanying passages and review the methods of Jesus. Which methods do you use? Which methods might you try?

CHAPTER 12

1. Write to various publishers and ask them to send you a statement of their philosophy of curriculum design and education.

2. Use the curriculum guide (Table 17) to evaluate three different curricular samples from various publishers for the same age group.

3. Write a two page paper on the pros and cons of using published curriculum.

4. Check to see when your Sunday school curriculum was last evaluated. Use the curriculum evaluation tool (Table 17) to evaluate your Sunday school's curriculum. Write a brief summary report for your Christian education committee, Sunday school superintendent, or the appropriate pastoral staff member overseeing Christian education in your church.

5. Call two or three publishers of Sunday school curriculum. Find out when they will be holding training sessions or conferences related to the use of their curriculum. Attend a conference, Sunday school convention, or a seminar to learn more about curriculum options.

CHAPTER 13

1. Think of a teacher who has had a significant effect on your life. Identify the characteristics of that teacher that made him or her so effective.

2. Review the material in this chapter that deals with credibility as a teacher. How strong is your credibility? How could you strengthen your credibility with your students?

3. Meet with two people from your class for a cup of coffee. Ask them this question: "If I could make one change in my teaching that would make me more effective, what would you suggest I focus on?"

4. Review the characteristics of great teachers presented in this chapter. Which characteristics represent strengths in your teaching ministry? Which are weaknesses?

5. Develop a plan for personal enrichment entitled, "Steps of Greatness." Identify things you plan to implement to become a great Bible teacher.

CHAPTER 14

1. Think of a student you would like to see more motivated to learn. What strategies can you identify to help motivate your student? Select one strategy to use in the next three weeks.

2. What have teachers done that have motivated or demotivated you as a student?

3. Compare the personal and structural factors of motivation. Which do you feel are more important? Why?

4. Do you agree that "motivating students to learn is largely a function of the student-teacher relationship"? Why or why not?

5. Look through books on motivation. Are the ideas presented appropriate to the Christian classroom? What ideas can you incorporate in your teaching?

CHAPTER 15

1. Evaluate three different publishers of adult curriculum. How effective are they in gaining attention? Do they present the biblical truth accurately and in a way that engages learners' interest? Are the applications relevant? Are students led to discover personal applications of the passage for daily living?

2. Different kinds of adult learners are identified at the beginning of this chapter. Which is most representative of your own nature as an adult learner? Describe your learning preferences as an adult student. Which style do you find easiest to teach?

3. Review the characteristics of adult learners. What do you believe is the most challenging factor in teaching adults? What is the greatest asset in teaching adults?

4. Design a lesson for adults using the HBLT structure. How does adult teaching differ from teaching youth or children?

5. If you are a teacher of adults, identify three new strategies for adult teaching that you will use in your next three teaching sessions.

CHAPTER 16

1. Why are relationships so important in teaching youth? Identify one student in your group that you can meet with in the coming week to strengthen your relationship. Briefly list that student's needs and ways you might be able to meet some of his or her needs.

2. Review two books on youth ministry. Identify three ideas from each book that you could try in your own ministry with youth.

3. In what ways must the HBLT structure be modified to work effectively with adolescents?

4. Several suggestions are made in this chapter concerning the nature of adolescents as learners. Which concepts are new to you? How might you change the way in which you teach to incorporate these ideas?

5. Several methods for working with youth are suggested. Which methods have you used successfully? Which have you not attempted yet? Select one method to incorporate into your teaching ministry.

CHAPTER 17

1. The authors indicate that the Bible is "an adult book, written by and for adults." What do they mean by this statement? Does this mean

that we should not teach the Bible to children? What must teachers do to make the Bible meaningful to children?

2. Evaluate three different examples of children's curriculum. How effective are they in gaining attention? Do they present the biblical truth accurately and in a way that engages learners' interest? Are the applications relevant? Are students led to discover personal applications of the passage for daily living? Is the material developmentally appropriate?

3. Other than the use of stories, identify a list of at least ten methods appropriate for teaching children the Bible. Which methods have you used? Which methods would you like to implement in your own ministry with children?

4. How must the HBLT structure be modified to work with early elementary children and later elementary children?

5. What concepts, doctrines, and Bible terms do you believe elementary children can understand? Later elementary children? Which concepts, doctrines, and terms are beyond their comprehension level?

CHAPTER 18

1. You have been asked to write an article for a newsletter dealing with the subject of Christian education of children. The article is to be one to two pages on the subject "Five Reasons For Making Preschool Ministry a Priority in the Church's Education Program." What would you communicate in your article?

2. Sit in on a two- and three-year-old Sunday school class. Make a list of observations about the developmental characteristics of this age group. Based on your observations, what implications can you draw for teaching two- and three-year-old children?

3. Observe children ages four and five. How are they different from the two- and three-year-old children you observed? What implications can you draw from your observations for working with four and five year olds?

4. How must the HBLT structure be modified to work with preschool children?

5. What concepts, doctrines, and Bible terms do you believe preschool children can understand? Which concepts, doctrines, and terms are beyond their comprehension level?

CHAPTER 19

1. Design a form to be used in evaluating your own teaching. If you work with a co-teacher, have him complete the evaluation form. If you teach adults, you might ask four or five people to evaluate your teaching as well.

2. Using the evaluation questions provided in this chapter, evaluate your last classroom teaching experience.

3. Why do you believe teachers resist evaluation? What could be done to encourage self-evaluation or responsiveness to evaluation by others?

4. If you are in a leadership role, arrange to visit one of your teachers' classes. Set up a meeting with one of your teachers to go over strengths and points of potential growth. If you are a teacher, ask someone in authority over you to evaluate your teaching. If you do not have someone to turn to for evaluation, talk to a fellow teacher and evaluate each other.

5. Based upon your evaluation, identify one area for personal development and one change that you can make to the class you teach. Be sure to be as practical as possible. Do not try to change everything that needs improvement at once. It is better to make one change that endures than to attempt ten that you ultimately do not implement.

CHAPTER 20

1. Identify one "success story" from your teaching ministry. What made this a successful experience or result? What can you learn from this incident for the future?

2. Identify one "teaching failure" from your teaching ministry. Why do you see this as a failure? How could you improve or change the outcome next time an incident like this occurs? What have you learned from this situation?

3. This chapter makes the point that teachers can have a profound impact on students. Name a teacher in your life who has profoundly affected you. Was it a positive or negative effect? Why did that teacher have such an effect? What can you learn from his or her teaching?

4. At the end of the chapter, the authors give ten suggestions designed to enhance your teaching ministry. Which of the suggestions will you employ, and why?

5. If you were to add five more suggestions, what would they be?